Notes from a

12
MAN

Notes from a

A Truly Biased History of the Seattle Seahawks

Mark Tye Turner

SASQUATCH BOOKS
SEATTLE

Printed in the United States of America
Published by Sasquatch Books
Distributed by PGW/Perseus
15 14 13 12 11 10 09   9 8 7 6 5 4 3 2 1

Cover photographs: David Belisle
Cover design: Rosebud Eustace
Interior design and composition: Rosebud Eustace
All interior photos credited to the Seattle Seahawks, with the exception of the
following photos: page 5 and page 113, courtesy Mark Tye Turner; page 175,
courtesy Greenstrat, 3/30/2007, 2:03 (UTC)

Library of Congress Cataloging-in-Publication Data
Turner, Mark Tye.
  Notes from a 12 man : a truly biased history of the Seattle Seahawks / Mark Tye
Turner.
     p. cm.
  Includes bibliographical references and index.
  ISBN-13: 978-1-57061-602-0
  ISBN-10: 1-57061-602-7
  1. Seattle Seahawks (Football team)--Anecdotes. 2. Sports spectators--Washington
(State)--Seattle--Anecdotes. I. Title. II. Title: Notes from a twelve man.
  GV956.S4T87 2009
  796.332'6409797772--dc22
                               2009017115

Sasquatch Books
119 South Main Street, Suite 400
Seattle, WA 98104
(206) 467-4300
www.sasquatchbooks.com
custserv@sasquatchbooks.com

For my father, Ned, who took me to my first Seahawk game, along with my first Husky football, Husky basketball, Pilot, SuperSonic, Sounder, and Mariner games.

CONTENTS

05: POP GOES THE CULTURE

06: MONSTER SCORES AND PHANTOM TOUCHDOWNS

07: IT WAS THE WORST OF CHAPTERS

08: YOU WIN SOME, YOU LOSE SOME, YADA YADA YADA

09: COMEBACKS, COMEDOWNS, AND A QUIZ

10: THAT WAS CLASSIC

11: WHAT A POSTSEASON!

12: ONE ERA CLOSES, ANOTHER BEGINS

INTRODUCTION

A few years back I had one of my many late-night epiphanies. Usually these epiphanies involve what I should be doing to better my life, such as trying food that doesn't come from a drive-through window. However, this epiphany was different. It told me I needed to write a book about my favorite team, the Seattle Seahawks. Seattle being one of the lesser-noted NFL franchises, the library of Seahawk literature is only slightly larger than the meat locker at a vegan restaurant.

Maybe you are a longtime fan of the team, going back to when the expression "Zorn to Largent" was heard almost as often in Western Washington as "It's just drizzling outside." Maybe you came aboard when Chuck Knox first brought the team to postseason glory. Or maybe you've only recently become a fan. If so, welcome. You are about to enter a sports time machine that will revisit some of the Seahawks' best (and worst) moments, with game stories, factoids, pop culture tidbits, and history dating back to the team's beginning. It's my intention to share with Seahawk fans (and NFL followers in general) my recollections of and insight about a team that's had a special relationship with its fans simply known as the "twelfth man."

Who am I and why am I writing this book? I've been a fan of the team since the Seahawks first set foot on the artificial turf inside the Kingdome. I am a "world's fair kid," born in Seattle during the city's Century 21 Exposition, aka the 1962 World's Fair. This means I'm as old as the Space Needle (soon this will be the Northwest equivalent of the expression "old as the hills").

The 1970s was a landmark time in Seattle sports history, and growing up during this period you watched the town transform into a major league city. You were old enough to remember when the area only had the Sonics and Huskies and was starving for both Major League Baseball and the NFL. Back then, we'd lost our baseball team when the Pilots moved to Milwaukee in 1970, and the NFL consisted of a couple of preseason games at Husky Stadium. If you were lucky, your dad would drive you 800 miles during the summer to see baseball games in the San Francisco Bay area. But the NFL? Forget it. Those games happened during the school year, and there was no way you were going that far on a weekend. However, when the Seahawks and Mariners finally arrived within a year of each other, a '70s Seattle kid could appreciate the privilege of being able to watch local NFL and MLB teams.

When I moved to Los Angeles after college in the late '80s, my fanaticism for the team didn't waver. If anything, it grew. I have spent my professional life working in television as a writer and producer, somehow earning an Emmy along the way. I'm really just a Seahawk geek, along with being a movie geek, a music geek, and a microbrew geek. My wife, Terry, wishes I were also a "make more money" geek.

What kind of Seahawk fan am I? "Devoted" is a good word to describe my fandom. Because I live in LA, I don't have season tickets, but I watch every game via the NFL Sunday Ticket on my DirecTV satellite dish. I am not one of those fans who paints their face or has turned their entire basement into a shrine to the Seahawks. Primarily because I'm allergic to body paint and I don't have a basement.

I'm a fan who records the highlights from ESPN's *NFL Primetime* and NFL Films of every Seahawk win. In recent years, I've also been clipping good plays directly from the game broadcasts for my own highlights reel. (Lest the NFL be alarmed, these are purely for my own collection, with no outside distribution.) I also have a number of full games that I can watch during the off-season to get my Seahawk fix. I am a fan who, at his wedding reception, had a table named "Seahawks." To appease the family and friends of Terry, who's from Pittsburgh, we also named one of the tables "Steelers." I am a fan who is something of a sports savant because I can recall obscure Seahawk knowledge and win many a sports trivia bet.

Until recently, when I would inform someone in LA that I was a Seahawk fan, it was not uncommon for the response to be "Huh?" or worse, "Why?" I think many longtime Seahawk fans, even those living in Washington state, have had their fandom questioned on occasion due to the team's lack of Super success. Years ago when I was a producer at E! Entertainment Television, I met Cowboy defensive back Larry Brown, who was getting a tour around the network offices. I told him that I was a Seahawk fan. He just laughed, shook his head like he was looking at some fool, and said he was sorry for me.

I think a number of Seahawk fans have chips on their shoulders because of what we feel is a lack of respect for the team around the league. There are a few reasons for this attitude. Despite the Hawks being around for over 30 years, the team still has a bit of the "new kid at school" image. Often the new kid isn't accepted, but rather, ignored. Until the Hawks win the Super Bowl or draft another "Boz," the team will always be somewhat under the radar. The late NFL Films narrator John Facenda (aka "The Voice of God") once said, "The Seahawks had been the team born on the wrong side of the tracks." He was actually making a dramatic play off an NFL Films shot that started from Seattle's railroad tracks before panning upward to the Kingdome, but you get the picture of how the rest of the league sometimes views the Hawks.

The team's geographical location has also made it the most remote franchise in the NFL. To give you an idea of how far away Seattle is from the rest of the league, compare it to

Chicago. In the distance between Seattle and its nearest NFL cities, San Francisco and Oakland, Chicago is closer to 17 teams. When you are not seen, you are not heard. Cable television coverage and the Internet have shrunk the metaphorical distance between the Seahawks and the rest of the NFL, but the physical distance will always exist.

However, being so remote does have its advantages. The Seahawks have always been more than just Seattle's team. They are really the Pacific Northwest's team. The Hawks are the most popular NFL franchise not just in Washington, but also in Oregon, Idaho, Montana, British Columbia, and Alaska. There are actually several large groups of Seahawk fans who fly 1,000-plus miles from all over the 49th State to Seattle for every home game.

More recently, the Seahawks have developed significant followings throughout Planet Earth. I know of fans in New Zealand, Norway, and every other country starting with the letter *N* (except North Korea, where overlord Kim Jong-il is a Raider fan, which means everyone in North Korea is a Raider fan).

A Seahawk fan hopes for success, savors victory, and doesn't take winning for granted. Longtime fans have also had to endure an evil owner, Ken "Over" Behring (last name pronounced BEAR-ing), who, after wearing down a once-proud franchise, nearly stole the team to Southern California. (Sadly, the SuperSonics were not spared a similar horrible fate.) Seahawk fans have rarely felt the true season lows that bring you ridicule on the late-night talk shows and a very high draft pick. However, we've felt even less the great elation of a championship. The middle is where the Hawks have been throughout most of their history. Consequently, in some NFL circles, the team has been known as the "epitome of average." I don't think it's meant as a compliment. Being average doesn't lend itself to the sort of Shakespearean drama that attracts most sportswriters, but it does carry its own kind of pain for fans. You know a great win against an upper-echelon team at home will be followed by a brutal road loss to a mediocre franchise in the Eastern Time Zone.

Many sports teams have books written by fans. There's a plethora of tomes by Boston Red Sox fanatics, including one by Stephen King. I am just providing equal time for the Seahawks. I mention this information lest anyone think I'm trying to fool the reader into believing I've created my own literary subgenre of fans and their memoirs known as the "fan-oir." Actually, I did Google the word "fan-oir" (and "fanoir") and nothing came up, so I will take credit for the creation of the word—but not the subgenre.

As I mentioned before, this book is filled with Seahawk game stories, history, and various nuggets of trivia. I have also added "time-outs": sometimes I go off topic to give the reader an extra bit of history or analysis. These time-outs are brief and, I hope, interesting.

I must note that many of the statistics and game facts in this book are derived from the Seattle Seahawks' media guides (or "facts books," as they were called until 1992). Often I went by my own notes and then confirmed them with other sources, including *The ESPN Pro Football Encyclopedia*, the *Seattle Times*, and *Seattle Post-Intelligencer* online archives, and the Web site Pro-Football-Reference.com. The numerous previously mentioned game tapes and highlights also proved to be invaluable. Hopefully, my accuracy rate is 100 percent, but if it isn't, I'm sure some of you readers will let me know with the subtlety of a Kenny Easley hit.

You may also notice that sometimes I refer to the Seahawks as "we" and "our." There has been debate as to whether it's appropriate for fans to use these words when describing their team. Some say it's improper, since the fans don't play, coach, or even work for the franchise. However, many fans claim their bond to their teams is so great that such language is valid. I am with the latter group. After all, we are the twelfth man.

IN THE BEGINNING

Well, you gotta start somewhere. I'm opting to begin this book with the actual creation of the team. Yep, that's me. Always thinking outside the box.

THE EGG HATCHES

My relationship with the Seahawks goes back to the team's inception and won't end until my physical being decides to take a knee. Team historians list June 15, 1972 as the official beginning of the Seahawks because it is the day Seattle Professional Football, a group formed by Puget Sound businessmen Herman Sarkowsky (who owned the Portland Trail Blazers of the NBA) and Ned Skinner (one of the original owners of the Space Needle), announces its intention to pursue an NFL franchise. In a bit of coincidence that screams providence, it's also my 10th birthday. (And an assistant football coach at San Francisco's Sacred Heart High School by the name of Mike Holmgren turns 24 that day.)

Construction of the King County Domed Stadium begins in early November 1972. Nineteen months later, the NFL gives notice that the city of Seattle will have a team for the 1976 season. This ignites interest among a few different ownership groups for the franchise rights. One of these groups is led by Hugh "The King" McElhenny, the former star running back at the University of Washington who went on to a Hall of Fame career with the San Francisco 49ers. McElhenny's enterprise wants to name the team the "Seattle Kings" for McElhenny's nickname (and for King County). Eventually, the NFL awards the franchise to the first pony in the race, Seattle Professional Football, now led by majority owners the Nordstrom family and including area businessmen Lynn Himmelman, Howard Wright and Lamont Bean, along with Skinner and managing general partner Sarkowsky. This saves the city from having the "Kings," a highly unoriginal nickname that is already being used in the NBA and NHL. Instead, the team owners invite the fans to help pick the name, receiving over 20,000 entries and

1,741 different suggestions. Scribbled on 151 submissions is the name "Seahawks." Thus is created one of the more lyrically alliterated team names.

In March 1975, the Seahawks name John Thompson as general manager. Thompson, formerly the executive director of the NFL's Management Council, starts to assemble the organization. His most crucial addition arrives on January 3, 1976, when Minnesota Viking assistant coach Jack Patera is named head coach of the Seahawks. The hiring of Patera is welcomed, partly due to his strong Pacific Northwest roots. He grew up in Portland and was an All-Pacific Coast Conference player at the University of Oregon. Thompson and Patera then embark on an association that will make the Seahawks one of the most successful expansion franchises in NFL history.

In order to stock an expansion team, the NFL holds a veteran allocation draft. Each existing NFL team is able to protect a certain amount of players, and the expansion franchise can pick from what's left over. In late March, the NFL holds the veteran allocation draft for the two new expansion teams, the Hawks and the Tampa Bay Buccaneers. The pool of available talent in the draft is composed mostly of marginal players and guys walking on one leg. However, Thompson and his staff are able to pick out a few gems, including Steeler defensive back Dave Brown, a No. 1 pick the previous year who was a victim of playing on a talent-rich squad in Pittsburgh. In all, 22 of the 39 players from the draft eventually make the regular-season roster.

A month later, the Seahawks participate in their first NFL college draft. With the second overall pick, they select Steve Niehaus, an All-American defensive tackle from Notre Dame. The college draft yields eight other players who would become charter members of the Seahawks, including wide receiver Steve Raible, safety Don Dufek, and Sherman Smith, a

The Seahawks' first head coach, Jack Patera. Those clothes better be from Nordstrom, or someone is getting fired.

quarterback from Miami University of Ohio who would be converted into a running back.

The Seahawks begin their playing history with a preseason game against the San Francisco 49ers on August 1, 1976, at the Kingdome. After a moribund first half, the team trails 17-0, and an unknown left-handed quarterback by the name of Jim Zorn takes over in the second half. Zorn, a rookie free agent who was originally signed and then waived by the Cowboys

A ticket from the very first Seahawk game ever. I wonder if the Pizza Haven coupon on the back is still valid?

two days before the start of the 1975 season, immediately brings exhilaration to over 60,000 brand-new Seahawk fans inside the Dome. His first pass is a 48-yard completion to Sam McCullum, a Northwesterner who went to high school in Kalispell, Montana, and college at Montana State University. Zorn then throws two more completions in a row to McCullum, the second one going for 12 yards and the first touchdown in team history. In the fourth quarter, Zorn hurls another touchdown pass and runs for a third score to bring Seattle back within seven points. The Hawks actually have a chance to tie the game in the waning seconds after recovering a fumble at the San Francisco 15-yard line. On the game's final play, Zorn doesn't see anyone open, so he takes off upfield from the 15. He makes it all the way to the 2 before being tackled just as the gun goes off. The Seahawks lose, 27-20, but they have found their starting quarterback and the face of a franchise that is soon known for aerial assaults, scrambling quarterback runs, and trick plays.

The Seahawks spent the first season in the National Football Conference before moving to the AFC Western Division the following year (where they remained until 2002). When the Seahawks came into the league, my father thought it was important to have season tickets to support the team. During the premiere season of 1976, he promised to take me to one game, a contest against the Atlanta Falcons. I then attended every home game with my dad from 1977 through 1979. I made an agreement with my two brothers: they got to go to the

Husky football games at the UW with the old man, while I had the Hawk games at the Kingdome. I think I got the better end of the deal, especially since there were more Seahawk games than Husky games. Even though my pop was more of a Husky fan than a Hawk fan, he nevertheless always made the trek from Bellevue to the Kingdome. When I went off to college in the early '80s, my younger brother, Milton, wasn't interested in going to every Hawk game, so my father got rid of his season tickets. I'm still mad at Milt.

THREE TRUE BUT BASICALLY IRRELEVANT FACTS ABOUT THE SEAHAWKS:

1. They have never tied a game, not even in preseason.
2. They are the only team to jump between conferences twice.
3. They are the only team to win division championships in both conferences.

GREAT SEAHAWK WINS: PART ONE

Obviously, there are no bad wins. Sure, there are the less-than-satisfying victories in which you struggle to beat an inferior team. There are also triumphs dampened by a serious injury. But a victory always makes the week go better. I absorb all coverage of a triumph, sometimes watching as many as five different sports reports on Sunday night. I also tend to read countless stories about the game either in print or on the Web, including the columnists from the opposing city's newspapers. I'm just a happier person following a win.

Often, producing television involves dealing with on-air talent. If a certain star I'm working with on a show is being a pain, I am less inclined to throttle them following a win. The blowouts are always fun, because the whole game is enjoyable and relatively stress-free. However, it's the comebacks and squeakers that make you feel more alive as the last second ticks off the clock. Road victories when the Hawks are huge underdogs are also extraordinarily satisfying. While the team has had a number of key wins, there are a few I think really stand out. Some are mentioned in depth elsewhere, but most are in the chapters I've ingeniously titled "Great Seahawk Wins." For your shopping convenience, I've listed them in chronological order.

SEAHAWKS 30, FALCONS 13
The Kingdome, November 7, 1976

It is the first Sunday of November during the bicentennial year of 1976. America has just voted in a peanut farmer named Jimmy Carter as president, while the state of Washington elects its first female governor, a scientist with the unlikely name of Dixy Lee Ray. I'm a teen venturing inside a brand-new sports palace known as the Kingdome, for my very first Seahawk (and NFL) game.

The seemingly always-injured Atlanta quarterback, Steve Bartkowski, is, once again, injured. That leaves backup quarterback Scott Hunter to start the game for the Falcons. Meanwhile, the Seahawks have no such problem, as their first-string quarterback, Jim Zorn, is healthy and at the controls. With touchdown passes to Sherman Smith and John McMakin, Zorn is clearly in control as the Hawks jump to a 14-3 halftime lead.

TIME-OUT Watching the excitement of 60,000 fans inside the Dome reminds me of going to my first Washington Husky game. It was opening day of the 1970 season at Husky Stadium as UW took on Michigan State University. The Huskies had a Native American sophomore quarterback named Sonny Sixkiller making his debut. The Dawgs and Sixkiller deep-sixed the Spartans 42-16. The sight of 50,000 Husky fans cheering was quite a rush for an 8-year-old. *Now back to the game.*

Early in the second half, Falcon Roland Lawrence tries to return a punt by running across the field inside his own 5-yard line. This is what coaches technically refer to as a "boneheaded decision." Dave Brown grabs Lawrence at the 2 and throws him into the end zone for the first safety in Seahawk history. A little later in the quarter, defensive back Al Matthews (celebrating his 29th birthday) steals a Hunter pass and takes it back 40 yards for the first-ever interception returned for a touchdown by a Seahawk.

Quarterback Hunter is then replaced by some guy named Kim McQuilken. (How's that for an unlikely name for an NFL player? To me, it sounds more like a woman playing a chimp in *Beneath the Planet of the Apes*. Actually, if you combine the names of the Falcon quarterbacks that day, you get actress Kim Hunter, who did play female chimp Zira in the *Planet of the Apes* movies.) The Kingdome goes nuts on another Hawk possession as Smith takes a handoff at the Seattle 47 and makes a few great cuts to avoid a number of Falcons. He is almost tackled at the Atlanta 20 but does an incredible 360-degree spin to shake off the defender, darting in for a 53-yard touchdown and a 30-6 lead. The Falcons score late in the fourth quarter when McQuilken throws a touchdown pass to Dr. Zaius.

Unlike their expansion brothers in Tampa, the Seahawks are able to give their fans the experience of a home win that inaugural season. In addition to it being the first regular-season win in the Kingdome, there were many other firsts in my first Seahawk game. It was the first time the team scored 30 points. It was Seattle's first win ever against an established team. And Sherman Smith became the first Seahawk running back to hit the century mark, rushing for 124 yards.

I think it's fate that my first live Seahawk game was a win. Who knows if I would've felt such limitless devotion for the Hawks if my first game had happened two weeks earlier, when Jim Zorn threw six interceptions and Seattle was killed 41-14 by a mediocre Detroit team? Or two weeks after the Atlanta game, when the lowly Saints came to town and won by 24? I like fate.

SEAHAWKS 56, BILLS 17
The Kingdome, October 30, 1977

The second-year Hawks are 1-5 after facing a brutal early schedule and going without Zorn, who missed the previous four games due to a knee injury. However, the Bills are also 1-5, and Zorn is healthy again. The Kingdome is psyched because there is a good chance for a Seahawk victory. The crowd also wants to get a glimpse of the single-biggest NFL star of the 1970s: O. J. Simpson. The Juice is in the twilight of his career, and this is our second (he'd played in the Pro Bowl the previous January)—and likely our last—chance to see him in the Kingdome.

The Seahawks score quickly and often in the first half. A Zorn to Largent touchdown reception is followed by a Zorn touchdown pass to Duke Ferguson. Then Zorn and Largent hook up again. Fans couldn't leave their seats for fear of missing a touchdown. Bills quarterback Joe Ferguson graciously throws interceptions, and the Hawks are more than willing to turn them into points. 21-3, 28-3, 35-3. It was becoming an old Atari Pong video game with the losing side's paddle frozen. The Seahawks walk to their locker room at halftime, leading 42-3 with the twelfth man in a frenzy, gorging on the football feast the team has provided.

In the second half the Hawks are in the unfamiliar position of killing the clock, as they are on the good side of a blowout. When fullback David Sims runs 17 yards through a nonexistent Buffalo defense, the scoreboard reads 49-3 Seattle. (The 46-point-plus differential still stands as the largest ever at any point of a Seahawk game.) The teams trade scores, and later Buffalo adds a finger bandage to the hemorrhaging wound when they score a second touchdown to make the final tally 56-17.

The Seahawks serve notice to the rest of the NFL that their offensive arsenal must not be taken lightly, establishing 15 team records that afternoon. Some of those records, including most points scored and most touchdowns in a game, have yet to be broken. The 56 points and 559 total yards are also the most by an NFL team during the 1977 season. Not bad for a franchise playing only its 21st game ever. (Equally impressive is that the second-year Hawks led the NFL in touchdown passes in 1977.)

What happened to Buffalo's fading superstar in the game? The defense limited O. J. Simpson to only 32 yards. The Juice did not play during the second half, due to injury and the fact that his team was getting blown out. I vividly remember seeing him through my binoculars sitting on the bench all by himself—I believe he was wearing a beard—looking down at the Kingdome sideline turf. It turned out to be O. J.'s last game played as a Buffalo Bill.

TIME-OUT Seventeen years after this game, Simpson became one of E! Entertainment Television's biggest stars, thanks to its highly rated coverage of his murder trial. One of the case's most memorable characters, Kato Kaelin, did a guest spot on E!'s *Talk Soup*, the comedy program that showed highlights of talk shows, where I worked as a writer and producer. When Kaelin took the stand during the trial, prosecutor Marcia Clark asked him about his *Talk Soup* appearance. We often replayed and goofed on this exchange, thus becoming possibly the first time a television program was mentioned during a murder trial and then used for comedic effect on said show. I don't know if I should be proud or ashamed. OK, I'm proud.

DREADFUL DEFEATS: PART ONE

Every Seahawk defeat hurts. Sometimes I can almost be ambivalent about a loss during seasons when all hope is lost, or when we lose on the road against a vastly superior team. But a particularly bad loss can affect your whole week. It wrecks your appetite. Your mood. Sometimes you go to the beach with your dogs and try to forget about the game. But often you can't forget. You stew over a loss. You think of every possible "what if?" scenario. *What if Darrell Jackson had held on to the ball? What if Terry Taylor hadn't slipped on the play?*

Blowout losses can be very embarrassing, but they are often less painful than close ones. You would think that if your team played hard and came up short, you wouldn't be as hurt as if they had just got stomped. But that's not the case. A good example is to compare the Hawks' back-to-back home losses during the 2004 season. Which game hurt more, the 38-9 beating by the Bills or the 43-39 loss on *Monday Night Football* to the Cowboys? Most Hawk fans would say the Dallas game. The close losses are usually worse. They allow you to think you had some control over the situation. If only you had sat in a different chair or wore a different shirt, the outcome would've been more favorable. It's ridiculous, but sports fandom rarely operates logically.

However, all types of losses can haunt you. At work. Driving in the car. Waking up that horrible Monday morning. It's a hangover staring at you in the sports pages. Sometimes I completely avoid TV, newspaper, and Web coverage of the game. I just don't want to be reminded of the loss. I'll admit I can sometimes be a miserable jerk after a defeat, and I should take the game less seriously. But what would be the fun in that?

In the early years there were big losses, scorewise, but those were to be expected. You can include the 1976 contest versus the Saints when we were routed 51-27. In 1980 the Cowboys pretty much pulled their own Wounded Knee on Thanksgiving against the Seahawks, 51-7 (still our worst blowout loss ever). But that was against a lousy Hawk team in the middle of a nine-game losing streak. The worst losses have been during seasons when the Hawks were competitive. Losses that affected our playoff position or effectively killed our chances at making the postseason. Or when we stunk so badly, it was historic. I have not included the excruciating losses at Kansas City's Arrowhead Stadium here, for those games are worthy of a chapter of their own (see "Arrowhead: House of 1000 Mistakes," page 174).

Why write about horrible losses? Because being a fan is not all about the good times when victory makes life better. Dealing with defeat helps mold you as a fan. If you didn't experience the bitter taste of losing, then you wouldn't have any humility. You wouldn't have a heart. You'd be a New York Yankees fan.

BRONCOS 37, SEAHAWKS 34
Mile High Stadium, September 23, 1979

It was either a Filipino philosopher or a Wisconsin water boy who once said, "A loss in September can keep you from the postseason in January." That phrase was never truer than when the Seahawks walked out of Mile High Stadium in this early-autumn contest.

The Hawks play well for a majority of the game. They have 10-0 lead after the first quarter. The halftime score is 20-10, Seahawks. When Sherman Smith scores in the third quarter, Seattle is up 34-10. But Denver's Craig Morton comes in to replace the legendary Norris Weese at quarterback and throws three touchdown passes in the period. The Broncos score the winning touchdown in the fourth quarter to complete the monumental Seahawk collapse.

The blown 24-point lead is still the largest in team history. But it is the ramifications of the loss that make it so painful. Denver finishes the season 10-6 and qualifies for the playoffs as a wild card team. The Hawks complete the season one game behind the Broncos and out of the postseason. This leaves the team with plenty of time to listen to Filipino philosophers.

RAMS 24, SEAHAWKS 0
The Kingdome, November 4, 1979

It's not often you are eyewitness to history, but sometimes it means witnessing something horrifying like the *Hindenburg* exploding, or in my case, the worst offensive display in the history of the NFL. Coming off a great win in their first appearance on *Monday Night Football* in Atlanta, the Hawks return home to drop a game in epic fashion against Los Angeles. The Seahawks have exactly one first down for the entire game. Yep, one. It is on a passing play from Jim Zorn to Steve Largent.

Seattle's zero rushing first downs ties an NFL record. We have the ball for exactly 14:28 of the entire game. Zorn completes exactly two passes. The Hawks gain a negative-30 yards in the air (due to sacks) and only 23 on the ground, to give the team a grand total of *negative-7* total yards, which is still an NFL record. Good Lord, the team would've had more total yards if it had just forfeited the game before kickoff.

I don't think anyone thought it was possible for a team that finished *fourth* in the league in scoring that year to be so putrid in a game. The Hawks had been averaging 350 total yards per game before this anemic display. It really is inexplicable. I remember the Kingdome faithful being more in a state of disgusted shock than all-out anger. I kept expecting the Seahawks to move the ball, but that was as futile as Linus waiting for the Great Pumpkin in the old Peanuts Halloween special.

TIME-OUT A few years ago I ran into former Ram defensive lineman Fred Dryer at a store that sells packing materials and boxes. Dryer is one of the few retired NFL players to have a successful dramatic career on television, as he was the star of the NBC show *Hunter*. However, I didn't want to talk to him about being a celebrity in two different fields. Nope, I wanted to ask him if he remembered playing in that blowout nightmare in 1979, to which he replied, "Oh yeah, we held them to negative yardage. It was fun." But he really didn't want to talk to me about the game. He wanted to talk boxes. He probably thought I worked there. He asked me what would be the best box in which to ship a bunch of football equipment. To me boxes are boxes, so I just pointed to the biggest one. As he sucked his teeth in annoyance and scouted the store for a real employee, I asked how it was playing for (former Ram coach) Chuck Knox. He said Chuck was a good guy and a great coach. Then, much to his relief, I left the store.

REQUIRED SEAHAWK HISTORY

Here's all the info old Seahawk fans may recall and every new member of the twelfth man needs to know. Key plays. Key seasons. Key players. Practically every key on the chain. Don't be scared by the academically imposing title of this section. There won't be a test after reading these chapters . . . or will there?

25 FORMER SEAHAWKS YOU SHOULD KNOW

I could actually make this list twice as long, but I am being limited by The Man! Who is The Man? I don't know. I suspect he lives in a townhome in Burien. For easy reading, I am using the innovative alphabetical-order method and including the years each man played for Seattle in parentheses.

Shaun Alexander (2000–07)

I'm sure everyone reading this book knows about Alexander. After all, he was the league MVP in 2005 and holds many team rushing records, including career yardage. But here's an amazing Shaun stat: he has more career rushing touchdowns in team history than the next two top players (Curt Warner and Chris Warren) *combined.*

Brian Blades (1988–98)

The second all-time leading receiver in team history. Took over the Largent mantle and became the team's main receiver in the early- to mid-1990s. He went over the thousand yard receiving mark four times in his career.

Dave Brown (1976–86)

Called "The Original Seahawk" because he lasted longer than any other player from the expansion draft. The cornerback is near or at the top of many franchise records, including most career interceptions. Only six players in the history of the NFL have intercepted more passes than Brown.

Keith Butler (1978–87)

An underrated linebacker who started most of the games during his decade with the Hawks. Still ranks second in tackles in the team record book. Technically the first Seahawk to appear on the cover of *Sports Illustrated*. I say "technically" because the cover really featured Marcus Allen. Butler was the guy trying to tackle him. I doubt he feels very honored about the appearance.

Dan Doornink (1979–85)

Nicknamed "Dr. Dan" because he earned his medical degree during the off-seasons while with the Hawks. Doornink was a solid performer with Seattle and is mostly remembered for his many clutch catch-and-runs out of the backfield. He once got into a scuffle with Steeler linebacker Jack Lambert, one of the meanest guys to ever play. But Doornink, possibly the smartest Seahawk ever, wisely walked away before Lambert yanked off his head and deprived Yakima County of a fine doctor.

Kenny Easley (1981–87)

One of the NFL's premier safeties in the 1980s. That's not just my opinion: he was named to the NFL's All-Decade team. Wide receivers would twitch in fear going across the middle whenever No. 45 was around. Easley was vicious but not dirty. There is a difference.

Chris Gray (1998–2007)

This right guard was part of the best offensive line in team history in 2005. Gray also started in a team-record 121 consecutive games. Think about it. That's nearly eight full seasons. Nearly eight years of constantly blocking oncoming defensive traffic that wants to kill your quarterback.

Jacob Green (1980–91)

He was Seattle's first great defensive lineman. During his career, only Lawrence Taylor and Reggie White had more sacks than Green. Unfortunately, Green was often overlooked in the Pro Bowl balloting. However, he is not overlooked by the twelfth man, who can always see Green's name on the Ring of Honor at Qwest Field.

Norm Johnson (1982–90)

The Hawks' longest-tenured kicker scored more points than any other player in team history. In 1986 Johnson tied an NFL record when he booted five field goals of 50 or more yards. He actually made more from that distance than he did from 40 to 49 yards. A fluky feat that most likely will never happen again in the NFL.

Cortez Kennedy (1990–2000)

The defensive tackle was the only Seahawk named to the NFL All-Decade team of the 1990s. Opposing quarterbacks were scared when Kennedy lined up against them. Little kids were scared when Kennedy dressed up as "Tez Rex" for Coca-Cola's Monsters of the Gridiron series of sports cards.

Dave Krieg (1980–91)

Currently holds most major Seahawk passing records (although it is only a matter of time before Matt Hasselbeck surpasses them). Beloved but also jeered during his time in Seattle. He has since become much more beloved due to all the duds who tried to replace him in the early '90s. Nicknamed "Mudbone"— I guess because he liked to eat bones covered in mud?

Steve Largent (1976–89)

Who? Only the guy who owned every major career receiving NFL record when he retired. I would like to thank all the coaches and scouts who thought Largent, coming out of the University of Tulsa, was too slow for the NFL. It was their "expertise" that led him to Seattle, where he became a Pro Football Hall of Famer.

Bryan Millard (1984–91)

Widely considered the team's best-ever offensive lineman until Walter Jones came along. He was also quite the character. I remember him once describing blocking out a certain defensive player as "trying to shave a bobcat in a telephone booth." Millard probably wouldn't use that expression today, primarily because phone booths are going extinct, like NBA fans in Seattle.

Joe Nash (1982–96)

No one has played in more Seahawk games (218) than defensive tackle Nash. He once blocked three field goals in a single season, a franchise mark that will be held by Nash until 8-foot robots are allowed to play on special teams.

Steve Raible (1976–81)

There are some Seattleites who only know Raible as the "KIRO-TV news anchor guy." However, first as a receiver and then as a team broadcaster, he has been affiliated with the Seahawks for their entire history.

Eugene Robinson (1985–95)

This safety is the all-time leading tackler in Seahawk history and once led the league in interceptions. Younger readers not familiar with Robinson should check out some of the old NFL Films footage of him. You will understand why he was the heart and soul of the Seattle defense for many years.

Michael Sinclair (1991–2001)

Like Cortez Kennedy, Sinclair was a great defensive lineman who unfortunately never tasted playoff victory in Seattle. In the mid-1990s he was one of the most dominant defensive ends in the NFL. In fact, he led the league in sacks in 1998. His total of 16.5 sacks that year is still a team record.

Sherman Smith (1976–82)

Seattle's first primary running back. He rushed for 805 yards in 1978 despite missing four-and-a-half games due to injury. Had Smith stayed healthy, he most likely would have been the team's first 1,000-yard running back that year. He recently reunited with Jim Zorn on the Redskins' coaching staff.

Mack Strong (1994–2007)

A classic overachiever. Strong was an undrafted free agent when he came to Seattle. The fullback is the only player to endure the horrible Tom Flores era and play in the team's Super Bowl season of 2005. He is also one of only three Seahawks to appear in 200 games. Unquestionably, he has the best football name ever.

Robbie Tobeck (2000–06)

It was a tough call to determine which center I should include on this list: Tobeck or Blair Bush. Both were quality veterans who came to Seattle and really helped steer the offensive line. And both played their college ball in Washington: Bush at UW, Tobeck at Washington State University. In the end, I gave the nod to Tobeck because he played in 10 more games and made the Pro Bowl in 2005, the only center in team history to accomplish that feat. (I know I'm going to hear it from my family for picking a Cougar over a Husky.)

Curt Warner (1983–89)

When I think of Curt Warner, I think of this great running back and not the quarterback who spells his name with a *K*. Only the strike of 1987 kept Warner from rushing for over 1,000 yards in five out of the six healthy seasons he played in Seattle. He now has a Chevrolet dealership in Vancouver, Washington. I wonder if he will ever mimic Seattle-area Chevy dealer Dick Balch, who used to smash cars with a sledgehammer in his TV commercials.

Chris Warren (1990–97)

A superb running back who unfortunately played during the lowest point in team history. Once held the team record for career rushing yards. His best year was 1994, when he led the AFC in rushing and was a first-team All-NFL selection.

John L. Williams (1986–93)

The fullback is the only Seahawk in the team's top five in both career rushing yards and career receptions. One of the most solid players to wear a Seattle uniform. Real Hawk fans refer to him as "John L." and never just as "John."

Fredd Young (1984–87)

Young began as a special teams monster. He blocked a punt and forced a fumble in his very first NFL game. He soon became a premier linebacker and went to the Pro Bowl all four years he played in Seattle.

Jim Zorn (1976–84)

A generation of Seahawk fans grew up thinking that a left-handed quarterback wasn't unusual. That a quarterback could scramble with ease. That a quarterback was always the holder who could fake a field goal and throw for a first down or touchdown. Zorn fooled us all.

1983: FROM POTENTIAL TO POSTSEASON

There are landmark seasons in Seattle sports history that bury years of disappointment and launch a team into the stratosphere of postseason glory. For the SuperSonics it was the 1977–78 season, when they went from a 5-17 start to seven points away from winning the NBA championship. For the Mariners it was 1995 and a comeback that brought them to within two games of the World Series. For the Seahawks it was 1983, when they were one game away from the Super Bowl.

The start of the '80s was a dismal time for the Seahawks. After winning seasons in 1978 and '79, the team went into the tank in 1980, losing their last nine games to finish 4-12. The next year was only slightly better, with the Hawks going 6-10. The pain of these two years was softened slightly for me by my newfound freedom in the dorms at Western Washington University. But I was still angry about the Hawks' tailspin. A part of me blamed myself for not being at the games to lend my "mojo" to the team.

The 1982 season also started badly. The Sam McCullum debacle during training camp, in which head coach Jack Patera and general manager John Thompson essentially fired Sam for his union activities, was an embarrassment to the team.

Patera also tried to reverse the team's recent fortunes by naming Dave Krieg as the starting quarterback at the beginning of the year. Krieg didn't last long, as a thumb injury sidelined him during the second game. Then a players' strike sidelined the entire team for seven games. During the strike both Patera and Thompson were fired, and director of football operations Mike McCormack was named interim head coach. McCormack reinstalled Jim Zorn as the starter, and the players responded well to the new coach as the team went 4-3 after the season resumed. However, a franchise-record-low crowd of 43,145 saw the final game of 1982 at the Kingdome. Clearly, something needed to be done to bring back respect and capacity crowds.

The day after the Hawks' last game, McCormack is promoted to team president and general manager. On January 26, 1983, the Seahawks name Chuck Knox as their new head coach. At Knox's initial press conference, the podium background is a hideous green curtain with an attached cardboard cutout of the Seahawks helmet (a far cry from the slick backgrounds of today's press conferences). Right after he introduces Knox, McCormack accidentally bumps into the helmet, causing it to move like some junior high drama department prop. But somehow this low-tech setup seems appropriate, because Knox is a rather old-school guy himself, with a propensity to use clichéd expressions that the press soon dubs "Knoxisms."

Three months later, the Seahawks trade their first-, second-, and third-round picks to Houston for the third overall choice in the draft, whereby they select Penn State running back Curt Warner. It is the first time the Hawks trade three picks for one, and some wonder if the team has given up too much for Warner. Training camp brings a new group of heady veterans, including Reggie McKenzie, Charle Young, Cullen Bryant, Harold Jackson, and former Husky All-American Blair

Head coach Chuck Knox. He introduced Seattle to the playoffs and his familiar "Knoxisms."

Bush. The Hawks need their leadership as they face the league's toughest schedule. Adding to the team makeover are changes to the Seattle uniform, the most significant being the Seahawk bird logo added to the sleeves.

On opening day at Kansas City, Warner introduces himself to the NFL as he races 60 yards on his very first play. Unfortunately, the team cannot sustain this momentum and loses at Arrowhead Stadium. The Hawks rebound in their second game, against the Jets in New York, where the temperature is a sweltering 95 degrees. The Seahawk offense, led by Warner, gains almost three times as much on the ground as they do from the air. Football wags coin this new offense "Ground Chuck."

The first half of the season is rather inconsistent, with the team going 4-4. Knox becomes increasingly frustrated with longtime starter Zorn. At San Diego, Zorn throws an interception that is returned for the game-winning score; to use a baseball analogy, it is strike one. The next week the Hawks beat the Raiders in the Dome, despite Zorn going 4 of 16 for 13 yards. Strike two. The following game against Pittsburgh, Zorn starts 1 of 8 for 2 yards with one interception. Strike three. He is pulled from the game, and Krieg, a fourth-year undrafted quarterback from now-defunct Milton College, steps up under center. Krieg throws for over 200 yards and two touchdowns and makes a game out of what had been a Steeler blowout.

TIME-OUT Coach Chuck's Knoxisms were so memorable that the team issued a special book of them when Knox was inducted into the Ring of Honor in 2005. Among my favorite Knoxisms are "If a hair on my head knew what I was thinking, I'd pluck it out," "Don't tell me how rough the water is, just bring the ship in," and "Never overload your butt with your mouth." *Now back to 1983.*

Krieg's first start is against the Raiders in Los Angeles. The Raiders terrorize Krieg early, sacking him three times. But he hangs on to lead the Hawks to triumph. Ironically, Zorn is one of the stars of the game when he completes a touchdown pass off a fake field goal.

With the win against the Raiders, the Hawks stand at 5-4. Fans are thinking playoffs, and I am sending my mojo in large batches from Bellingham. The Seahawks return to the Dome and beat the Broncos as Warner breaks Sherman Smith's single-season team rushing record while Krieg continues to impress. Playoff talk builds throughout Puget Sound. Two weeks later in Denver, Krieg becomes the first Hawk quarterback to pass for over 400 yards in a game when he slings for 418 and three touchdowns. But there's also the first real glimpse of the tragic Krieg, as he also throws four interceptions in the loss. The twelfth man continues to talk about the postseason, just not out loud. Meanwhile, I frantically search for more mojo.

In previous years the breaks needed to get to the next level seemed to escape Seattle. Help from other teams didn't materialize, and Lady Luck never landed a wet kiss on the Seahawks' beak. But it is different in 1983. Week 15 is the most significant example of getting the right breaks. The Seahawks come into the week at 7-7 but are behind Buffalo, Cleveland, and Denver, all at 8-6, in the fight for the two wild card playoff berths. Denver beats the Baltimore Colts at home, but the Browns and Bills both lose. The Brown loss is especially fortuitous, as they stumble against the worst team in the league, the Oilers, who score one of only two wins for the season.

At the same time the Bills and Browns are losing, the Seahawks are at Giants Stadium, clinging to a 17-12 lead as New York stages a late fourth-quarter comeback. With only 0:31 remaining, the Giants appear to score a miraculous game-winning touchdown, sending the stadium crowd into mass euphoria. But the aforementioned Lady Luck smooches the Hawks as a Giant lineman is flagged for holding. The euphoria inside the stadium is quickly replaced by something uncommon for New Yorkers: mass silence. Thank you, mojo. And thank you, Lady Luck. You are one sexy dame.

The following week the Hawks host New England in the regular-season finale. It's the 117th regular-season game in the history of the Seahawk franchise, and none of the previous

116 can rival it for importance. Seattle has control of their destiny. Win, and they're in the playoffs for the first time ever. The Hawks respond by putting on one of their best performances of the year. The defense allows only a single touchdown, and the offense, behind the mighty trio of Krieg, Warner, and Largent, scores in every quarter. The Seahawks dispatch the Patriots 24-6. After going to the locker room, many players return to the Kingdome field for a curtain call in front of the twelfth man, a glorious moment that I and all other Hawk fans have been waiting for since 1976.

It's interesting that the team makes it into the postseason dance with a 9-7 record. The Hawks had gone 9-7 twice before but failed to enter the playoffs. As a bonus, the Seahawks have home-field advantage for the wild card round against the Broncos; because they were blown out at Kansas City in the final week of the regular season, Denver won't play at Mile High Stadium. This is huge, because the temperature in Denver is zero degrees with a wind chill factor of minus 22, while within the Kingdome it's the usual 72 degrees for this Christmas Eve contest.

The din inside the Kingdome is monstrous when the Hawks strut onto the field. It's a party atmosphere as concessionaire/cheerleader Bill "the Beerman" Scott, decked in a white tux, leads the Seahawk faithful in the Wave while holding up blue placards. In their ever first playoff game the Hawks look like a team that has lived in the postseason, winning by a score of 31-7. Krieg throws an almost perfect game, going 12 of 13 for 200 yards and three touchdowns. The city of Seattle receives a very nice Christmas present, as it tastes NFL playoff victory on its very first attempt. The Beerman toasts victory with a celebratory King Cup. I toast to my Seahawk mojo.

The following week the team shocks the world by beating the defending conference champion Miami Dolphins (see "Great Seahawk Wins: Part Three," page 81). Unbelievably, the team is now one win from going to the Super Bowl. In the AFC Championship game against the Raiders in Los Angeles, the greatest season in the team's eight-year history sadly ends with a gigantic thud. Warner is stopped cold, and Krieg has the worst game of his career. In a weird twist that recalls an opposite move earlier in the season, Knox replaces Krieg with Zorn in the second half. Zorn has two picks, but he also throws two touchdown passes to make the final score a slightly more respectable 30-14. Those are Zorn's last two touchdown passes in a Seahawk uniform.

Like the 1995 Mariners, who brought baseball back from the bitterness of the 1994 players' strike, the 1983 Seahawks reinstate a sense of fan pride that had been missing in the three previous years, which had been ravaged by poor play and labor strife. The team finishes the season leading the AFC in take-aways, with a nice balance of 26 interceptions and 28 fumble recoveries. The Hawks also become only the second team in NFL history to lead the league in both punt and kickoff coverage in the same season. Curt Warner proves he is worth three draft picks by becoming only the second rookie to lead the AFC in rushing and is named AFC Offensive Player of the Year by many publications. Chuck Knox is tabbed coach of the year by a number of organizations as well. Easley and Warner become the first Seahawks ever to start in the Pro Bowl. The 1983 Seahawks brought national prominence to pro football in the Northwest and set in motion a winning tradition throughout the '80s.

A FLUKY SEAHAWK HISTORICAL NOTE

Despite playing in only 20 games in 1981 and '82, defensive tackle Mike White holds the team record for most career blocked extra points (three) and is third in blocked field goals (two).

THE MATURATION OF MR. HASSELBECK

In March 2001 the Seahawks trade their first-round pick (at No. 10 position) and a third-round choice for Green Bay's first-round pick (No. 17 position) and Packer backup quarterback Matt Hasselbeck. Coach Mike Holmgren is familiar with Hasselbeck from his Green Bay days, when he drafted the Boston College quarterback in the sixth round. Having lost faith in Jon Kitna, Holmgren tabs Hasselbeck as the quarterback for the present and future of the Hawks. I, along with many other members of the twelfth man, am skeptical. The quarterback position has been a revolving door ever since Dave Krieg left a decade earlier. No less than nine different players started as the team's signal caller during this time, and none had any real sustainable success. Compare this to the first 15 years of the franchise, when Krieg and Jim Zorn were the only real starting quarterbacks.

Hasselbeck struggles mightily in his first year in Seattle. He does not throw a touchdown pass in his first three games and suffers a groin injury that forces him to miss two starts. In his place, veteran Trent Dilfer leads the Seahawks to consecutive victories over the Jaguars and Broncos. When Hasselbeck

Matt Hasselbeck, Seattle's most beloved bald guy since Jay Buhner.

returns from the disabled list, his play does not improve. Seattle loses to Miami and at Washington (where Matt is benched). However, Holmgren retains his faith in the young quarterback by keeping him as the starter. Hasselbeck continues to toil in his first season. Mistakes mount, and calls grow at Husky Stadium for Holmgren to put in Dilfer. These fans get their wish when a shoulder injury ends Matt's season in the 14th game of the year. Dilfer again leads the Seahawks to two wins to close out 2001.

The following season Dilfer is named the starter in camp but suffers a sprained knee in the first preseason game. This leaves Hasselbeck to play with the first string for the remainder of camp and start opening day of the regular season at Oakland. Although he plays respectably, the Raiders kill the Hawks. Dilfer returns as the starter the following week and remains in that position until he tears his Achilles tendon against the Cowboys in week seven. Hass enters the game and helps the Seahawks to a victory in Dallas.

With Dilfer gone for the season, Hasselbeck now has a chance to demonstrate he is the man to lead the Seahawks. It starts horribly in an 11-point home loss to the Redskins. Although Hasselbeck doesn't throw an interception, he has two fumbles and is sacked twice on the fourth down when the Hawks have the ball inside the red zone. But soon he is fully grasping Holmgren's West Coast offense. He twice breaks the Seahawk team record for single-game passing yardage within a month. The first time is in a loss to the 49ers when Matt throws for 427 yards, eclipsing Krieg's 19-year-old record.

The offensive fireworks in San Francisco are only the preliminaries compared to the final game of the year at San Diego. The Seahawks come into the Charger contest riding a two-game winning streak, including a solid 30-10 victory against the Rams the previous week. A win in San Diego would give the team a final record of 7-9, which looks a lot better than the dreaded double-digit-loss tally of a 6-10 mark. It would also send every twelfth man into the off-season on a high note, removing some of the sting of what had been a disappointing first year of the new Seahawk era (new conference, new uniforms, new stadium).

During the first three quarters, Hasselbeck throws for nearly 250 yards, but the Seahawks can only manage a single touchdown, thanks to an interception and fumble in the red zone. Early in the fourth quarter, the Hawks cut the lead, but the Chargers answer with their own touchdown to make the score 28-14 with only 8:37 remaining. Yet Hasselbeck and Holmgren know a comeback is very possible, thanks to the porous Lightning Bolt defense. One touchdown drive comes rather quickly as Hass punctures the Chargers secondary as if he is an over-anxious voter in a polling booth.

The next Seahawk drive is not so easy. They are 88 yards away from tying the game and have only 3:30 to do it. On one play, Hasselbeck hurts his nonthrowing arm when an unfriendly Charger slams him to the ground. Another setback occurs when running back Shaun Alexander is bent like one of those old Gumby dolls by a San Diego defender. This forces Alexander to the sideline for the rest of the game.

Undeterred, Hasselbeck picks up first downs via his arms and feet when he scrambles on fourth down. After a couple of clutch passes, Matt has the Hawks at the San Diego 1-yard line but with only 0:05 to play. The Bolts are expecting a pass, especially since the Seahawks line up five receivers and an empty backfield. But Holmgren brilliantly calls a quarterback sneak, and Hasselbeck pushes himself into the end zone to tie the game. A hushed silence strangles the Qualcomm Stadium crowd. As Hass tries to get up from the end zone, a Charger restricts his balance, and he falls back down. When he finally gets up, he triumphantly raises the ball above his head.

Unfortunately for San Diego and its tired defense, the Seahawks win the coin toss in overtime. On the first play from scrimmage, Hasselbeck breaks his own team passing yardage record. The momentum is clearly with Seattle as they quickly move into San Diego territory. The Chargers try everything to thwart the drive, including safety Rodney Harrison taking a late shot at Hasselbeck that is wrongly not flagged. (If you Google "NFL's dirtiest players," Harrison is one of the first names to pop up. According to an interview with the *Seattle Times* dated September 4, 2003, Hasselbeck said he told Harrison, "My mom hits harder than that.")

The Seahawks are in long field goal range when Hasselbeck flings a pass that is intercepted at the San Diego 20. I'm sickened but not entirely surprised. It's the type of mistake that has doomed the Seahawks a number of times under Hass' helm. He walks back to the Seattle sideline, not relishing the earful he will receive from Holmgren's vocal cords.

The Seahawk defense, which had been much maligned all season, forces a quick series from the Lightning Bolts. This provides Hasselbeck with a chance at redemption. Facing a third and long near midfield, Hass drops back to pass but sees an open field in front of him, so he takes off, scurrying all the way to the Charger 33 before being popped again by Harrison. Matt immediately gets up and tosses the ball to an official as he gets a different sort of earful from Harrison's vocal cords.

After a few Mack Strong running plays, Rian Lindell knocks through the game-winning field goal to send a disappointed Qualcomm crowd into the darkness of Mission Valley. Never has a 7-9 record felt so good.

The game is one to start Seahawk historians pounding the calculators. The Hawks set team records for total yardage (591) and plays run (90) in a single game. This contest was even more beneficial for Hasselbeck: he established team records for passing yardage (449) and completions (36) that helped him reach performance clauses earning him millions of dollars.

However, this game meant much more than numbers and money to Hasselbeck. It was the intangibles that demonstrated to his teammates and fans that he could lead them to a comeback win, even in the absence of their star running back. While his arm contributed greatly, it was his feet that helped at the most crucial of times. He was also able to overcome an irresponsible interception that could've ruined the contest.

Over the course of two seasons, Matthew Hasselbeck had endured the boos of the twelfth man, the scowls of Mike Holmgren, and even the cheap shots of Rodney Harrison. He was able to take the momentum from the Charger game into the off-season and lock up the starter job on a more permanent basis. I and other members of the twelfth man were skeptical no more.

FAMILY BUSINESS

Hasselbeck and Tatupu have both scored against the Seahawks. Don Hasselbeck and Mosi Tatupu, that is. Don, father of Matt, caught touchdown passes for the Patriots against the Hawks in 1977 and 1980 (the game winner, actually). He also grabbed a touchdown versus the Hawks while he was with the Raiders in '83. Mosi, Lofa's dad, had a pair of touchdowns in '84 versus Seattle when he was a Patriot. Additionally, former Seahawk Shawn Springs' father, Ron, scored a touchdown as a Cowboy against the Hawks in 1980.

OUR KINGDOME: THE FUTURE IS OBSOLETE

The ceiling tiles fell. The aluminum urinal troughs had a nasty smell. The game results could be hell. I saw the Seahawks play before 64,000 and the Mariners in front of 4,000. I caught The Who and The Stones from the floor for big money and the world-champion SuperSonics from the 300 level for three bucks. I was fortunate to see my all-time favorite baseball player, Lee May, hit a home run in the place. I also saw a guy take a leak in a bathroom sink during a concert. All at the Kingdome, the Seahawks' home for nearly a quarter of a century.

I remember when the Kingdome was being constructed in the early 1970s. It started out as a cleared area south of downtown, but over time it started to grow like it was this magnificent creature that would bring us Major League Baseball and the NFL when it was born. When you drove into the city at night, there was the amazing sight of lighted roof beams slowly being laid into place. When you are a kid, patience is an uncommon virtue. However, the building of the Kingdome was especially agonizing, because it took nearly four years to complete. I wanted it done *now* so I wouldn't have to settle for watching Class A minor league baseball at Sicks' Seattle Stadium.

During the construction of the Kingdome, other changes were happening around Seattle. One of the most notable was the city becoming Hollywood North for the major movie studios. Before the '70s, it was very rare for a film to be shot in Seattle. But as the hammers were banging on the Dome site, film productions were banging out scenes on the streets of

Jet City. Among the movies shot in Seattle at this time were the bittersweet *Cinderella Liberty*, starring James Caan; *McQ*, an action movie with John "The Duke" Wayne; the political thriller *The Parallax View* (which included a memorable scene on top of the Space Needle); and the made-for-TV movie *The Night Strangler*, featuring one of my all-time favorite TV characters, Carl Kolchak, played by Darren McGavin. However, none of these movies used the creation of the Kingdome for dramatic effect. I thought The Duke should've at least plugged some hoodlum on one of the Dome's newly built ramps.

Disneyland used to have a "City of the Future" exhibit you would see while riding the PeopleMover in Tomorrowland. One of the focal points of this utopian metropolis was a domed stadium. To me, the Kingdome represented Seattle's entry into the future. Being a huge fan of Stanley Kubrick's *2001: A Space Odyssey* and other futurist fare, I envisioned flying cars arriving at the Kingdome in the 21st century. Too bad the stadium was obsolete by the time the new millennium arrived.

Baseball purists hated it. Opposing football teams feared it. Basketball players were befuddled by it. It opened with Billy Graham. It closed with Dan Marino. Its official name was the King County Domed Stadium, but it was really known as the Kingdome. We locals often just called it "the Dome." The Kingdome was one of those "cookie-cutter" multipurpose stadium designs but with a twist: it had the largest concrete roof on earth. This design made for awful concert acoustics but held an incredible advantage for the Seahawks: when the twelfth man was roaring, the decibel level would be similar to a jet taking off—in other words, loud. (*TV Guide* once ranked it the loudest sports stadium in the country.) In fact, there were times when you couldn't hear the person sitting next to you. This was troublesome for Seahawk opponents. Denver head coach Dan Reeves and others even had the novel idea of blaring crowd

The Kingdome's roof was perfect to squeeze the juice from a 400-ton orange.

noise over loudspeakers during practices for Seattle games. Reports that Raider owner Al Davis teamed up with Satan to construct (unsuccessfully) a giant mute button for the Kingdome crowd are unconfirmed.

During the Seahawks' early years you could see local radio personality Wayne Cody soliciting interviews from the Hawk faithful during his pregame show outside the stadium. Fans could also hear the trumpet stylings of Richard Peterson, a street musician who, in the 1970s, seemed to have the smallest repertoire ever: one song ("When the Saints Go Marching In"). Inside, the place echoed with the shouts of stadium vendors such as Rich the Peanut Guy and Bill the Beerman (who always encouraged adult fans to "give your tongue a sleigh ride" with some suds).

I used to think the roof looked a little like Gamera, the giant turtle of Japanese sci-fi movie fame, but upon further review, I concluded it bore only a passing resemblance. It's more accurate to say it looked like a giant hand juicer. During every Hawk home game, the Dome would be dressed with various homemade signs, plus more-professional (and uniform) banners from the many chapters of the Sea Hawkers booster club.

Pelé was the first of many sports superstars to appear inside the concrete cavern. Bo Jackson can lay credit to being the only player ever to both hit a home run and score a touchdown inside the Dome. Walter Payton played three times inside the place and threw two touchdown passes, yet never scored a touchdown himself. There were three NCAA Final Fours and two no-hitters (both by the Mariners) thrown in the Dome. It is the only stadium ever to host All-Star games for each of the big three: Major League Baseball, the NBA, and the NFL.

For pure sports history, few moments can rival what happened on April 10, 1989: 19-year-old Ken Griffey Jr. stepped into the batter's box in the Kingdome for the first time, returning the very first pitch he encountered into the left-field bleachers for home run number one in his soon-to-be Hall of Fame career. A decade later, Griffey hit the last home run ever inside the Kingdome.

The ol' beast weathered many an insult from visiting sportswriters, but its worst moment occurred during the summer of 1994, when ceiling tiles came falling down prior to a Mariner game. This forced the team to move 15 home games to opposing stadiums. Ironically, the M's were saved from playing the last two months on the road when the players' strike cancelled the season. The Dome closure also forced out the Seahawks, but they had Husky Stadium across town as an alternative. The following year, the stadium experienced arguably its finest moment when Edgar Martínez doubled home Griffey Jr. in the bottom of the 11th inning to beat the Yankees in an amazing playoff series. (I say "arguably" because this is a Seahawk book, after all.)

For nearly a quarter of a century, the Kingdome was as much a part of Seattle's cityscape as the Space Needle, Smith Tower, and Pike Place Market. But the economics of pro sports ultimately doomed the Dome: it was destroyed one day before its 24th birthday. ESPN Classic aired the Kingdome's implosion live. It partially felt like the network was airing a live execution. Dave Krieg, along with former Sonics Slick Watts and Jack Sikma, joined ESPN anchor Kenny Mayne for the Dome's final minutes. It was appropriate that local boy Mayne delivered the eulogy for a dying stadium. I have to admit I shed a tear as I watched a significant place in my life be reduced to chunks of concrete and dust in a matter of seconds.

The Kingdome had all the charm of a Days Inn room in Everett, but it was Shangri-la to Seattle sports fans. Without the Kingdome, there would be no Seahawks, no Mariners, no giant Marlboro Man on the scoreboard. Actually, there was no Marlboro Man once a law was passed that prohibited cigarette advertising on government buildings. The old cowboy was replaced by a giant McDonald's pennant. It looked ridiculous.

THE GREATEST PLAY THAT DIDN'T OFFICIALLY COUNT

SEAHAWKS 42, BRONCOS 14
The Kingdome, December 11, 1988

There was some bad blood between the Hawks and the Broncos in 1988. On opening day in Denver, Bronco defensive back Mike Harden delivered a vicious hit on Steve Largent that knocked No. 80 out cold. Largent also chipped a tooth and bent his face mask. As Steve laid on the Mile High Stadium grass, Harden yelled some smack mere inches from his unconscious head. Although he wasn't penalized on the play, Harden was later fined $5,000 by the league for the hit.

The teams didn't play each other again until a critical week 15 contest, but no Seahawk had forgotten Harden's actions. Immediately after scoring a Denver touchdown in the second quarter, one of the Broncos tries to spike the ball, but Hawk safety Paul Moyer slaps away the pigskin as if to say, "Not in our house!" This causes all sorts of shoving between the teams.

During the following Seattle drive, Brian Blades lays a nice low block on defender Jeremiah Castille that forces both of them to the ground. However, Castille takes exception to the block and starts shoving Blades. Brian tries not to engage, but then the two lock into each other and start rolling around like a couple of pro wrestlers. Three officials cannot break up the melee. Then the side judge is dragged to the Kingdome turf. When the fight finally ends, Castille is called for a personal foul, while Blades is unfairly flagged for retaliating. This sends a very upset Largent to scream at the ref that it wasn't retaliation on Blades' part. Hearing an angry Largent voice (caught by the ref's microphone) shocks me as if I were listening to an outburst by a mellow uncle.

On the very next play, Dave Krieg lofts a pass near the goal line, but it's intercepted in the end zone by Harden, who then takes off the other way. As Harden nears the 25, Largent seemingly comes out of nowhere to lay a hard but totally legal pop on him. The hit capsizes Harden, causing him to fumble. As if some great equalizing force is at work, Largent dives to recover the loose ball at the Denver 29. Steve gets up and has a few choice words for a dazed Harden before walking away. The twelfth man and Seahawk players are howling over this act of redemption. At first I'm flabbergasted. Largent?! He usually seeks revenge by toasting a defensive back with his feet, not his shoulders. Soon this emotion is replaced by laughter as I watch the replays. Largent?!

However, Castille is flagged for defensive holding on Blades, which wipes out the interception. Hence the play does not *officially* count. But try telling that to Harden or Largent.

The Hawks eventually score touchdowns on their first six possessions en route to a 42-14 Denver destruction. The victory is crucial for Seattle, as they go on to win their first AFC Western Division championship. But these facts take a back seat on a day the greatest Seahawk of them all was remembered for a defensive play.

FULL CIRCLE

In 1988 against the Chargers, Steve Largent broke Charlie Joiner's record for career receiving yards. It was two years earlier that Largent had seen Joiner set the record against the Hawks in the Kingdome. Now it was Joiner's turn to watch. However, this time Joiner was up in the

Charger coaches' booth. Sitting next to him was San Diego offensive coordinator Jerry Rhome, Largent's original wide receiver coach with the Seahawks and his coach at the University of Tulsa. Rhome was probably the most responsible for the trade with the Houston Oilers that brought Largent to Seattle.

THE 1984 DEFENSE DOESN'T REST

George Orwell's novel *1984* warned the world about a potential future run by a totalitarian government. When the actual year 1984 arrived, NFL offenses were *totally* monitored by the ball-swiping Seattle Seahawk defense. I know, I'm stretching to make a literary reference, but the Hawks' defense in 1984 was truly dominating.

Some football fans wonder how the Seahawks could lose star running back Curt Warner in the first game of the season and still go 12-4, the fourth-best record in the league that year. A lot of credit goes to the head coach, who converted the offense from "Ground Chuck" to "Air Knox," allowing Dave Krieg to set numerous team passing records. (I believe Knox used the Knoxism "You play the hand you're dealt" almost as often as he said hello that year.) However, it was their defense that enabled Seattle to become one of the premier teams in the NFL. With essentially the same group from 1983, the team went from 27th to 6th in total defense. They had 63 takeaways, by far the most in the league and still the second-highest total in NFL history. Included in this tally are 38 interceptions, which means they averaged more than two picks a game. To put this in perspective, the closest the team has come to this record is 30 in 1999 and 26 in 1983.

Along with the special teams, the defense scored or set up 188 points. One example of this high-scoring defense is when the first-place Chicago Bears venture inside the Kingdome. In the first quarter Chicago quarterback Bob Avellini hangs a screen pass that Hawk cornerback Keith Simpson easily snags and runs back 39 yards for a touchdown. Bears head coach Mike Ditka is seen stewing on the sidelines over the errant pass.

In the third quarter the Bears are at their own 7 when Avellini dumps a screen to Matt Suey. Awaiting the fullback is linebacker Keith Butler, who pops the ball free and into the end zone, where Joe Nash lands on it for his first career touchdown to put the Hawks up 31-7. Meanwhile, coach Ditka looks like he's going to chop Suey on the sidelines. In the fourth quarter Ditka decides he's seen enough of Avellini and sends in some guy named Rusty Lisch to finish the game. With 0:20 remaining in the contest, ol' Rusty is picked off by cornerback Terry Jackson, who returns it 62 yards to the house for the Hawks' third defensive score of the day. Ditka has his pet goat finish off the game at quarterback.

In a battle between two monster defenses, the Seahawk D proves to be the more opportunistic. Despite the offense being outgained by 100 yards and having only 12 first downs all day, the 38-9 final score has the appearance of a blowout win.

The Seahawk defense also recorded three shutouts and didn't allow a touchdown in two other games in 1984. At one point in the season, the Hawks didn't give up a score in 10 straight quarters.

Included in this stretch is a record-setting game against Kansas City at the Kingdome. The assault starts in the second quarter when the Chiefs have the ball at the Seattle 14. Quarterback Bill Kenney tries to hit his receiver at the 5, but Dave

I don't know what I liked better, Kenny Easley's punishing hits or his ability to steal the ball.

Brown steps in front and after bobbling the ball for a few yards, fully gains possession at the 10 and sprints 90 yards down the sideline to give the Hawks a 10-0 lead. A few minutes later, Kenney again has the Chiefs driving into Seattle territory, and once again he is picked off. This time the thief is Keith Simpson, who returns it 76 yards for a touchdown.

Kansas City head coach John Mackovic replaces Kenney in the second half with Todd Blackledge, but it doesn't make any difference. On one play Blackledge barely avoids a sack by Kenny Easley, only to be intercepted by Brown, who races 58 yards to the end zone for his NFL record-tying second return for a touchdown in the game. Not wanting to let his teammates have all the fun, Easley finishes off the larceny in the fourth quarter when he snags a Blackledge pass and returns it 58 yards to make it a 45-0 annihilation. The Seahawks set an NFL game record with four interceptions returned for touchdowns. The 325 interception return yards are also an NFL record, which remains to this day.

The 1984 defense was anchored by super-safety Easley. He led the league with 10 interceptions, including two for touchdowns. More importantly, his punishing hits made receivers think twice before going over the middle. Easley was also a model team player. When wide receiver/punt returner Paul Johns suffered a career-ending injury early in the season, Easley volunteered to return punts. Knox told NFL Films it was the first time in his coaching career a starter volunteered for such action. Easley's punt return average of 12.1 was fourth best in the NFL that season.

Easley was named the NFL Defensive Player of the Year by most publications. He and fellow defensemen Nash and Brown were voted to the Pro Bowl. Jeff Bryant, with 14.5 sacks, and Jacob Green, with 13, should've been voted in as well. But it really was a team effort orchestrated by defensive coordinator Tom Catlin, defensive line coach George Dyer, defensive backfield coach Ralph Hawkins, and Knox (who was named NFL Coach of the Year by many organizations). In a year when our All-Pro running back went down in the first game, the defense put together one of the best seasons in team history.

2005: A MILLION MONKEYS OFF OUR BACKS

I love monkeys. They are funny, lovable, amazing creatures. In 2005, for the first time in my life, I was able to witness capuchin, howler, and spider monkeys in their natural habitat in Costa Rica. The Seahawks, on the other hand, were dealing with a different type of monkey, a far more sinister breed: the kind that stays attached to your back. For those not familiar with the expression "a monkey on your back," it is a phrase that refers to the monkey as a problem or burden that hinders one's ability. The previous two years saw the team haunted by monkeys that kept a talented group from going to the next level. But in the off-season of 2005, the Seahawks made a few key management changes, most notably firing Bob Whitsitt and hiring Tim Ruskell as team president. This was the beginning of the Hawks removing many monkeys off their back during their Super Bowl–bound 2005 season. Enough to fill the primate house at Woodland Park Zoo.

The Ram Monkey

In 2004 the Hawks lost to their division rivals three times in agonizing fashion. But in '05 they swept their series with the Rams. In St. Louis special teams gave up an opening kickoff touchdown but redeemed itself with a critical fumble recovery late in the fourth quarter. In Seattle, Marcus Trufant turned the game around when he snuffed out a fake field goal.

The Dropped Catches Monkey

Seattle receivers were infamous for dropping key receptions in 2003 and '04. Prior to the 2005 season, the Hawks signed

Joe Jurevicius as a third receiver to complement starters Dar-rell Jackson and Bobby Engram. Jurevicius turned out to be the most important free-agent signing of the year. Both Jackson and Engram missed significant time, but Joe not only filled in incredibly, he also provided a steadying influence that helped eradicate the drops that had troubled the team.

The Cowboy Monkey

In a miraculous comeback against Dallas (see "15 Freakin' Fantastic Finishes," page 58), the Hawks erased the previous season's "Monday Night Meltdown," where they'd lost to the Cowboys in heartbreaking fashion on national TV.

The Blown Lead Monkey

The 2004 season saw a number of late-game leads vanish. Early in the '05 campaign, Seattle withstood a Falcon comeback and then put away the Cards in the second half the following week. Against the Rams at the Qwest, St. Louis pulled within eight points in the fourth quarter, but the Hawks answered with a clock-killing touchdown drive to ice it. These games gave the Hawks much-needed confidence, which carried throughout the year.

The Game After a Bye Week Monkey

The Holmgren-coached Seahawks had never won following a bye until we beat the Cardinals in the desert. Credit Shaun Alexander's spectacular team-record-tying touchdown run of 88 yards as the play of the game.

The Early Eastern Time Zone Monkey

The Hawks had lost their last seven games held in the Eastern Time Zone starting at 1 p.m. That changed when they came back from 10 points down in the fourth quarter to defeat the Titans in Tennessee.

The Playoff Monkey

Twenty-one years of postseason despair ended with a triumph against the Redskins. The following week the Hawks doubled their playoff win total since 1984 with a victory in the NFC Championship game (see "Great Seahawk Wins: Part Six," page 265).

The 2005 season was filled with so many seminal moments and events, my editor would have to order a giant pot of Tully's coffee and a new pair of scissors if I tried to include them all. Here are just a few that are not mentioned elsewhere in the book: Sweeping the NFC West division. The numerous delay-of-game penalties produced by the twelfth man. Shaun Alexander scoring his record 28th touchdown at Lambeau Field. Outscoring opponents 83-3 in early December. Setting a team record for rushing yards with 320 against Houston. Fullback extraordinaire and all around good guy, Mack Strong, finally making the Pro Bowl. The Hawks Alexander named NFL MVP and becoming the first Seahawk to grace the cover of *Sports Illustrated* (it's about time!).

STRIPPED OF STREAK

On September 26, 2004, the Hawks snapped the 49ers' NFL record of 420 consecutive games without a shutout when they crushed San Fran, 34-0. It was the first time the Niners had been held scoreless since October 9, 1977. To give you an idea of how long ago that was, Jimmy Carter was in his first year as president, only the affluent owned microwave ovens, and the Seahawks were just 18 games old.

Most importantly, the Seahawks knocked the aforementioned monkeys off their back. Too bad "less-evolved" primates couldn't have officiated the Super Bowl: they would've done a better job than the Homo sapiens assigned to the game.

GREAT SEAHAWK WINS: PART TWO

SEAHAWKS 29, VIKINGS 28
The Kingdome, October 8, 1978

Minnesota quarterback Fran Tarkenton and the famed Purple People Eaters defense make their first and only appearance at the Kingdome in 1978. I'm excited to see one of the premier teams of the '70s in person. Head coach Jack Patera is excited, as he coached the Eaters for seven years. The Vikings are only a season removed from winning their fourth NFC Championship, and while they are on the decline in '78, they are still contenders and big favorites in this game.

The first half is alternately exciting and frustrating for the Hawks. Jim Zorn throws a 44-yard touchdown pass to Sam McCullum to give the team an early lead. However, Efren Herrera's extra point is negated by a false-start call against Seattle. Backed up 5 yards, Herrera's second attempt is blocked. The future Hall of Famer Tarkenton is known for his incredible scrambling abilities. However, in this game, it is one of his disciples, Zorn, who has a great scrambling touchdown run to make it 13-0. Late in the second quarter, fullback David Sims runs 8 yards for a touchdown on a nice draw play. (Sims would go on to lead the NFL in touchdowns scored in 1978.) Unfortunately, the Vikings again block the extra point. One block is a mistake; two blocks is a trend. A trend that will have some Hawk fans thinking the team should forgo kicking extra points and have Herrera run it in instead. (Mind you, this is before the two-point conversion was introduced to the NFL.)

Things get worse in the third quarter as Minnesota scores two touchdowns to go up 28-19. When Zorn throws his second interception of the game at the Viking 31 early in the fourth quarter, life is very bleak inside the Kingdome. The popcorn seems stale. The Pepsi tastes flat. But the defense steps up to play possibly its best quarter in team history (up to this point) as it limits Tarkenton to only 8 more passing yards and, more importantly, allows no more Viking points or first downs. Meanwhile, the Hawks put together a solid drive and close the gap when Zorn, seeing no open receivers but an open lane on the right side, darts 22 yards for a touchdown. The extra point once again is an adventure as the Hawks are flagged for a false start after Herrera's kick is successful. However, this time Efren is able to convert the second attempt, mere milliseconds before another Viking comes in from the side to block it. The score now stands 28-26, Minnesota.

After the defense holds the Vikes to three and out, the offense gets the ball back with 7:04 remaining. Early in the drive on third down, Zorn is stopped just short of the first-down markers at the Seattle 38. Patera decides to go for it on fourth down, knowing:

1. If he punts it back to Minnesota, the offense may not see the ball again.

2. Picking up a few inches represents the best way to beat his old boss, Bud Grant.

3. What did a third-year expansion team have to lose, since they were not expected to win anyway?

Patera's knowledge pays off as Sims lunges a good 36 inches for the first down. Another key play occurs just inside the two-minute warning when Zorn avoids the sack by dumping a pass off to Sherman Smith, who scampers to the Minnesota 16 to put the Hawks in makeable field goal position. The Hawks eat up more clock and get all the way to the Viking 2 before calling their last time-out with 0:03 left. My dad, wanting to avoid the rush out of the stadium, drags me out of our seats. He tells me we can watch the field goal from a monitor on the 200-level concourse. Reluctantly, I exit our row. As Herrera comes onto the field, three things are going through my mind and the minds of thousands of other Hawk fans:

1. Efren had been a shaky 2-6 in field goal attempts this season.

2. This field goal was exactly the same distance as an extra point, and he already had two blocked today.

3. Why would Fran Tarkenton go on to host *That's Incredible!?*

As I sit at the top of our section, I risk the wrath of my father by running back down the steps so I can watch the field goal in person. Incredibly, just as the Hawks are ready to snap, flags come out for the *fourth* time on a kicking attempt in the game. The call goes against the Vikings, moving the ball near the 1. Rather than hear my dad tell me we need to watch the kick from a concession stand near an exit, I decide to stay on the stairs and watch the next attempt. Then, in almost anticlimactic fashion, Herrera makes what could possibly be the shortest game-winning field goal that will ever happen in team history. I quickly run up the steps, where my dad gives me a semi-stern look before we hustle out of the Dome.

The win is very significant in the story of the Seahawks because it is the first time Seattle beat a team that finished the season with a winning record. Minnesota was 8-7-1 in 1978 (and NFC Central Division champ), which, incidentally, was not as good as the Hawks' 9-7 mark. By finishing above .500, Seattle becomes the fastest NFL expansion team to have a winning record. Consequently, Patera is named NFL Coach of the Year by many organizations, while general manager John Thompson is honored as the NFL Executive of the Year by *The Sporting News*. Steve Largent leads the AFC in receptions and is the team's first Pro Bowl selection. Zorn himself figures prominently in postseason lists. After leading the conference in completions and yardage, he is named AFC Player of the Year by the Touchdown Club of Washington, D.C. He is also named second-team All-Pro by the Associated Press and runner-up for offensive player of the year by United Press International. Incredibly, he is passed over for the Pro Bowl in favor of Miami's Bob Griese, who didn't have nearly as good a season as Zorn. Some Pro Bowl voters obviously suffered from a rare brain condition that prevented them from making an intelligent decision.

SEAHAWKS 31, FALCONS 28
Atlanta-Fulton County Stadium,
October 29, 1979

Fall 1979. The SuperSonics are defending their NBA championship. I'm a Bellevue High School senior. Radio is my extra-curricular love, as I am fortunate to have a 10-watt station, KASB-FM, to use at my school. (Before anyone complains about Bellevue High students being spoiled, I must point out that we did share the station with the three other high schools in the district. It was good we interacted with students from Sammamish, Newport, and Interlake high schools.

Thankfully, we were spared the riffraff from Mercer Island.) For the first time in their history, the Seahawks have the nation's undivided attention on *Monday Night Football*. Just hearing famed announcer Howard Cosell talk about Largent and Zorn in the show's opening with the classic "dun dun dun da" music underneath makes me feel as though the team has finally arrived in the NFL. As with almost every place that hosts a game on *Monday Night Football*, the atmosphere inside Atlanta-Fulton County Stadium is part football game, part Mardi Gras.

The game begins badly as the Falcons jump out to a 14-0 lead. The second touchdown occurs early in the second quarter on a turnover. As Seahawk punter Herman Weaver drops the ball to his kicking foot, a Falcon defender comes in and deflects the ball backward, whereby another Falcon picks it up and runs 40 yards for a touchdown. Officially, it's ruled a fumble recovery. In reality, it's in its own bizarre category: neither a block nor a fumble. A blumble, perhaps.

On the Seattle's next possession, a rainstorm hits the stadium. It doesn't affect the Hawks as Jim Zorn marches the team into Atlanta territory. The drive appears to stall when they face fourth down and six at the Falcon 34. However, coach Jack Patera goes for it. With Atlanta expecting a pass, Zorn brilliantly picks up the Falcons' noted "Grits Blitz" defense and scrambles all the way to the end zone. Football fans everywhere are amazed by a guy whose name sounds as though it came from a comic book dash like a superhero on the soggy grass.

Halloween is only two days away, so Seattle pulls off a few tricks that are treats for Hawk fans. First, under the aegis of new special teams coach Rusty Tillman, they sneak an onside kick (after their second touchdown) that completely catches Atlanta off guard. It also gives the Seahawks the ball at the Falcon 43. Three plays later the drive stops, and Patera sends in Efren Herrera to attempt a 55-yard field goal. Zorn's name may sound like a comic book character, but on the field he's more like a Hollywood actor. As special teamer Art Kuehn comes in and whispers the play to Zorn, the quarterback appears agitated, and his body language toward the Seattle bench screams "angry." Falcons witnessing this demonstration no doubt think Zorn is mad that he won't have a chance to pick up the first down like he did earlier in the quarter. But as my old drama teacher Georgie Johnson would say, acting is all about the sale. And on sale tonight: famously fooled Falcons. As Atlanta completely expects the field goal attempt, the stocky Herrera fakes the kick and runs up the middle. Zorn, who is the holder, lofts the ball into Efren's awaiting arms for a 20-yard reception.

Cosell goes nuts, saying this is the sort of innovation the NFL needs. Seattle takes advantage of this innovation and snags the lead when Dan Doornink bowls his way 8 yards for a touchdown. Fulton County Stadium is stunned, feeling like the Union Army's General Sherman has come to Atlanta and trashed the city all over again.

The Seahawks have a number of opportunities to put the game away in the second half, but turnovers prove to be the great equalizer. Doornink has two fumbles, and Zorn adds a third. There's more Seahawk trickery when Weaver fakes a punt and throws it to wide receiver Jessie Green, who gains 9 yards. Problem: the Hawks need 12 yards. Cosell derides this kind of "innovation." (Note to self: Make sure your innovation always picks up the first down.) With great field position, the Falcons are able to drive deep into Seahawk territory as the rain-soaked crowd starts showing life again and Patera looks like a candidate for Gamblers Anonymous. However, the Seahawk defense keeps the Falcons out of the end zone, and rookie defensive end Manu Tuiasosopo blocks a field goal attempt.

Late in the fourth quarter the Seahawks finally hold on to the ball, and Doornink atones for his fumbles, scoring on a

26-yard touchdown run with 1:55 remaining. The Seahawks now have what seems to be a safe 10-point lead, 31-21. Emphasis on *seems*.

With many of their fans having already folded up their umbrellas and headed for the parking lot, the Falcon offense comes alive and scores in less than a minute to make it 31-28. Incredibly, Atlanta recovers the onside kick, and those folks still remaining inside the stadium are screaming for a miracle comeback. Seahawk fans, meanwhile, are wondering how this 10-point lead with less than two minutes left to play suddenly became so shaky? It gets worse as Falcon quarterback Steve Bartkowski successfully launches a 43-yard bomb. Now the worry of overtime is replaced by the sickly feeling of defeat as the Falcons have the ball at the Seattle 12 with 0:35 and two time-outs remaining. On the very next play Bartkowski floats the ball to his tight end near the left edge of the end zone, but Seahawk cornerback Dave Brown jumps up and grabs the ball to push the miracle meter back on Seattle's side. A turnover, the one thing that could secure a victory for the Hawks, occurs.

This is the game that introduced the Seahawks to many parts of the country and gave America something to talk about Tuesday morning. It didn't matter if you lived in Tukwila or Tulsa, you were going to remember this game. Has there ever been another NFL contest that featured two successful onside kicks, a fake field goal, a fake punt, a blocked field goal, and a bungled punt returned for a touchdown? Maybe in a Marx Brothers movie.

03

HERE'S ONE FOR THE BOOK

What do Bo Jackson, the Krieg-to-Skansi touchdown, the guy who drove O. J.'s Ford Bronco, the paranormal, and one of the NFL's greatest postseason upsets have in common? You'd better guess "the Seahawks" or you're reading the wrong book.

15 FREAKIN' FANTASTIC FINISHES

Occasionally, a football game won't be decided until very late in the contest. When the Hawks win with little time to spare, there's an adrenaline rush inside me that is so good, it almost feels illegal. Here are 15 Seahawk games where the outcome wasn't determined until the final minutes—or in many cases, the final seconds. A few games such as the 1995 "Mile High Comeback" in Denver are not listed here and are instead included in other chapters.

15. Kitna Comeback

Vs. Tennessee (11/29/98): Here's the scenario: The Hawks are down 18-17. They start their final drive at their own 28 with only 0:28 remaining. And they have just one time-out. Did I mention this is only Jon Kitna's second start as an NFL quarterback? On Seattle's first play, Kitna hits James McKnight near the 50. The Hawks benefit from the officials' generosity and the Oilers' stupidity as a personal foul and an unsportsmanlike call give them the ball at the Tennessee 38. Two plays later the inexperienced Kitna lets the play clock run out, resulting in a 5-yard penalty. Maddeningly, it forces the Hawks out of field goal range. But on the following play Mike Pritchard makes a catch at the Tennessee 31 and wisely gets out of bounds with 0:06 to play. This sets up Todd Peterson with a 48-yard kick that sails through. Tacoma native Kitna is named AFC Player of the Week for his performance.

14. Brownout

At Kansas City (11/19/78): With 0:15 to go at the Seattle 1, the Chiefs are 36 inches away from taking a 17-13 lead. KC quarterback Mike Livingston pitches to running back Tony Reed.

The "Original Seahawk," Dave Brown. He was one of three former Hawks
to also coach the team.

Cornerback Dave Brown bounces off a blocker and flings himself onto Reed, forcing the Chief to cough up the ball. The pigskin bounces backward like a toxic hot potato, in and out of the hands of various Seahawks and Chiefs, before Brown himself recovers it at the 18-yard line to preserve the 13-10 win.

13. Rogers and Rian Rescue

At San Diego (12/30/01): After the Chargers tie it at 22 with only 0:16 seconds remaining, Seahawk returner Charlie Rogers has an incredible 64-yard return to the San Diego 36. As the clock only has a mere 0:06 on it, the Hawks don't have enough time to run a play. Holmgren sends out kicker Rian Lindell. The kid from Vancouver, Washington, promptly nails a 54-yarder for the win. It's Lindell's third game-winning field goal against the Chargers in two years. That night San Diego coach Mike Riley searches the Net for Lindell voodoo dolls. It doesn't matter, as Riley is fired the next day.

12. Saved By the Boulware

Vs. Miami (11/21/04): This had the makings of another one of our 2004 meltdowns. After blowing a 10-point lead, the Hawk defense looks flustered in the final minutes as Miami, led by an interim head coach, marches down the field aiming for the big upset. With 1:05 to go and the score tied at 17, Miami has a first and 10 at the Seattle 42. Rookie safety Michael Boulware perfectly reads A. J. Feeley's pass and returns it 63 yards for the touchdown. Upon leaving the Qwest, the twelfth man's emotion is a mixture of exuberance and relief.

11. A Record-Breaking Finish

Vs. Cleveland (12/18/77): Seattle was fourth best in the NFL in sacks allowed in 1977. One reason was the mobility of Jim Zorn. He demonstrates his backfield prowess in the final game of the year against the Browns. The Hawks trail 19-13 with a mere 0:52 remaining. Sitting at the Browns' 15, Zorn creates a nice play-action fake, then quickly rolls out to his left and hits Steve Largent falling down in the left front corner of the end zone. The score gives the Seahawks a fifth win for the season, the most ever by a second-year expansion team.

10. Welcome Back, Mr. Krieg

Vs. Houston (11/13/88): In a 24-24 game, the Seahawks start their winning drive at their own 20 with 4:50 remaining on the Taco Time clock. (Taco Time is a local Mexican fast food chain with the best crispy burritos. It used to sponsor the game clock on the Kingdome scoreboard.) Dave Krieg, in his first game since separating his shoulder two months earlier, methodically moves the team down the field, eating as much of the taco clock as possible. Key plays include a 16-yard pickup by Largent and a crucial third-down catch by John L. Williams. Chuck Knox makes an interesting decision after Williams rushes to the Houston 28 with 0:33 left. Instead of taking one of the Hawks' three time-outs and then running at least another play to make the field goal attempt shorter, Knox decides to let the game clock run down to 0:05. Evidently he has complete faith in kicker Norm Johnson to make the 46-yard field goal. The only question concerning the kick is the holder. Normally, backup quarterback Jeff Kemp has been holding for Johnson this season. But with Krieg's return, Kemp is inactive for the game. Logic states the player with the best hands should be the holder, and that would be Largent. Knox is a logical person, so Largent is on the field. Knox's logic and his faith in Johnson are rewarded, as a perfect hold allows Norm to nail it. The Taco Time clock reads all zeroes. It's now time for one of those crispy burritos.

9. Failed to Be Foiled By the Flag

At St. Louis (10/15/06): When receiver Torry Holt makes a spectacular touchdown catch to give the Rams the lead, 28-27 with only 1:44 remaining, it appears the Seahawks have blown the game. However, Matt Hasselbeck, despite having no time-outs left, expertly drives the team into field goal range. After getting the Hawks to the St. Louis 32 with 0:14 left, Hass brings them up to the line and spikes the ball with four seconds remaining to set up a 49-yard field goal attempt. But there is a flag against Seattle on the play. Ram coach Scott Linehan thinks it's offside, which would bring a 10-second runoff and end the game. Linehan, a Washington native (born in Sunnyside), is all excited, believing he's won. But ref Ed Hochuli explains that the call is illegal formation, a type of penalty that does not necessitate a runoff. Instead, it's a 5-yard penalty, making the field goal attempt 54 yards. Linehan calls a time-out to ice Hawks place-kicker Josh Brown, but it only helps settle him down. The snap and hold are perfect, and Brown boots it right down the middle with plenty of yardage to spare. Linehan doesn't have a sunny-side disposition afterward. It is one of four last-second game-winning field goals by Brown in 2006. Yeah, that's a team record.

8. Burleson's Redemption

Vs. Cincinnati (9/23/07): One of the great "goat to hero" stories in Seattle sports history involves Mariner right fielder Jay "Bone" Buhner. In the eighth inning of game two of the 1995 American League Championship series against Cleveland, Buhner failed to catch a very playable fly ball. His error led to the Indians scoring the tying run. However, in the 11th inning, Bone atoned for his mistake when he blasted a game-winning home run.

Against the Bengals, wide receiver Nate Burleson dropped a few critical passes, including a certain touchdown in the fourth quarter of a tight game. But he achieves some Buhneresque redemption on the Hawks' final possession, with the team trailing 21-17 and only 2:42 remaining on the clock. It starts when Burleson makes a nice 15-yard pickup as he is falling out of bounds to ignite the drive. Later, the Hawks convert a critical fourth-and-one call at the Cincinnati 37. On the very next play, Matt Hasselbeck lays a perfect pass to Burleson between two defenders at the Cincy 3. Nate is then able to make it inside the left front pylon for the touchdown. The twelfth man cranks it up to the *Spinal Tap* volume of 11 at the Qwest, and Burleson's redemption is complete.

However, I'm worried the Hawks scored too quickly because there's still a minute to play and the lead is only three points. The Bengals have Carson Palmer, an arsenal of killer receivers, and three time-outs. What's the best way to keep Palmer from beating you? Keep him off the field. How? Have special teamer Lance Laury cause a fumble by the Bengal kick returner and have Deon Grant recover said fumble. Game over.

7. Largent Finally Gets Loose

Vs. Denver (12/8/79): The Seahawks should have the lead, but a fake field goal in the third quarter backfires when kicker Efren Herrera can't handle the pass from Jim Zorn. Instead, the Hawks trail 23-21 with 3:55 left in the contest. The team starts their last drive at their own 21 with only one time-out left against the very tough Bronco "Orange Crush" defense. A roughing-the-passer penalty on Denver moves Seattle 15 yards, and a Zorn scramble gives the Hawks another 9. The Broncos are flagged again as a pass interference call gives the Seahawks the ball at the Denver 43.

Steve Largent has been frustrated most of the day by Bronco All-Pro Louie Wright. However, on second down and with 1:48 on the clock, Largent puts on a little move that fools the Denver cornerback into thinking he's going to the outside. Then he quickly cuts to the inside, leaving behind a very toasted Wright. Zorn, who has rolled to his right, pumps once before airmailing a perfect pass to Largent at the 5. A few Tulsa trots and it's touchdown Seahawks. Largent then uncharacteristically spikes the ball.

I go nuts from my 200-level perch. The twelfth man's reaction is possibly the loudest inside the Dome in the team's four-year history. Amazingly, Largent broke his wrist during this nationally televised Saturday game but continued to play and score the winning touchdown. (He would also lead the NFL in receiving yardage in 1979 despite missing the final game due to the broken wrist.) It is the Seahawks' first-ever win against the Broncos.

6. The First Victory is Preserved

At Tampa Bay (10/17/76): It is dubbed the "Expansion Bowl" as the two newest members of the NFL battle on a very hot October afternoon in Tampa—a pair of winless teams fighting to exit the absolute gutter of the league. After taking a 13-3 halftime lead, the Seahawk offense sputters in the second half, while the inept Buc offense manages a touchdown. With 0:42 remaining in the game, the Buccaneers have a chance to tie the score with a field goal. However, linebacker (and Brylcreem pitchman) Mike Curtis comes in from the left side and gets a hand on the ball, which causes the kick to fall way short of the uprights. The block preserves a 13-10 win and the first regular-season victory in team history. One dubious note about the Expansion Bowl: it featured a total of 35 penalties, the most in an NFL game in the last half century. Ugh.

5. The Silver-and-Black Turn Blue

At Oakland (11/26/78): After stopping the Raiders on fourth down, the Hawks take over at their own 21 with 2:27 left in regulation and trailing 16-14. On their second play, Jim Zorn misses Steve Raible with a pass, but Jack Tatum's vicious forearm doesn't miss Raible's head. (It's the type of hit that made

Tatum infamous. He paralyzed Patriot Daryl Stingley with a nasty shot in an exhibition game that season and wrote a book titled *They Call Me Assassin*. Tatum's tactics would later be outlawed by the NFL.) Raible cannot recover and slumps to the grass, where he is down for a good two minutes. He looks absolutely catatonic as he is held up by two trainers and taken to the sidelines.

With Raible on the bench trying to remember his own age, the Hawks continue to drive down the field. On one play, Zorn scrambles backward almost 20 yards to avoid the Raider rush but is still able to hit Sam McCullum for a first down at the Oakland 43 with 0:42 left. Later, a crucial fourth-down conversion gives Seattle the ball at the Oakland 28. Then, with only 0:07 left, kicker Efren Herrera coolly walks out on the field. He ignores the taunts of the Coliseum crowd and knocks a 46-yarder through the uprights for the game. The Seahawks become the first team to beat the Raiders twice in one year since 1965. Oakland head coach Madden quits at the end of the season and becomes a video game.

4. A Foxborough Explosion

At New England (9/21/86): The Seahawks are staring at another East Coast loss, down 31-21 late in the game. A Norm Johnson 33-yard field goal trims the deficit to seven points with just under three minutes to play. With 2:20 remaining, Jeff Bryant sacks Pats quarterback Tony Eason at the New England 10-yard line on third down. The sack forces punter Rich Camarillo to kick halfway back of his own end zone. The former Husky, who early in the game had a punt blocked for the first time in his career, is snakebit again as Patrick Hunter comes in untouched to deflect the kick. The ball bounces around the end zone before it takes a fortuitous skip into Seahawk Paul Moyer's waiting hands to tie the game. The crowd at

Foxborough Stadium is dumbfounded. That is, all except the few hundred happy Hawk fans, including the three guys in the first two rows right in front of Moyer's recovery. Actually, two of these dudes could've been drunkards from Providence with no vested interest in the game but who dug the incredible play.

New England uses little of the game clock on their next series, as the Seahawk defense forces Eason to throw off target. The Hawks get the ball back with about a minute and a half to play. On second down at their own 33, Dave Krieg spots receiver Ray Butler beating two defenders and lofts a perfect pass to him at the Patriot 24. Butler easily sprints into the end zone for the game-winning score. The Hawks score 17 points in 1:39 to win, 38-31.

3. The Block

Vs. Houston (11/03/96): When the Seahawks nearly move to Los Angeles in the winter of 1996, it takes a brutal bite to the team's box office. Crowds in the Kingdome drop below the 40,000 mark for a number of games; the absolute bottom in attendance (minus the 1987 strike games) comes when the Houston—soon to be Tennessee—Oilers visit Seattle. For the record-low 36,320 fans that venture inside the Dome that afternoon, a most improbable ending occurs.

With the score tied at 16 and 3:30 remaining in the game, the Oilers drive from their 20 to the Hawk 20 in just under three minutes. Oiler head coach Jeff Fisher calls a time-out to set up his field goal unit for a 37-yard game winner. Wisely, he drains the clock, so when the ball is snapped, only 0:16 remains. Oiler kicker Al Del Greco had made 12 straight field goals and had not had a kick blocked in 10 years. But his 13th kick yields to its unlucky image as Michael McCrary comes zipping in untouched and not only blocks the kick, but also recovers the ball on a generous Kingdome turf bounce at the

33. He displays good sense and teamwork as he laterals to Robert Blackmon at the Seattle 40. Blackmon darts up the field while my friend Bob watches in amazement as I do a Nestea plunge onto my hardwood floor just as the Hawk safety crosses the goal line for the game-winning touchdown.

The next day I call someone at the NFL headquarters to find out how many times a team has blocked a game-winning field goal in the closing seconds and then returned it for a touchdown and the win. The NFL rep guesses it had happened only three times previously in the 77-year history of the league. I guess the league doesn't keep such stats within reach when geeks like me call the office to inquire about obscure trivia.

Sadly, the comeback was probably seen by the fewest number of Seahawk fans to ever watch a (nonstrike) regular-season game. It was blacked out, which meant the game wasn't broadcast anywhere in Western Washington. It is reasonable to deduce that only the lucky Hawk fans outside the blackout zone or those, like me, who had the NFL Sunday Ticket satellite TV package could have seen this most unlikely of Hawk endings.

2. Bluebirds Blast, Bledsoe's Blunder Blamed

Vs. Dallas (10/23/05): Down 10-3 with 2:01 to play, Seattle moves 81 yards in 81 seconds to tie the game. Both Jerheme Urban and D. J. Hackett make incredible catches, and Shaun Alexander passes Chris Warren as the all-time team rushing leader on the drive. The touchdown occurs when Hasselbeck hits tight end Ryan Hannam, who makes the reception while sliding in the end zone.

The special teams unit allows Dallas to return the kickoff to its own 41. Fortunately, the defense gives up only 3 yards on first and second down. As the Cowboys huddle on third and seven with 0:14 left, announcer Dick Stockton says the game is headed for overtime unless "something amazing happens." When Cowboy quarterback Drew Bledsoe brings his team to the line, I scream "interception." Many times when you yell out something like "interception," your prophecy falls short. However, if you do it often enough, the odds are bound to hit in your favor. Sure enough, Bledsoe rolls out and throws into the flat, where Jordan Babineaux intercepts. Babineaux returns the ball 25 yards just inside field goal range and then smartly goes out of bounds. Josh Brown immediately runs out onto the field. With no time to mentally prepare for the kick, Brown slams a 50-yarder for the win.

The twelfth man is in a state of epic euphoria. Brown manages to take off his helmet before being mobbed by his teammates. Meanwhile, I'm screaming loud enough for anyone within a two-block radius of my house to hear me. I think the only one who didn't was the old guy down the street with the broken hearing aid.

1. Krieg to Skansi

At Kansas City (11/11/90): The setting is Arrowhead Stadium, usually a miserable place for the Seahawks (see "Arrowhead: House of 1000 Mistakes," page 174). But for one glorious November afternoon, it is the site of the most rewarding comeback in team history.

During the majority of the game, it's your typical Seahawk display at Arrowhead: a few highlights and lots of futility. Actually, it's more like historic futility, as Chief linebacker Derrick Thomas just has his way like a Republican in Florida. Nobody can block him, and consequently he sets the NFL record for sacks, with seven in the game. Seven?! That's a good *season* of sacks for most linebackers. But the Chief offense doesn't do well, and after our defense makes Kansas City go three and out late in the game, quarterback Dave Krieg has one last chance in the final minute, down 16-10.

Back at my apartment in Hollywood, something possesses me to grab a rubber football, point it at the television, and exclaim, "I have faith in my Seahawks!" The game is one of those rare regular television Seahawk broadcasts in Los Angeles, and I take full advantage of my fanaticism. No need to feel self-conscious about sneering looks from other patrons at a sports bar.

The Seahawks have 0:48 and 70 yards to go with no time-outs. On first down, Krieg is able to dump off a screen pass to John L. Williams right before Thomas sacks him again. John L. catches it at the 30 and zips up to midfield, where he is stopped. But he doesn't get out of bounds, so the clock keeps ticking. There's 0:38 left as Williams furiously gets up. It's frantic as the Hawks try to make it to the line while the Chiefs take their sweet time. I continue to hold tightly to the ball and scream, "I have faith!" Krieg gets the snap off when the clock clicks 0:22 and proceeds to hit Tommy Kane at the KC 38; Kane then gets to the 25 before he is tackled with 0:17 on the clock. Krieg, with cool urgency, directs the team to the line and spikes the ball with 0:04 left to give the Hawks one last play.

The spike acts like a mini time-out for both teams. Coach Chuck Knox is slimmed down in 1990; in fact, he is a spokesman for the Slim·Fast diet drink. But he is swallowing a lot of air as he screams out instructions to his offense. On the Chiefs' sidelines, head coach Marty Schottenheimer and his defensive coordinator Bill Cowher tell their players to make sure no Seahawk has even a remote chance of scoring a touchdown.

An audience of 71,285 screams for a Chief stop. The Seahawks come to the line of scrimmage. Only six Chiefs await them. The other five are in or near the end zone. A constant chant of "I have faith!" flows from my lips. Krieg operates out of the shotgun. He takes the snap at the 31 and rolls back to the 37, where he is very aware Thomas is coming toward him untouched to add to his NFL sack record.

Maybe it's fate. Maybe it's luck. Maybe it's that he is tired of being slammed to the concrete like Arrowhead artificial turf, but Krieg somehow steps up in the pocket slightly, which forces Thomas to spin around him. Dave gets away from the linebacker long enough to spot receiver Paul Skansi, who inexplicably is all alone in the end zone. Krieg's pass—which he throws with all zeroes on the clock and going against his body—hits a leaping Skansi right in the "I" in the "CHIEFS" end zone marking. Skansi, a Gig Harbor native, catches it in between four Chiefs, who suddenly realize they have been burned. In my elation I nearly squeeze the air out of the ball. In Kansas City the aforementioned 71,285 go into collective shock. There's a certain beauty to the silence inside the stadium. It sounds like defeat.

Skansi's catch only ties the game at 16, but Norm Johnson knocks through the extra point to give the Hawks a 17-16 victory. My faith in the Hawks is rewarded. In the aftermath on the field, Eugene Robinson gives Knox a big screaming soul shake. Krieg also accepts congratulations while blood drips from his throwing elbow. Meanwhile, the public address announcer at Arrowhead says without the slightest bit of irony, "We hope you've enjoyed the game."

Krieg's final numbers for the day: 16-23 for 306 yards, two touchdowns, no interceptions, and nine sacks. In a twist that hasn't happened often, if ever, in NFL history, the AFC offensive and defensive players of the week are awarded to opposing players in the same game: Krieg and Thomas. Two seasons after this game, Krieg was a Kansas City Chief. Ten years after this game, Thomas died due to complications from a car accident in which he wasn't wearing his seatbelt. His NFL sack record remains. In 1999, a poll of NFL writers picked the top 75 touchdowns from an estimated 41,000 in league history. Krieg-to-Skansi was ranked 59th. It should've been higher.

REPEAT WHEN NECESSARY

In 1990 kicker Norm Johnson is the hero on consecutive weeks. These back-to-back games are nearly identical as the Hawks force fumbles in overtime to set up Johnson with a 40-yard winning field goal against the Chargers and a 42-yarder versus the Oilers. The Hawks win both games 13-10. There is a better chance of Dick's Drive-In adding a veggie burger to its menu than the Hawks duplicating this exact consecutive feat.

THE TWELFTH MAN VERSUS A GHOST

SEAHAWKS 35, REDSKINS 14
NFC WILD CARD PLAYOFFS
Qwest Field, January 6, 2008

There seemed to be an almost supernatural battle at the Qwest during this playoff game: the twelfth man versus the ghost of Sean Taylor. Announcers Cris Collinsworth and Tom Hammond noted the presence of the recently deceased Taylor after Hasselbeck threw his first interception. It occurred just after Washington scored its first points of the day early in the fourth quarter. Collinsworth credited Taylor for the Redskin inspiration, and then, right on cue, the Redskins took the lead, 14-13. The Skins scored 14 points in 2:15 after going the first 45 minutes empty.

Possibly the wackiest kickoff in Seahawk history and no doubt one of the scariest then takes place. The winds in the southern end of the stadium send the ball on a fluky flight that prematurely makes its descent. Nate Burleson frantically moves up to field the ball, but it lands in front of him and takes a 45-degree bounce. A Redskin special teamer is able to scoop up the ball and run it into the end zone. I am truly in sports shock: did the Skins just score again?! I didn't think the kicking team could advance the ball, but I'm not positive. However, the referee announces to the crowd that the ball cannot be advanced. Relief. Some Redskin players and fans will say it was Sean Taylor who caused the bizarre kickoff. The cynical side of me thinks it's ridiculous to believe a dead football player can suddenly control the wind in Seattle. The spiritual side of me wonders if they are right.

Luckily, the Redskins totally botch the gift that has been bestowed on them by Mother Nature (or a ghost). After starting at the Seattle 14, they gain only 2 yards on their first two plays. Fullback Mike Sellers (an actual Washingtonian who graduated from North Thurston High School in Lacey) had earlier in the week called out the twelfth man as being "manufactured." On third down Sellers manufactures his own screwup when he lines up in the wrong place. This forces quarterback Todd Collins to call a time-out. A frustrated Collins heaves a few choice words Sellers' way. Dissension. That can kill any ghost. After the time-out, the Skins are diffused when Patrick Kerney forces a bad pass from Collins. It now brings up a chip shot field goal for the Redskins.

The twelfth man has witnessed a number of critical missed field goals by opponents. In 2005 alone, there was the Jose Cortez miss in the Dallas game, Jay Feely's three-peat with the Giants, and Washington's then-kicker John Hall missing a field goal in the fourth quarter of the playoff game after the Skins had recovered a fumble on a kickoff. Add to this list the name Shaun Suisham (say that five times). With every twelfth man screaming at full volume, Suisham hooks the 30-yard kick to the left. Is it a nervous leg, the wind, or the power of the twelfth man that causes the miss? The logical side of me believes it's one of the first two options. The spiritual side of me thinks it's the third.

Despite all the problems the Hawks encounter in the fourth quarter, I have this calm confidence that everything will turn out all right. The Redskins only lead 14-13, and there is plenty of time remaining. Even after Hasselbeck throws another interception, I know the Hawks will prevail. The team and the twelfth man will keep Washington and their ghost from victory. The defense, which plays one of its best games of the season, forces a three and out, aided in part by a false-start penalty courtesy of the twelfth man. When the Seahawks get the ball back, there is still eight minutes left, ample time to take the lead. Just as important is the fact that the drive starts at the Washington 42, thanks to a wind-hindered punt of 33 yards. Then Burleson's clutch third-down catch puts the Hawks in field goal range, but I was thinking we were going to get the touchdown. Sure enough, Hasselbeck hits D.J. Hackett for the go-ahead score. I am still confident, but am I calm? No, I'm jumping up and down, as I'm wont to do when the Hawks score a huge touchdown.

Before the Redskin game, the Hawks had never returned an interception for a touchdown in the postseason. Only once (1984 against Kansas City) had the team returned two picks for scores in one quarter. However, within the span of 5:12 in the fourth quarter, Marcus Trufant and Jordan Babineaux each return interceptions for scores and rewrite history. These touchdowns effectively put the game, in the words of the late great announcer Chick Hearn, in the refrigerator. After going

21 years between playoff victories, the Hawks win a postseason game for the third straight year.

A FLAG-FREE FEELING

The 2007 Seahawks averaged the fewest number of penalties in the NFL in 34 years. Holmgren has always run one of the more disciplined squads in the league, but the '07 edition of the Hawks was especially impressive in avoiding the flags. Maybe every Seahawk was allergic to the color yellow.

DREADFUL DEFEATS: PART TWO

BRONCOS 31, SEAHAWKS 14
The Kingdome, December 15, 1984

It is the final game of the regular season in what had been the franchise's most stellar campaign. Both teams come into the Dome with identical 12-3 records, battling for the AFC Western Division crown. Beforehand, Seattle management officially retires no. 12 in honor of the fans. It's the first time such acknowledgment has been bestowed on the fans of a sports team. However, the twelfth man wanted a refund after this loss. John Elway spoils the lovefest, and the Broncos celebrate a division championship on Kingdome turf. Elway runs for one touchdown and throws for another. But the killer score is in the third quarter, when Dave Krieg is intercepted by Steve Foley, who returns it 40 yards to make it 24-7. Instead of having a week off and then facing the 9-7 Steelers at home, the Hawks had to meet the world-champion Raiders at the Dome and then travel on the longest road trip in the NFL—Seattle to Miami—to face the eventual conference champion Dolphins.

To further my grief, my college roommates Bri, Jay, and I have to move out of our rental house immediately after the game. The place had been sold, and naturally we waited until the last minute to move to our new digs. It's a special kind of pain to have the image of Elway happily jumping up and down burned into your memory while you haul boxes of your life to a new location.

PATRIOTS 20, SEAHAWKS 13
The Kingdome, November 17, 1985

The Seahawks are poised to snap their "two wins in a row, two losses in a row" routine as they lead the Patriots 13-7 after three quarters at the Kingdome. Curt Warner is on his way to another 100-plus-yard rushing game, and the defense has effectively shut down the New England offense. But with 10:35 to play, Pats quarterback Steve Grogan hits Craig James with a 23-yard touchdown pass. The Hawks catch a huge break when kicker Tony Franklin, who had made 70 consecutive extra points, hooks it wide left to keep the score tied at 13. Later, Seattle is in position to take the lead, but a pass from Krieg is tipped, and Patriot safety Fred Marion intercepts it at the New England 2 and returns it 83 yards to the Seattle 15. My friend Richie screams that Krieg tried to force in a pass to continue his 28-game streak with at least one touchdown throw (the fourth longest in NFL history). Two plays later I'm able to take my hands away from my face just long enough to watch wide receiver Irving Fryar grab the game-winning touchdown pass. Krieg's streak is stopped. More importantly, the Hawks' record drops to 6-5 and basically kills their shot at the playoffs in a year when even the 11-5 Broncos fail to make it to the postseason. However, for the Patriots, the game proves pivotal to beat out said Broncos for the final playoff spot, and they parlay that postseason berth into an AFC championship. Krieg should've at least received a thank-you note from the Pats.

BENGALS 34, SEAHAWKS 7
Riverfront Stadium, November 16, 1986

A real mess. After starting the season 5-2, the team is on a three-game losing streak when they arrive at Riverfront Stadium. The Seahawk misery continues, as they constantly shoot themselves in the foot in this contest. Norm Johnson misses three field goals. Krieg is sacked five times. He throws only one interception, but it is returned 36 yards for a touchdown. And then there is the fumble in the Seattle end zone that is recovered by the Bengals for a touchdown. The loss puts us in the unrecoverable position of 5-6. I saw this game at a restaurant in Olympia with one of my old Bellevue friends, Tom, who was going to school at Evergreen State College. I have never watched a game in Olympia again.

RAIDERS 37, SEAHAWKS 14
The Kingdome, November 30, 1987

I hate this game. I hate it because it was against the Raiders. I hate it because it was on *Monday Night Football.* I hate it because it spoiled our chance at a division title. But mostly I hate it because the media will show "highlights" of Bo Jackson running down the Kingdome turf for the rest of my life and beyond. It's known throughout the sports world as the "Bo Game." See Bo run right over a lame Brian Bosworth and into the end zone. See Bo run into the Dome tunnel, as Al Michaels says, "all the way to Tacoma." See Bo run for 221 yards, still the most against the Hawks in team history.

Our dominance against the Raiders in the Dome was shattered. The Hawks had stomped on the Silver-and-Black in Los Angeles earlier in the season, but this time they somehow lay a big egg to a weak Raider team that would eventually have its worst year since 1962. Coming into this game, Seattle was in control of the AFC Western Division with a 7-3 record, but the loss gives the Broncos the lead for good. I swear that if I make it to heaven and I see that clip of Bo running down the sidelines, I'm going to smash every monitor in the afterlife.

CHARGERS 17, SEAHAWKS 6
San Diego Jack Murphy Stadium, September 18, 1988

The Seahawks are looking to start the year 3-0 for only the second time in team history, but this disastrous game in San Diego changes the course of the season. The Chargers, enduring an eight-game losing streak, take an early Krieg interception 55 yards for a touchdown. Krieg moves the Hawks on their next possession but is picked off in the San Diego end zone. On their next drive, Norm Johnson misses a 30-yard field goal when the ball hits offensive lineman Edwin Bailey in the back. With the Hawks down by only four points in the fourth quarter, it goes from awful to downright horrifying when Krieg separates his shoulder after being sacked. Dave can be seen wincing in major pain on the sidelines. Hawk fans don't feel much better. The Chargers, who had gone 58 straight possessions without an offensive touchdown, put the game away on a fake reverse that goes 25 yards for six points. Backup quarterback Jeff Kemp tries to rally the Seahawks late but is intercepted at the San Diego 1-yard line. The loss is especially costly, as Krieg is gone for seven games. This forces a talented Seahawk team to struggle with Kemp and Kelly Stouffer at quarterback.

REDSKINS 29, SEAHAWKS 0
The Kingdome, December 23, 1989

Seattle comes into this season finale on a three-game win-ning streak with a chance to avoid the first losing year dur-ing the Chuck Knox era. It is also the predetermined last game in Steve Largent's brilliant career, and he becomes the first inductee in the Seahawks' Ring of Honor. With these factors on their side, the Hawks proceed to get shut out for the first time under Knox. The offense manages to pick up a mere dozen first downs and turns the ball over four times in this nationally tele-vised Saturday contest. In what was also to be his final game as a Seahawk, Curt Warner has one of his worst games, rushing for only 8 yards. Largent, in his swan song, has 41 yards on two receptions. It had been 13 years, 3 months, and 11 days since his NFL debut in this very stadium, when he caught five passes for 86 yards. The team's tepid performance is very puz-zling because the Redskins' defense is only average in giving up points, ranking 13th in the NFL in 1989. Seattle finishes with a 7-9 record, their first losing season in seven years. A really crummy way to send off Largent. Couldn't they have given him a gold watch instead?

NASH BRIDGES THE COACHES

Nose tackle Joe Nash is the only Seahawk ever to play for five different head coaches in franchise history. He signed as a rookie free agent in 1982 when Jack Patera was still the coach. Nash quickly had a new boss when Patera was fired during the players' strike that season and Mike McCormack took over on an interim basis. His next new head coach, Chuck Knox, came aboard in 1983 and lasted nine years. However, Nash lasted longer. He survived the following three years under Tom Flores before finishing his career with Dennis Erickson at the helm. He should have held on for a few more years so he could have played for Mike Holmgren and completed the set. Instead, he retired in 1996 after playing only 15 years. Wimp.

HE WAS A SEAHAWK?

You may recognize these guys, but chances are you don't remember them as Seahawks:

Al Cowlings

Most infamous for being the guy who steered O. J. Simpson's white Ford Bronco the day The Juice was arrested in front of the entire world. Cowlings played defensive end for the Hawks in exactly one game during the 1976 season. Not to be confused with former Mariner Al Cowens, who never chauffeured a suspected murderer 200 miles around Southern California.

Jeff George

The No. 1 overall pick of the 1990 draft was known for his clashes with coaches as much as for his rocket arm. After Trent Dilfer went down with a season-ending injury in 2002, the Seahawks signed George as Hasselbeck's backup. George never did anything more than hold a clipboard with the Hawks. In defense of George, he did an excellent job holding that clipboard. He never let it drop below his waist and always kept it at a 90-degree angle.

Ed Marinaro

Best known as Officer Joe Coffey on the television show *Hill Street Blues*, Marinaro appeared in one game at fullback for Seattle in 1977. He didn't have a single carry or reception. Before being drafted in the second round by the Vikings in 1972, he had a stellar career at Cornell University in the Ivy League. This means he was a pretty smart jock. So why on earth would he become an actor? (I kid, my thespian friends.)

Sean Salisbury

If you follow the NFL on ESPN, then you are familiar with Salisbury's analysis. Salisbury started his pro career by signing a free-agent contract with Seattle in 1986. Although he never saw any regular-season action during his one year with the Hawks, he beat the odds by making the roster and becoming the third-string quarterback. Believe it or not, he never tires of being called Salisbury Steak.

Gino Torretta

Torretta holds the distinction of being the only former Heisman Trophy winner to play for the Seahawks. In his one and only Seattle appearance, occurring in 1996, he helped the Hawks to victory over the Raiders. However, calls for a "Gino Torretta Day" in Seattle still go unanswered.

GREAT SEAHAWK WINS: PART THREE

SEAHAWKS 27, DOLPHINS 20
AFC DIVISIONAL PLAYOFFS
Orange Bowl, December 31, 1983

The Orange Bowl stadium in Miami has been the site of three great Seattle-area football games. The 1985 Orange Bowl game featured the Washington Huskies against the Oklahoma Sooners. Oklahoma had a flashy freshman linebacker named Brian Bosworth, but the school also had a horse-drawn-wagon mascot called the "Sooner Schooner" that had a propensity for getting penalties. Consequently, the Dawgs stunned OU. There was also the 1994 Huskies, who went to the the stadium and snapped the University of Miami's NCAA record home-winning streak. But for me, the biggest game occurred on New Year's Eve 1983 when the Seahawks faced the Dolphins in the AFC divisional playoffs.

Competing in only their second playoff game ever, the Seahawks come in as massive underdogs to the defending AFC Champion Dolphins. Miami had gone 12-4 in 1983, including finishing the regular season by winning 9 of 10 and their last five in a row. Miami's "Killer B" defense (so called because seven starters had last names beginning with the letter *B*) has allowed the fewest points in the league. On offense, the Fins are lead by rookie quarterback Dan Marino, who sparked the team's winning streak when he took over the starting job earlier in the season. The battle of two veteran coaches also favors Miami, with Don Shula holding an 8-3 record over Chuck Knox. Most of the Dolphins have playoff experience, as the team went to the Super Bowl the previous season. For most of the Hawks, their playoff experience is limited to the win a week earlier against Denver. Playing at home, the Dolphins are almost unbeatable for the last three years, going 20-3-1. The team is also 7-2 in playoff games at the Orange Bowl. These are the facts all football analysts bring up to give the Seahawks absolutely no chance of winning this game. I too am not optimistic. I'm just hoping the Hawks don't get killed.

The weather is overcast and a moist 51 degrees at kickoff. It had rained all night and into the morning in Miami, leaving the stadium damp, looking like Seattle instead of the sunsplashed environment normally associated with south Florida. The first half also plays a little soggy. At the intermission, the Dolphins lead 13-7 with Marino having another stellar game. Meanwhile, Seahawk quarterback Dave Krieg is struggling. He is missing his targets with poor passes. Steve Largent, thanks to Miami's double coverage, is shut out in the first half. Still, it's only a six-point deficit, and I'm just hoping the Hawks don't get hammered in the second half.

Early in the third quarter, good fortune comes to the Seahawks as the defense recovers a fumble at the Seattle 45. Twice, Krieg converts on third-and-long situations (including a great Paul Johns reception) before Warner muscles his way into the end zone to give the Hawks the lead. The fear I have about the Hawks being killed is slowly evolving into optimism.

The Seahawk defense continues to shut down the Dolphins. On one drive, pressure on Marino results in an interception by cornerback Kerry Justin at midfield just as the third quarter ends. The Seahawks again are able to cash this turnover into points, with a Norm Johnson field goal. Seattle now leads 17-14, with 10:42 remaining. On the other side of the country, hundreds of thousands of Seahawk fans, including myself, are cautiously optimistic. This optimism grows as the defense, thanks to utilizing seven defensive backs, continues to thwart Air Marino on consecutive drives. The steady rain, especially in the second half, and lack of Dolphin fireworks subdue the crowd of 71,000 at the Orange Bowl.

The Seahawks take possession with 4:44 to play at their own 27 and leading by four. On first down, just as announcer Marv Albert talks about the Seahawks looking to pull off the big upset, Krieg throws out to the flat, where Dolphin defensive back Gerald Small is alone to find a gift waiting for him. He returns the interception to the 16-yard line. The Orange Bowl erupts. Krieg, trying to force a pass to Largent (still shut out for the game), grossly miscalculates the route. On the sidelines, Chuck Knox is livid. He is a conservative coach who takes no chances when holding the lead. Also on the sidelines now stands Krieg. With no one around him, he looks like God's Loneliest Man, no doubt contemplating the magnitude of his mistake. When Dolphin running back Woody Bennett scores the go-ahead touchdown, my heart sinks. We were on the verge of one of the NFL's greatest postseason upsets, and now I'm looking at a stadium full of Dolphin fans dancing in their rain ponchos. This feels far worse than if the Hawks had just been killed.

The suddenly jubilant crowd is thinking the status quo has been restored. The Seahawks are thinking there is still 3:43 remaining in the game, and they are only down by three. Krieg, thinking about a long flight back to Seattle, returns to the field, only a few feet from where he made the biggest blunder of his career mere minutes earlier. Starting at their own 34-yard line, Knox calls two running plays that gain 8 yards. It's now third and two. Miami rushes five guys. The offensive line protects Krieg. The quarterback spots Largent, who has eluded two defenders. Krieg's pass is low, but Largent slides to make a great catch at the Miami 42. Mr. Largent's first reception of the day comes nearly 58 minutes into the game. It is the most important third-down conversion in the Seattle Seahawks' eight-year history.

Largent's catch brings the game to the two-minute warning. On the first play after the break, Krieg goes over the top to hit Largent with a bomb at the Miami 9. Steve then runs upfield before being pushed out of bounds at the 2 as screams of terror spew from the Orange Bowl bleachers. The play is beautifully executed as Largent fakes out the cornerback on the short route and then goes long. Krieg is equally perfect, as his pass lands in the 1-square yard where Largent can catch it out of reach of the defenders. After being shut out the entire game, Largent has two receptions for 56 yards in 30 seconds.

On first and goal, in the noisy closed end of the Orange Bowl, Warner takes the pitch to the right and outruns everyone to the corner. He gets past the pylon while the Fins' defense can only watch helplessly. I start screaming. Seahawk nirvana has entered my body. With the extra point the Hawks now lead 24-20 with 1:48 left.

Twice Miami is given an opportunity to come back, and twice Dolphin kick returner Fulton Walker capsizes the opportunity. First he fumbles the kickoff after the Warner touchdown. This leads to a Seahawk field goal and a 27-20 lead. Miami is able to save most of the clock during the Seahawk possession, thanks to Shula's judicious use of time-outs. With Marino always a threat to make the big play, the Dolphins still have a chance to tie the game. But once again Walker fumbles the kick return, and Dan Doornink recovers for Seattle. I and every other twelfth man can now comfortably rejoice over the victory. As the clock nears zero, Seahawk Reggie McKenzie and others lift Coach Knox and carry him across the muddy field in front of a stunned Orange Bowl crowd. In a rare display of positive public emotion, Knox shakes a rolled-up play call sheet.

Afterward, sports pundits across the land call it one of the biggest NFL upsets in postseason history. Most will say the Hawks won it on guts and not by a fluke. Curt Warner is the offensive star of the game with 113 yards rushing and two touchdowns, but Krieg is the one who triumphs over adversity that afternoon. Up to this point and for many years to come, it is the biggest win in team history. That night I celebrate the victory on New Year's Eve in downtown Seattle with my friends Richie and Jay. At one point I'm screaming "Seahawks" so loudly out of Richie's car window in Pioneer Square that he is pulled over by Seattle Police. Richie tells the cops he had one drink at midnight (which is the truth). He then tells them I am just excited about the Seahawk victory. They say it was an amazing win and let us go.

SEAHAWKS 31, COWBOYS 14
Texas Stadium, November 27, 1986,
Thanksgiving Day

One of my funniest memories of Thanksgiving while growing up involves my Grandpa Bud. He was quite a character, frequently using the expression "That's the stuff!" to describe myriad positive situations. He was also fascinated with the latest gadgets and gizmos (as he was wont to call them). One year he bought an electric carving knife to use on the Thanksgiving turkey. He thought it was going to make the carving easier and more efficient. Unfortunately, the knife had one not-so-insignificant problem: it was loud. I mean *really* loud. From the living room, it sounded like a chain saw was attacking the bird. On Thanksgiving Day, 1980, the Seahawks must've felt like the Cowboys were carving them apart. The Hawks endured their biggest blowout loss ever, a 51-7 massacre in front of the entire nation.

Now six years later, they face Dallas again in the national holiday spotlight. Seattle, at 6-6, is trying to keep its slim playoff chances afloat after a four-game losing streak deflated their promising start. Dallas at 7-5, is also fighting for a postseason berth. The Cowboys have won six straight and 9 of 10 on Thanksgiving coming into this game. It's this sort of holiday domination that makes them favored by more than a touchdown.

The game starts poorly for Seattle. The Cowboys, with former Husky (and Bellevue's Interlake High School product) Steve Pelluer at quarterback and the Heisman Trophy backfield of Tony Dorsett and Herschel Walker, take the opening possession and march 78 yards for a touchdown. But Seattle answers with a nice drive of their own. Facing third and one at the Dallas 6, the Seahawks run a quarterback draw, and Dave Krieg dives headfirst into the end zone to tie the game.

The second quarter belongs to the Hawks. Largent continues his NFL record streak by making a reception in his 136th straight game, when Krieg hits him with a 37-yard pass to the Dallas 12. Two plays later, Steve makes a diving catch in the end zone to put the Seahawks on top. Seattle takes advantage of good field position on their next drive and scores on a 19-yard pass play when wide receiver Byron Franklin beats his man to the end zone. The Seahawks close out a nearly flawless first half with their fourth score on four possessions as Norm Johnson boots a 42-yarder to make it 24-7 at the half. The three first-half touchdowns represent a nice reversal for the Hawks, who had only scored one touchdown on offense in each of their last five games.

The game gets a little more interesting in the third quarter for the casual football fan enjoying some pigskin on Turkey Day. I personally call it more agonizing as the Cowboys, riding the hot hand of Pelluer (who completes his first 14 passes), score on Walker's 1-yard touchdown run. The Hawks then waste a nice drive of their own when Johnson misses a chip shot field goal to keep fans at Texas Stadium thinking about more than just how many gallons of gravy they will consume later that evening.

The fourth quarter doesn't start much better, as Krieg, trying to throw the home run ball to Largent, is picked off in the end zone. But the Seahawk defense and a critical offensive holding call force a Cowboy punt that is returned by Paul Skansi to the Dallas 40. From there, it becomes The Curt Warner Holiday Show. He piles up yards like I pile up food on my plate at Thanksgiving dinner. On first and goal at the 10, Warner goes to the left side, barreling past two defenders and into the end zone.

The 31-14 final score no doubt had Cowboy fans choking on their pumpkin pie. It also sent Dallas on a slide, leading to its first losing season in 22 years. For the Seahawks it was a great showing for a huge national television audience. As my Grandpa Bud would say, that's the stuff!

RETURN TO SENDER

In 1998 the Seahawks set an NFL record for most total returns (interception, fumble, kick, and punt) for touchdowns in a single season, with 13. The year's first score was a harbinger when Shawn Springs intercepted a Bobby Hoying pass and returned it 42 yards for the touchdown as the Hawks spoiled the Eagles' home opener, 38-0. Another seven interceptions were returned for 6, including two by Darrin Smith and a career one by Springs. Cortez Kennedy's only touchdown was one of two fumbles taken back for scores. Joey Galloway had a team-record two punts returned for a touchdown, while Steve Broussard scored the fastest touchdown in Hawk history when he ran the opening kickoff against the Redskins 90 yards to the end zone. To put this season's feat in perspective, the Hawks only had 25 returns for touchdowns the other nine years of the decade combined.

04

NOTES ABOUT A TWELFTH MAN

It was either Benjamin Franklin or my wife who said, "Football makes you act like a freak!" Since Ben never heard of football and has been dead for a couple of hundred years, I'm guessing it was my wife who made the comment.

TO LIVE AND DIE IN L.A. AS A HAWK FAN

When I moved from Washington to Los Angeles in 1987, the hardest adjustments were not being able to buy all those great Northwest microbrews and not seeing the Seahawks on regular television every week . . . and, uh, missing family and friends.

For my first eight seasons in Southern California, I had to contend with two NFL teams vying for local attention. Each week one of the two networks with the rights to the Sunday afternoon games (at this time it was CBS and NBC) would schedule a national doubleheader. NFL rules state that if the home game of a local NFL team does not sell out, it will be blacked out. Consequently, the local television market will not have access to both games of the doubleheader. This meant that rarely was there ever a football doubleheader on the tube in Los Angeles, because one team was usually at home. The Rams, playing in Anaheim Stadium, would sometimes, but not often, sell out. The Raiders, who had their home games in the cavernous LA Coliseum, would never be filled to capacity. The lack of doubleheaders irked most football fans in Southern California because it wasn't often the big national games were available locally. For me, fewer doubleheaders further reduced my chances of seeing the Hawks on local television. It was just one of the problems facing a Seahawk fan in LA.

There was also the problem of color, namely the Seahawk color of blue. Los Angeles had two rival gangs, the Crips and the Bloods, which based their looks on certain colors. For the Bloods, it was red, because . . . um . . . they were really committed to plasma donations. For the Crips, it was blue. Not just blue, but a blue that was very similar to the Seahawks' blue.

Eazy-E, part of the famed rap group N.W.A., would occasionally be seen wearing a Seahawk cap. I could be wrong, but I don't think it was because he just loved Dave Krieg. I also remember watching local television newsman Paul Moyer (not the former Seahawk safety) talk about meeting some gang member who was wearing a Seahawk hat. Moyer asked the guy why he had a Seahawk cap when the Raiders and Rams were the local teams. The young hoodlum cited the color, not the team, as the reason he sported it. I thought to myself, "Great, I could get shot by a Blood if I wear my Seahawk hat in public." Then I realized I'm just a skinny white guy who would never be mistaken as a member of the Crips.

To watch most Seahawk games usually involved seeking out a sports bar with a satellite dish that would be willing to show the Seattle contest. This wasn't an easy task. Unlike in other cities, there were few sports bars in Los Angeles, especially in the Hollywood area where I lived. There were some places that had access to games, but often these establishments catered to the more popular teams. As the Seahawks' fortunes plummeted in the early '90s, so did their fan base in LA. As often as a sunny Southern California day or a Hollywood flop, I'd start watching the Hawks at a bar, only to have the television switched to a Cowboy or Giant game because there were suddenly more Dallas or New York fans in the joint. It didn't matter that I was there first; the bartender would always reason simple economics while hitting the remote just as Krieg was dropping back to pass.

By the mid-1990s, my sports prayers had been answered. A small round object called a digital satellite system (DSS) was introduced to the public. Through the DSS service DirecTV, you could purchase the NFL Sunday Ticket package. Sunday Ticket allowed viewers to watch all the out-of-market NFL games that were not available locally. In 1996 the DSS had become affordable enough for me to purchase, and I plopped it onto the roof of my San Fernando Valley house.

For me, the NFL Sunday Ticket was a godsend. No more begging sports bar owners to put my Seahawks on their preemptive televisions. No more ordering overpriced onion rings. No more enduring the endless mockery from arrogant Cowboy fans. I can still recall the joy of flipping through all the games that first Sunday of the season and realizing that it was me and not some sports bar joker who had control of the remote. Even though the Hawks lost that opening game to the Chargers, I was ecstatic.

I hadn't been ecstatic seven months earlier when my biggest sports nightmare became a reality. Mankind's equivalent to a rotting tub of margarine, Seahawks' owner Ken Behring, announced he was moving the team to Los Angeles. My personal apocalypse came one day when I opened up the sports page of the *Los Angeles Times* and saw six pages devoted to the move, including a timeline of Seahawk history. Those who didn't know me well would comment how great it was that my favorite team was coming to my adoptive city. Those who knew me better understood the anger I felt about the move. In fact, I wrote a letter to the *Los Angeles Times* sports page that was published on February 10, 1996:

> As a Seahawk fan since the team's inception and an L.A. resident for the last eight years, I am totally disgusted that the team is trying to move to Southern California. Ken "Over" Behring, a man who did his best to destroy a classy organization, has forgotten the Seahawks really belong to Seattle. If they do indeed move here, the people of the Southland should boycott this franchise. No moral person would buy a car if they knew it was stolen. The same applies to football teams.
>
> MARK TURNER, North Hollywood

The *Times* printed 12 letters concerning the move and not one of them was in support of the team coming to Los Angeles. Some slammed Behring. A few were critical of the transient culture that was pervasive in the NFL thanks to the Cleveland move. And there were some that bagged on the Seahawks by stating they didn't want *that team* in Los Angeles (admittedly, those letters did hurt).

I will never forget watching the footage of a moving van leaving the Seahawk complex in Kirkland while some fans yelled, held signs in protest, and even tried to block the truck's departure. I always thought there should've been more people out there, but I understood it was part of OverBehring's evil plan to make the team so unappealing that no one would care if they moved. But he was wrong. Many people did care. There was a guy named Mark Collins who started a grassroots movement called Save Our Seahawks. Collins spent a year and a half of his life trying to gather support to keep the team in Seattle. He even filed a class-action lawsuit against Behring. And there was someone else who cared. Paul Allen. A local guy who made a few bucks helping to start up a little company called Microsoft.

On June 17, 1997, I awaited the results of Washington Referendum 48, which took a vote on whether to approve public funds to build a new stadium for the Seahawks. Defeat would mean no Paul Allen ownership; it would also signal the Hawks' move to Los Angeles. My brother Milt phoned me throughout the evening with election updates. The referendum was winning, but it was close. I couldn't celebrate, because there were a number of mail-in ballots that had yet to be counted. A few days later, I heard Referendum 48 had really passed. It was as if I had just received some critical good news from the doctor: I was happy, but I had an equal feeling of relief.

Since then it has been a lot better to be a Seahawk fan in Los Angeles. As I mentioned earlier, I've been able to watch every game at my house since 1996. Also, Redhook and Pyramid ales have been available at Southern California grocery stores for many years (not that you need to drink Northwest microbrews to be a Hawk fan, but it helps). And thanks to this thing called the Internet, I am able to follow the local Seattle coverage of the Seahawks and discuss the team on various forums. I do dream of the day that I have enough disposable income to fly up to Seattle for every Hawk home game, but until then, I think I can survive just fine as a Seahawk fan in LA.

A LICENSE TO KILL

Personalized license plates are a good way to show Seahawk spirit. Most of the obvious choices are already taken in many states, including SEAHAWK, SEAHWKS, SEEHAWK, CHAWKS, and C HWKS. Try some more unusual spellings, such as C HOCKS or the French-sounding C HAQUES. Some people won't have any idea of your intent and will look at you with puzzlement or ridicule. However, those in the know will applaud your creative gumption.

VIEWING BUDDIES

For some, watching a Seahawk game is a solo experience. They don't want to be bothered by anyone or anything. Others have special groups of friends and/or relatives to share the excitement and/or misery. Sometimes I watch games at home, but this can create a problem because my wife gets mad when I yell or get too excited during a game. She thinks our dogs, Molly and Hana, get scared, but I personally think they like it when the Seahawks do well. Fortunately, I can watch many games at my best bud Stan's house because he also has the NFL Sunday Ticket package. Stan is a fellow Northwesterner, having partially grown up in Coeur d'Alene, Idaho. While he's not as avid a fan as I, he nonetheless occasionally indulges in a primal scream on a big play.

With the dawn of the Chuck Knox era, I started watching games with my friend Richie. I met Rich when he was a DJ and I was the music director at my college radio station, KUGS-FM, at Western Washington University. We used to hang out a lot, playing intense games of Wiffle ball. Richie was also the genius behind a band called the Stinkbugs that achieved semicult status in the Bellingham area. I was one of the many part-time members who would play with him during a recording session or live, either on KUGS or at a venue such as the "world-famous" Up & Up Tavern in downtown Bellingham. Rich always described the band's style as neo-inspirational progressive cocktail music.

Dave Krieg's unlikely success during the 1983 season perked interest in Richie, a former Air Force brat who didn't have ties to any one particular NFL team once Johnny Unitas retired (Rich is nine years older than I). For the next few years while I was in school, Rich and I would watch games together. During a telecast, we'd always "low five" each other over a good play or if a penalty went our way. We were superstitious that if we didn't do this ritual, the good plays would evaporate. Rich also had a penchant for calling games won a little too early for my tastes. I'd flip out if he said the game was in the bag if we were up by only 10 points with five minutes to play.

Rich was fascinated by and frustrated with Krieg's incredibly consistent inconsistency. As everyone who followed the Seahawks during this period can attest, Krieg could look like

Joe Montana one game and Joe Pisarcik the next—sometimes during the same game. Krieg would infuriate you with a costly turnover but later turn cat vomit into chicken cordon bleu with an amazing play.

At the start of each game, Richie would look for Krieg warming up on the sidelines to see which mask he was wearing. If Rich thought Dave was wearing the "good" mask, we knew it was going to be a Hawk win. But if he saw the "bad" mask, then we were doomed to lose. His prediction rate was pretty good. Of course, Rich did use standard deductive reasoning: if the game was on the road against an NFC opponent, or played in Kansas City or in cold weather, Rich would usually say Dave was wearing the bad mask.

Rich is known as the Jacques Cousteau of garage-saling in Whatcom County. He scours garage sales throughout the region in search of musical instruments and pop culture memorabilia. Once he bought me a Seattle Seahawks board game for a buck (see "Seattle Seahawks: The Board Game," page 112). Another time he found a Dave Krieg action figure in which Dave is wearing a beard. Krieg looks an awful lot like Dan Fouts. I'm sure the manufacturer just used the old Fouts mold, painted a Seahawk uniform on the figure, and called it Krieg.

When Krieg was let go after the 1991 season, Richie was crushed. It was very hard for Rich to watch Seahawk games for a few years. He would find himself instead following the team Krieg played for during a particular season. I know he watched a few Lion games when Krieg was the quarterback in Detroit. Rich and I occasionally still watch Seahawk contests together. When we do, the low fives are always part of the game.

NEW SPORTS MATH

I may have been mediocre in math at school, but I can still use it to advance an argument that the average NFL game is five times as important as an NBA game, and 10 times as crucial as a Major League Baseball game. The numbers back up this statement: there are 16 regular-season NFL games, 82 NBA games, and 162 baseball games. A four-game losing streak in baseball or basketball isn't good, but it won't kill a season. However, a football team could play only four games and be virtually eliminated from the play-offs by early October if they start 0-4. This is the sort of data football fans need to explain why they sometimes yell at the television during a seemingly insignificant play.

UP IN THE HAWKS' NEST

SEAHAWKS 30, BEARS 23
Qwest Field, November 18, 2007

Among my inspirations for writing this book was Nick Hornby's *Fever Pitch*. Hornby is an English author (he also wrote *High Fidelity* and *About a Boy*) who chronicled his own fanaticism for the Arsenal Football (soccer to us Yanks) Club. One of the points he makes in *Fever Pitch* is that as a fan of a particular team, you belong to an extended family. However, unlike a real family, whose members can have their own agenda, this extended family has the same goal: to experience a championship. Fans come from a range of social classes and political viewpoints, but they rally around their team.

Can you spot me in the Hawks' Nest? I'm next to Waldo.

The twelfth man is my extended family, and against the Bears, I sat in the Hawks' Nest at Qwest Field (not to be confused with the great Hawks Nest Bar & Grill in Seattle). This may be the most unique section in the whole stadium from which to view a game. With its metal benches, the seating is more like the 300 level of the Kingdome than the rest of the Qwest. The grandstand is cone shaped, with open space between it and the other parts of the stadium. You are literally perched, overlooking the field: "a bird on the wire," in the words of poet/singer Leonard Cohen. Not surprisingly, the fans are quite boisterous and passionate in the Nest. If you are not standing during key plays, you are missing the action. Players, including Patrick Kerney and Leroy Hill, gestured to the crowd in the Nest when the Bears were backed up near the north end zone. This always inspired fans to play their part in the game as members of the twelfth man.

The energy and buzz at the Qwest are equal to, if not greater than, that inside the Kingdome during the Hawks' peak years in the 1980s. Many major league and college teams have vocal fans whose enthusiasm creates a home field advantage; however, there's something intangible about the twelfth man. It can really freak out opponents, as evidenced by the extraordinary amount of false-start penalties by visiting teams. The Bears had four in this game, including three during critical drives in the fourth quarter.

The twelfth man may have been at its loudest when Josh Brown tackled the always-dangerous Devin Hester during a kick return. Who could have thought a kicker was capable of a hit that would've made Kenny Easley proud?! The Hawks scored 30 points on the tough Chicago defense, but Brown's tackle may have been the biggest highlight of that victorious day.

10 A.M. KICKOFFS ARE A CRIME AGAINST NATURE

Possibly the biggest thing that irks me about the NFL are the 10 a.m. Pacific Time Zone starts for the Seahawk (and other West Coast teams) games in the Eastern and Central Time zones. These games, which begin at 1 p.m. ET, are hard on the players and fans. For the players, a cross-country flight on Friday or Saturday leaves them no time to adjust their body clocks. This means they're playing at 10 a.m. because they're still on Pacific Time. It's a clear advantage to the East Coast players, who are starting the game at 1 p.m., or the Central Time players, who are beginning play at noon. How many players grew up playing games at 10 in the morning? Unless you're in the first game at a peewee football jamboree, I would say none.

AN EXPLOSIVE MOMENT

Just prior to the second half of the Seahawk-Saint game in 1979, someone threw a lit M-80 firecracker onto the King- dome floor near the New Orleans bench. The loud explosion jolted the crowd, not to mention the Saints themselves. The kickoff was delayed momentarily as Seattle Police went into the stands and apprehended the joker responsible. This was one of the weirder large-scale public event moments I experienced in Seattle. It was clearly topped less than a year later when I saw the great British rock group The Kinks play at the old Seattle arena. As Ray Davies sang "All Day and All of the Night," I witnessed a flailing body fall from the ceiling and crash into the crowd on the floor. Apparently, a guy had crawled through the overhead air ducts to watch the sold-out show, when a portion of the channel collapsed, causing him to fall some 60 feet onto a few shocked con- certgoers. Although there were some injuries, miraculously no one was killed. Do you suppose the guy who threw the M-80 was the same person who fell from the ceiling? Nah. But maybe they were cellmates.

10 a.m. The only thing I do well at that hour is drink coffee and pretend to work. It's hard enough to actually *watch* a game at that hour. I can't imagine playing against premier players at such an early time. It's just unnatural, like margarine. For East- ern and Central Time Zone players, starting West Coast games on their late-afternoon body clocks is not nearly as much of a disadvantage, because most grew up playing late afternoon and night games. You won't often hear players or coaches com- plain about this fact, because they abhor excuses, but I am

convinced these 1 p.m. ET/10 a.m. PT kickoffs have cost the Hawks a number of games over the years.

The 10 a.m. kickoffs also affect two distinct and very different groups of Seahawk fans. There are those who go to church on Sunday mornings and miss much of the first half, if not the whole game. There are also those more wild fans who like to stay out late on a Saturday night and have trouble getting up for a 10 a.m. start. Sure, both groups could watch the game on tape or TiVo, but I would think the NFL would want to discourage viewers from watching games in this manner because it prompts most fans to fast-forward through the commercials, therefore hurting the NFL's biggest cash cow, television and its sponsors. For fans taping the game, there is also the risk of hearing the score from a radio, television, or the obnoxious guy who screams out the result in the middle of a church service like Homer Simpson.

TIME-OUT Speaking of Homer Simpson, the Seahawks have been mentioned in one episode of *The Simpsons*, when daughter Lisa becomes very adept at forecasting pro football games and picks Seattle because they have something to prove. *Now back to my rant.*

Usually the NFL schedules some Eastern and Central Time Zone games at 4 p.m. ET, but rarely do those involve the Seahawks. Take, for instance, week one of the 2008 season. The Hawks played at Buffalo at 1 p.m. ET/10 a.m. PT on Fox. It was actually one of four games scheduled at that time on Fox. Now, there was no good reason why that game could not have started at 4 p.m. ET/1 p.m. PT. Fox only had three games slated for that afternoon, including Dallas at Cleveland (another 4 p.m. ET start). Fox may claim that the Cowboy-Brown game was the "national" game, but it was not being broadcast across the country, because Carolina at San Diego and Arizona at San

Francisco were on at the same time on Fox in significant parts of the United States. I'm sure the Seattle market would forgo the Dallas and Cleveland game if the alternative was having the Hawks on at 1 p.m. I could make the same argument for every other Hawk game that started at 10 a.m. PT. So, Commissioner Goodell (if by the remotest chance you are reading this), understand that NFL teams and fans on the West Coast should not be subjected to the 10 a.m. starts. It simply is not fair, especially in light of the fact that these teams fly more air miles than other franchises. I also bet television ratings would be better if they played their East Coast games at 1 p.m. PT.

WORST SEAHAWK FAN EVER

During the Sunday night game against the Saints in 2007, an NBC camera caught a guy at the Qwest wearing a paper bag (with a spray-painted frown) over his head. If the team were 3-12 I could almost understand this tired act of fan disgust. But the Hawks were 3-2 coming into the New Orleans game. It was just an unoriginal and beat display. To make matters worse, he was wearing a Largent jersey. Plus, the bag wasn't made from recycled paper.

A FEW NOTES FROM SUPER BOWL WEEK

Written during the week of January 30–February 4, 2006

All this Seahawk coverage is incredible. It's almost like I'm getting famous myself. It's very surreal. When your team lives under the radar for most of its history, it's overwhelming when

NOTES ABOUT A TWELFTH MAN

they are propelled into the Super Bowl spotlight. There are numerous articles every day about your team, and their name is thrown into the pop culture zeitgeist. I saw the Seahawks mentioned in *Entertainment Weekly* for the first time. All this interest isn't entirely comfortable to me.

Why do I have some fear of the Hawks winning the whole thing? Is it because Super Bowl champs are sent into a whole other exposure stratosphere that changes the team forever? They stop being just your club and start becoming a tool for national advertising executives. She is not your girlfriend anymore: she is America's sweetheart and here comes the breakup. "Uh, Mark, I know you've been with me for 30 years, but I really want to be in 1,000 Coors Light commercials." Winning a Super Bowl would bring in a lot of new fans, but this is a double-edged sword for us longtime Hawk followers. While we despise some of these so-called bandwagoners, we also know they are a product of winning. And winning is a good thing.

Interestingly, it was 10 years ago this week that OverBehring announced he was moving the Seahawks to Los Angeles. A decade between the Hawks' darkest hour and their brightest era. Sometimes it seems like the move might've happened a hundred years ago. Sometimes it seems like only yesterday.

I sent my brother-in-law Tony, who lives in Pittsburgh, an e-mail this week about the Super Bowl.

Hey Tony,

It's your brother-in-law, Mark, here. Can you believe it's a Pittsburgh–Seattle Super Bowl?! I think it's hilarious that my team finally makes it to the big dance, and it's against the Steelers. What are the odds of that? Your sister has been able to watch the Steelers this year because I have the dish with all the NFL games. It could get ugly over here next week. I hope everything is well with you.

Mark

And here was his entire response later in the day:

> It's a shame that Seattle's first trip to the Super Bowl is going to end with a very lopsided defeat. Pittsburgh by 12.

That was it. No "Hey, how are you doing? It's great to hear from you." Nothing but those two sentences, which displayed about as much charm as a Christmas card from Al-Qaeda. What a brother-in-law!

ANOTHER FLUKY SEAHAWK HISTORICAL NOTE

The Hawks have played the Dolphins in the postseason more often than any other team (three games). If you include all the regular and postseason games against Miami, nearly a quarter of them have been in the playoffs. Dan Marino faced the Seahawks more times in the postseason than he did in the regular campaign. His first playoff loss and last playoff win came against the Seahawks.

THANK YOU, PAUL

Out of the depths of Behring Hell came a local savior named Paul Allen. Seeing that Seattle was on the verge of losing the Seahawks, Allen bought the team and saved it from a horrible fate in Southern California. For this, all Seahawk fans owe Allen an amount of gratitude the size of Mount Rainier.

Sure, Allen theoretically could have built the Seahawk stadium on his own. However, as I understand it, the public funding was spread out through lotteries and taxes generated by the stadium/exhibition center and the existing hotel tax, not money from the state's general fund. Allen himself spent more than $130 million on the stadium and agreed to pay for all

Paul Allen after the NFC Championship. Can you imagine Ken Behring holding this trophy?
Neither can I.

cost overruns, a huge deal considering the extra costs on the Mariners' new stadium. Allen, along with his team at Football Northwest and First & Goal (including Bert Kolde, Jody Patton, and Bob Whitsitt), laid a secure future for the Hawks with the new stadium. He has also spent millions of his own money making the Seahawks a first-class operation. From the team's jet to paying players and personnel to building a new Seahawk headquarters and practice facility, the franchise has become the envy of the NFL.

One of the things I like about Allen is that he's the only team owner I know who had similar childhood sports experiences as I. He sometimes mentions going to Husky football games as a kid with his dad. I did the same thing. There is something cool about this fact. I also like that he created the Experience Music Project/Science Fiction Museum and Hall of Fame in Seattle. Those are the sort of projects I'd build if I had a few extra billion dollars. (Another thing I would build: a Seahawk-themed miniature golf course with Mirror Pond Ale flowing through the hazards instead of water.)

Ownership is possibly the biggest key to a successful pro sports franchise. It is also the hardest to change. You can't fire, cut, or trade an owner. The Seahawks went from having quality local owners in the Nordstrom family to Ken Behring, a callous Californian who wanted to steal the team from Seattle, then back to another local owner, Allen, who has restored success to the organization.

I know all this must sound like I'm kissing Allen's butt, but he is the guy who rescued this team from its darkest period. Plus, are you really a sycophant when you sincerely mean what you write? I've been fortunate enough to personally meet Pete Townshend and thank him for making music that has meant a lot to me. I'd like to extend a similar appreciation to Allen. So hey, Paul, er, Mr. Allen, thanks for saving the Seahawks. I'd like to buy you one of our home state's great microbrews sometime.

NEVER GONNA WORK WITH TWO

The Hawks had two fullbacks named John Williams in camp in 1986. The one with the *L* in the middle stuck around.

05

POP GOES THE CULTURE

It's been said the NFL is in the entertainment business. I don't know if I totally agree with that statement. After all, I don't feel very entertained when the Hawks lose. Watching Hasselbeck throw an interception or the defense give up a big play has as much entertainment value to me as viewing the Ben Affleck/ Jennifer Lopez disaster known as Gigli. However, the Seahawks have occasionally seeped into entertainment mediums and popular culture has never been the same.

AT THE MOVIES

When it comes to Hollywood, the Seahawks unsurprisingly have not had a lot of attention. You can't include *The Sea Hawk*, the 1940 swashbuckler starring Errol Flynn (a party animal who could put Lindsay Lohan/Amy Winehouse/the latest celebrity train wreck to shame). Nor can you include *Submarine Seahawk*, an obscure thriller that has nothing to do with one of Dave Krieg's patented sidearm throws.

However, you can include *Harry and the Hendersons*, a movie about a Sasquatch that moves in with a Seattle family. Some of the characters, including the dad, played by John Lithgow, wear Seahawk garb. Personally, I think the movie would've been better if bigfoot Harry had worn a Largent jersey. There's also *Man of the House*, a family comedy in which Chevy Chase's character wears a Seahawk hat. I can't vouch for the quality of this movie since I've only seen clips, but just the phrase "Chevy Chase family comedy" is enough for me to avoid it like the avian flu (National Lampoon's *Vacation* being the exception in his oeuvre).

The film to most prominently feature the Seahawks is *Twice in a Lifetime*, a 1985 drama starring Gene Hackman as Harry, a Seattle-area mill worker who loves the team. The movie opens with Harry wearing a Seahawk cap as he strolls through town. In the next scene he's wearing a Seahawk shirt at his 50th birthday dinner as he listens to a poem composed by his wife, played by Ellen Burstyn. The ode mentions how important the Hawks are to him. Next he's watching the Mariners losing on the tube while his son-in-law says the city would be nothing without the Seahawks.

Harry attends his birthday party at a local bar, where the walls are adorned with Seahawk pennants; photos of Warner,

Easley, and others; a Seahawk dry erase board; and two big handmade banners, WE ❤ THE HAWKS! and GO HAWKS! When we first see Harry's future love interest, Audrey, played by Ann-Margret, an Olympia Beer Seahawk schedule is in the background. His pals at the bar give Harry a new Seahawk hat and jacket like the one Coach Knox would wear to the frigid confines of Riverfront Stadium. Harry sports the Hawk attire during the rest of the party, including when Audrey gives him a big birthday kiss.

The film then shifts to the love story between Harry and Audrey and the brutal collapse of his marriage. There's a nice scene shot in the Beacon Hill neighborhood featuring the couple with the Kingdome in the background. Audrey asks Harry about going to Seahawk games; he replies that he never misses them. They are the reason he gets up in the morning. He then takes her to a game, and as they stand outside the Dome, Harry tells her to keep "an eye on No. 32, Curt Warner." I remember when I first saw this film, I had to hit the rewind button to make sure I heard Hackman correctly. Yep, after all this setup that Harry is a big Seahawk fan, the filmmakers screw it up by misidentifying Warner's No. 28.

The filmmakers do redeem themselves once Harry and Audrey are inside the Kingdome watching the game. According to the film's director, Bud Yorkin, in his DVD commentary, they shot this scene during an actual game. You see the real Seahawks coming out of the tunnel before the 1984 opening day game against Cleveland. Even more impressive is the game footage with Hackman and Ann-Margret in the stands watching the Hawks and Browns in action. It isn't some Hollywood trickery involving phony players. They actually stuck a hand-held camera right behind the pair and just shot their reactions to the authentic action on the field. The film also has some great shots of the twelfth man doing the wave while the Sea

Gals and the old Seahawk mascot strut their stuff on the field. It's cool to see this great era of Hawk football having a role in a major motion picture.

However, there isn't a scene of Harry coming out of the Kingdome demoralized because "No. 32" Curt Warner suffered a season-ending injury during the game (which really happened). Instead, we see Harry dump his wife and shack up with Audrey. The question that remains on my mind: did Harry keep his season tickets in the divorce settlement?

THE SEAHAWK CAR

During the late 1970s, the Seahawks teamed up with a few local Datsun (now known as Nissan) dealers to issue a special car that was called the "Z Hawk." It was a silver 280Z with blue and green racing stripes that flowed into the Seahawk bird logo just like on their helmets. There is no truth to the rumor that the basement-dwelling Mariners of the '70s issued a special version of the AMC Gremlin.

SEATTLE SEAHAWKS: THE BOARD GAME

The Seahawks are featured in a number of video games these days, but you have to go back more than 20 years to witness the team's introduction into the world of board games. In 1986 a company called Pipeline Productions created the Seattle Seahawks Trivia Game. Their reasoning? Why shouldn't the Hawks join Candy Land, Chutes and Ladders, and The Game of Life as a subject to be immortalized in a board game? Seemed like a pretty good idea to me. I don't remember this

The Seahawks' game didn't put Milton Bradley or Parker Brothers out of business.

game hitting the market. It wasn't until about 10 years later that my friend Richie found it at a garage sale. Richie surprised me with it when I visited him in Bellingham. I was happy that someone had combined my love of board games and my love of the Seahawks to form one competitive concoction.

The game board is a replica of the Kingdome's football field, complete with a Seahawk helmet at the 50-yard line and the word "Seahawks" written in the official team font on both end zones. To play the game, you need two contestants on either side of the field. One player is the blue team; the other is the green team. Just like regular football, players alternate being on offense, and they "drive" down the field by answering a question from a game card given by the opposing player. The questions are all about Seahawk history from 1976 to 1985. The cards are divided into decks 1–5 and ranked, with 1 being the easiest questions and 5 the toughest. Correctly answer a No. 1 question and you advance 1 yard on the game board. However, if you miss the question, you lose 5 yards. It follows this pattern up to the No. 5 cards, which are 5 yards ahead for the correct answer and 1 yard back if you are wrong. Players stay on offense as long they advance the ball 10 yards within four downs. If not, the ball is "punted" 40 yards to the other player. Once a player makes it into the end zone, they score six points.

The main game piece is a cardboard football, which moves downfield as you answer the questions. Also included is a 30-second game clock, which means a player needs to answer the question within a half a minute or be penalized 5 yards. According to the rule book, the game is divided into four 20-minute quarters with "a half-time intermission of 15 minutes." What you are supposed to do during this 15-minute break is anybody's guess. Create your own locker room where you can scream at yourself for playing lousy? Imagine you are waiting in the beer line at the Dome by standing in front of the fridge for 14 minutes and then grabbing some suds? Go act like you're paying attention to the wife before quickly getting back to the game for the second-half kickoff?

I was very excited to play this game. After all, I knew a lot of Seahawk trivia and I thought I could do well. However, once Richie, my brother Milt, and I started playing, I realized why I had never heard of the game before. It's kind of a dud. I understand someone (or a few people) spent a lot of time creating it, but many of the questions are inane, bordering on the absurd. For example, some of the supposedly easy No. 1 questions are ridiculous: "Who is the current ticket director of the Seahawks?" Equally comical are a portion of the No. 5 questions: "What is the first name of former Seahawks general manager John Thompson's wife?" (For those of you dying to know, it's Mimi.) Not that I have anything against ticket directors or general managers' wives, but even the most lunatic of fans would be hard pressed to know these types of answers. In fact, if you know the name of a former GM's wife off the top of your head, then you're probably a stalker.

Soon, Richie, Milt, and I got tired of answering queries such as "Who held the position of equipment manager for one year only?" (Yep, a real question.) The game did contain a lot of legitimate questions, but it wasn't enough to keep us interested. Today, it sits on a bookshelf gathering dust. The only function it serves is as a collector's item. If I'm really bored, I may pull out the game cards and ask myself, "Who was the Seahawks business manager from 1977 to 1982?" As we all know, the answer is Bob Anderson.

OFF THE CHARTS

One sign your team has captured the imagination of a city is when someone pens a song about the franchise. The Chicago Bears had probably the most famous (or should I say, infamous) football song when "Super Bowl Shuffle" was released in 1985. It is most noteworthy because it featured actual members of the team performing on the song and in the music video. The song received a Grammy nomination, which meant a lot of the voters were either Bear fans or tone-deaf. However, before the Bears did their little shuffle, there was "The Blue Wave Is on a Roll," a music video produced at Seattle's KING-TV prior to the 1985 season. The video featured some Seahawks, including Edwin Bailey and Mike Tice, "singing" in a locker room. Sharing lead vocal duties was linebacker Michael Jackson. Using Jackson was a shrewd move on the record producer's part to get a few extra sales from boneheads who thought they were getting a tune from the guy who had just sold a billion *Thriller* albums. The song itself was basically a knockoff of The Coasters' hit "Yakety Yak." Imagine if the Seahawks had won the Super Bowl following the 1985 season: it would've been "The Blue Wave" that exploded onto the pop culture scene, not the "Super Bowl Shuffle." (Thanks to YouTube, you can watch "The Blue Wave" online.)

The Seahawks have had a number of songs written about them, especially in recent years when digital home studios and near-instantaneous song downloading has made it very easy for artists to release their topical tunes to the listening public. Back in the early 1980s when the team was making its first playoff run, it wasn't so easy. You would have to go into a real recording studio and cut a song. The next step would be to have the song pressed into vinyl for the 7-inch single. Then you'd send this little 45 rpm ditty to local radio stations in hopes of getting some airplay while it still had relevance.

I'm not sure if it was the first Seahawk song ever released, but the initial one I can recall came out in 1983 when I was the music director at my college radio station, KUGS-FM, at Western Washington University. Going by the highly original title "The Seattle Football Song," it was made by a group that called themselves The Bench Warmers. The song was a take-off of the Peter Tosh pop-reggae hit "Johnny B. Goode" and featured a singer referring to Curt Warner as "Curtis." The song also mentioned "Jimmy," apparently in reference to Jim Zorn. This quickly made the song outdated since Dave Krieg had taken over the starting job midseason. It didn't get much airplay at KUGS, partly because no one had heard of "Curtis" or "Jimmy."

There was another song that came out in the mid-1980s called "The Seahawk Wave" by Robbie Frantz. It was a poppy tune featuring one of those snazzy sax solos that had been popular 10 years earlier. Unlike "The Seattle Football Song," it wasn't a takeoff of an existing hit, and it didn't mention any Seahawk players. However, the song is notable for using almost every marine metaphor imaginable. Frantz's label ViVi Records appears to have spent some real money on the project. The single had its own custom jacket cover, complete with a Seahawk helmet graphic. It was even an officially licensed NFL product. I always wondered how that came to be. Must've been the marine metaphors.

MILK IT

Before the milk mustache became the dairy industry's advertising signature, Jim Zorn and Steve Largent pitched the white beverage throughout the Northwest. The duo even sang in the commercials. Milk may do a body good, but their singing did damage to my ears.

BLUE–AND–GREEN MONDAY NIGHTS

"The Seahawks. The NFL's most interesting and unorthodox team."
—Howard Cosell on *Monday Night Football*, November 26, 1979

"Here in the Kingdome in Seattle. Fans coming from all over the Northwest. They even have season tickets that they've sold in Seattle."
—Frank Gifford on *Monday Night Football*, November 26, 1979

Monday Night Football. It's the one game that all of America (including other NFL players) has a chance to see and one of the great mergers of pop culture and pro sports. Early on, it starred Howard Cosell and his 75-cent words. "Dandy" Don Meredith and his homespun songs. Play-by-play announcer Frank Gifford and his head-scratching mistakes.

If you watched *MNF* in Western Washington from the 1970s through the mid-1990s, then you know it usually started on an hour delay at 7:00 p.m. (Seahawk games excepted). This could prove troublesome when you were a kid, because the games would go past your bedtime. (For you younger readers, a "bedtime" was an established schedule parents set so kids would go to bed at a regular hour each night. If my niece Ginny and nephew Quint are any indication, bedtimes have gone the way of record turntables in the last 20 years.)

Monday Night Football was ABC's longest-running prime time show, and it usually beat the competition from the other networks. When the Seahawks first appeared on *MNF* in 1979, the game in the West Coast viewing region was up against such network fare as *Little House on the Prairie* on NBC and *WKRP in Cincinnati* on CBS. The delightfully boring Ingalls clan and a wacky radio station were no alternative for Seattle sports fans. Since then, the Hawks on *MNF* have entertained both the nation and the twelfth man with a mixture of trickery, drama, and some NFL history that has often led to victory for Seattle.

Our first-ever Monday night game was at Atlanta, when a fake field goal became a Jim Zorn pass to kicker Efren Herrera that had every football fan in America talking on Tuesday morning (see "Great Seahawk Wins: Part Two," page 49). A month later, the *MNF* carnival came to the Kingdome for the first time as the Hawks took on the New York Jets. Even before the Seahawks existed, I'd wished for a *MNF* game in Seattle. I likened the situation to the NASA space program. At the beginning of the '60s, President Kennedy said there would be an American on the moon by the end of the decade; when Neil Armstrong set foot on lunar soil in 1969, Kennedy's proclamation came true. *Monday Night Football* on ABC began in 1970, and by the end of the decade there was a game in Seattle. (All right, maybe I'm overstating it—slightly.)

Walking inside the Kingdome that Monday evening, you could see every twelfth man was ready for prime time. The Dome was filled with posters awaiting their shot at television fame, including one that read "VIVA HERRERA" with a drawing of the Seahawk kicker looking like the Frito Bandito (political correctness had not yet made its way inside the stadium). There was another that read "JETS FALL PREY TO THE SEAHAWKS," featuring a sketch of a Seahawk bird with its talons wrapped around an airplane, presumably not a Boeing aircraft.

CHANGE THE CHANNEL! I hold a special fondness for the Jets because the first football bet I ever made was on "Broadway Joe" Namath's gang. I wagered my older brother Hank five cents that New York would beat the Colts in Super Bowl III. Sure enough, the Jets won, and as I held out my hand in front of Hank expecting a nickel, he dropped five pennies in my palm. I kicked myself for not making the bet an actual *nickel*. Even back then I hated pennies.

As we await the kickoff, my dad points to the announcer's booth and wonders "if Howard is on the sauce tonight." "The sauce?" I ask. "Alcohol," my old man replies. This is the first time I hear alcohol referred to as "the sauce." To me as a kid, Howard Cosell was the old guy who would sometimes use words I didn't understand and narrate the highlights of Sunday games at halftime. I didn't know he was a boozehound. So I have my father to thank for this illumination.

The Seahawks set up their first touchdown of the game when Cornell Webster blocks a punt with his *foot*. Yes, his foot blocked the kick when the Jet punter was too slow. That is rarer than having your kicker catch a pass. Quarterback Zorn is simply brilliant this evening. At one point he completes 14 passes in a row. Archie Bunker and every other Jet fan must have shut off their Zeniths before the end of this 30-7 rout.

CHANGE THE CHANNEL! During the 1980 fall television season, CBS battles Monday Night Football with Flo, a spin-off of the sitcom Alice. The show stars Polly Holliday as Flo, the sassy waitress who always utters "Kiss mah grits!" This is a perplexing line for viewers in the Pacific Northwest, since exactly three people in the area know what grits are.

I think if Jack Patera hadn't been a football coach, he would've had a fine career as a TV producer. He certainly had an eye for what makes good prime time television. During Seattle's Monday night appearance against the Raiders in 1980, Patera calls another successful fake field goal in which Zorn hits Herrera for a first down. This leads to laughter and cheers from Dandy Don and Cosell, and an eventual touchdown for the Hawks. The next season San Diego comes to the Kingdome for a Monday night affair. You would think Charger head coach (and Seattle native) Don Coryell would've made sure Patera wasn't able sneak in another fake field goal, but you'd be wrong. However, this trick play is a little different: Zorn throws a little shovel pass to Sherman Smith instead of to Herrera. The play goes for a touchdown, which helps the Hawks beat San Diego for the first time in team history.

The Seahawks again take on the Chargers during their next Monday night appearance in 1984 at San Diego/Jack Murphy Stadium. It really is a game of threes for Seattle: three Largent touchdown receptions and three interceptions by Kenny Easley (a Seahawk team record). These threes add up to a 24-0 victory and NFL Defensive Player of the Week honors for Easley. For the Chargers, it's the first time they've been shut out in five years. It's so bad in San Diego that Shamu, the killer whale at nearby SeaWorld, is seen pouring Smirnoff down his blowhole.

Two weeks later the Seahawks are back on Monday night, this time in the Dome against the defending world-champion Raiders. The buildup all over Western Washington for this brawl is incredible. The defense is on a nine-quarter scoreless streak, and the team has won six in a row. A record crowd is on hand to see the 8-2 Hawks against the 7-3 Silver-and-Black. As with most games from this era, I watch it 90 minutes north of Seattle in Bellingham, along with my friends Bri, Jay, and Richie, and a few 11-ounce bottles of Rainier beer. It seems like every single rail inside the Kingdome is covered with a homemade poster. One enterprising person has even made T-shirts that read "Raider Busters," complete with a slash over the Raider logo to mimic one of the year's biggest movies, *Ghostbusters*. The shirts are a big hit: the lot of 40,000 reportedly sold out before the game. Radio station KUBE even put in rotation a parody of the *Ghostbusters* theme song, called "Raider Busters."

A dismal first half sees the Hawks down 7-0 at halftime and the twelfth man somnambulant. However, in the third quarter the team finally lives up to their Raider Buster status. Seahawk rookie special teamer Fredd Young hammers returner Dokie Williams on a kickoff. The hit is part locomotive, part *Rollerball*. More importantly, it inspires the Hawks. Seattle takes the lead when Krieg threads the ball between two defenders to Byron Walker in the back of the end zone. Announcer Frank Gifford originally says it is Largent with the touchdown reception, a natural mistake since Largent is 5 feet 11 inches and white, while Walker is 6 feet 4 inches and black.

On the Hawks' next drive, Daryl Turner beats Raider Lester Hayes to the end zone for a touchdown reception, and the once-dormant Kingdome crowd erupts in epic fashion. Only slightly less screaming is emitting from my house on Forest Lane in Bellingham as bottles of Vitamin R rattle on the coffee table.

However, two Dave Krieg mistakes keep East Coast viewers from switching the channel to Johnny Carson. An interception leads to a Los Angeles touchdown to make it a 17-14 game. Later, a Krieg fumble gives the Raiders the ball in Seattle territory. Fortunately, the defense denies the Silver-and-Black any more points, and the record Kingdome crowd is rewarded with a victory. Up the I-5 corridor in Whatcom County, we celebrate this huge win with another Raiiiiiiiii-nieeeeeeeer-beeeeeeeer.

CHANGE THE CHANNEL! Going against Monday Night Football in 1985 in the Seattle area is *TV's Bloopers & Practical Jokes* on NBC, in which host Ed McMahon plays hidden-camera practical jokes on unsuspecting celebrities, much like Ashton Kutcher would do on his MTV show *Punk'd* nearly 20 years later. In other words, Kutcher owes his entire career to McMahon. Meanwhile, CBS offers its mostly female viewers an alternative to football called *Scarecrow and Mrs. King*. The program doesn't feature an actual scarecrow, much to the dismay of farmers expecting a romance between a straw-stuffed dummy and one of Larry King's ex-wives.

The Hawks lost twice on Monday night in 1985, but the team did provide America with some entertainment on one particular play against the Rams. With Seattle at the Ram 3, Krieg can't hold on to a shotgun snap at the 8-yard line. The ball scurries backward, aided by not one, but two Ram defenders, who not only fail to recover the ball but also send it back to the 20-yard line. Krieg, who hasn't given up on the play, manages to be in position as one of those sweet Kingdome turf bounces plops the ball right into his hands. Dave, no doubt thinking there's no way he can waste this bit of good fortune, heaves a pass to receiver Danny Greene in the back right corner of the end zone for the score. Just your typical 3-yard touchdown pass. Unfortunately, the Hawks lose the game to a quarterback named Dieter Brock—actually, we lost to running back Eric Dickerson. Dieter is the stiff who handed him the ball.

Sportscaster Al Michaels thankfully took over the play-by-play duties in 1986 from Frank Gifford (who remained in a commentating role). However, Michaels is calling the World Series for ABC and misses out when Steve Largent puts himself in the NFL record books during the Seahawks' 33-7 victory over the Chargers. In the second quarter, league history is appropriately made on a third-down conversion, when Krieg finds Largent over the middle for 17 yards. The reception extends Largent's consecutive-game streak with at least one reception to 128 games, breaking Harold Carmichael's record. The game is stopped for a brief ceremony as the Kingdome denizens give him a standing ovation. Sadly, this is Largent's only major NFL record-breaking catch to occur in Seattle (his records for career receptions, yardage, and touchdowns all happened in road games). Later Largent *completes* an 18-yard pass to Byron Franklin; it's one of two complete passes thrown by Largent in his 14-year career.

The following year the Hawks visit the Jets in New Jersey. The electronic marquee outside the Meadowlands Sports Complex looks like it'd be more at home on Broadway in nearby Manhattan:

JETS/SEATTLE
APPEARING TONIGHT:
THE BOZ

New Yorkers are able to witness one of only 25 performances of The Brian Bosworth Show before it closes for good. But for the Seahawks, this game is more like a theatrical flop that shuts its doors after opening night. The team loses 30-14, leaving The Boz with zero chance of scoring a Tony Award.

CHANGE THE CHANNEL! A television writers' strike in 1988 delays most of the original programming on NBC and CBS toward the end of the football season, forcing the networks to air movies opposite *Monday Night Football*. ABC's lone scripted Monday show, *MacGyver* (which aired after *MNF* on the West Coast), doesn't suffer from the strike: the ever-resourceful *MacGyver* manages to create scripts out of toilet paper, toothpicks, and huckleberries.

One of the Seahawks' most competitive Monday night games comes in 1988 against the Raiders in the Kingdome. The Hawks had lost their last 15 games in a row when trailing at halftime. But a Paul Skansi touchdown reception with a mere 0:30 remaining before the break gives Seattle a 21-20 lead. Now the Hawks don't have to worry about their losing streak when behind at the half—or do they?

Norm Johnson kicks off to the rookie Tim Brown, who takes it at the 2-yard line. The reigning Heisman Trophy winner proceeds to cut through the middle of the Hawk coverage team before heading to the outside, where it looks like he'll go all the way for a touchdown. Melvin Jenkins appears to be the last Seahawk to have a chance to bring him down, but his diving attempt is just short. Miraculously, rookie cornerback Dwayne Harper is able to catch up to Brown and tackle him just 3 yards shy of the end zone. Despite stopping the touchdown on the return, the Hawks still almost certainly face being down at halftime. But after a holding penalty nullifies a Raider touchdown on the ensuing play, kicker Chris Bahr hooks a 31-yard field goal. This sends the twelfth man into delirium and a crestfallen Brown searching for some Xanax as one of the longest kick returns ever against the Hawks comes to naught.

The halftime lead is secured. No worries about the 15-game losing streak. Thanks to Curt Warner and John L. Williams becoming the first pair of Seahawk running backs to rush for over 100 yards in the same game, Seattle eventually wins this critical battle in the war for the AFC Western Division championship, 35-27.

CHANGE THE CHANNEL! When Frank Gifford was part of the announcing crew for *Monday Night Football*, he would always say, "Live from the Kingdome in Seattle, Washington," before every Seahawk home game. It's always been a pet peeve of mine when broadcasters add "Washington" right after "Seattle," and Gifford was one of the worst offenders. No one says "Los Angeles, California"; it's just "Los Angeles." You don't hear "Live from Soldier Field in Chicago, Illinois"; it's "Live from Soldier Field in Chicago." The same should hold true for Seattle. No one will be confused about Seattle's location. There is no "Seattle, New Jersey," or "Seattle, Wisconsin." In fact, Seattle is one of the few major U.S. cities to have a truly indigenous name. The city is named after a Native American tribal leader from the Pacific Northwest, Chief Seattle (also known as Chief Sealth). Why spell it out for those who are geographically challenged? Make 'em look at a map.

In 1989 the Hawks face a Buffalo Bills team that features a future Hall of Fame backfield with Jim Kelly and Thurman Thomas. However, it is the Seahawks' future Hall of Famer, Steve Largent, who provides the play of the game. After the Seahawks score the first touchdown on a Curt Warner run, they attempt the extra point. But the snap is low, and holder Largent wisely picks up the ball and runs it in for a point (the two-point conversion had yet to exist in the NFL). Largent was doing the holding because regular holder Jeff Kemp was inactive for the game. His heads-up play turns out to be critical. Largent's second-ever point after touchdown is the last point he would ever score inside the Kingdome and the difference in the 17-16 victory.

CHANGE THE CHANNEL! ABC's competition for *Monday Night Football* in 1990 in the Pacific Time region includes *Uncle Buck* on CBS and NBC's *Ferris Bueller*, both of which, coincidentally, are based on films by the king of the teen movie, John Hughes. *Bueller* is canceled in December despite featuring a pre-*Friends* Jennifer Aniston as one of the leads. *Buck* lasts a year and a half, most likely because it features a character named Skank.

The twelfth man displays its classy and forgiving nature to a Monday night television audience in a game against the Bengals in 1990. Early in the contest, a beleaguered Norm Johnson comes out to attempt a 51-yard field goal. Johnson had been the goat a week earlier when he missed two game-winning field goal attempts at Denver. One would expect at least a smattering of boos to rain on Norm, but the Kingdome crowd gives him a very good ovation. The positive energy works as Johnson knocks it through, and the Hawks prevail in their 31-16 upset over first-place Cincinnati.

The Cincy game also features some interesting linebacker-on-quarterback violence when Seahawk Rufus Porter fails to hear a whistle and body-slams Boomer Esiason. The Bengal quarterback doesn't appreciate his shoulder being taken down into the hard Dome turf and tells Porter he did a very bad thing. Rufus, no doubt disliking a quarterback telling him how to do his job, takes a swing at Esiason. And then another swing. The Hawks are assessed a 15-yard penalty, but Porter is not thrown out of the game. This is huge, because the Seattle defense had been dominating the contest. On the next play Esiason's pass is batted down by, you guessed it, Rufus. He yells another pleasantry at the quarterback's face. (If this happened today, no doubt he would be flagged for taunting.) The Kingdome is screaming during all this action, which causes Esiason to commit a delay-of-game penalty on the following play. After the Bengals fail to convert on third down, both Boomer and Rufus return to their sidelines. Esiason vows never to name a dog Rufus, while Porter promises himself to never call one of his pups Boomer.

Inexplicably, the brass at ABC thought it was a good idea to put the 1992 Hawks on the schedule in a game at the Dome against the Broncos. By the time this affair rolled around in late November, the network was surely regretting it. Seattle came into the game with exactly one win and possessing one of the worst offenses of all time. The Broncos were faring a bit better, but John Elway was hurt, so rookie Tommy Maddox got the start for Denver.

In a game that it seemed no one wanted to win, it takes a 3-yard touchdown pass from Stan Gelbaugh to Brian Blades on the last play of regulation for Seattle to tie it at 13. On their second overtime possession, the Hawks drive down the Denver 16, whereupon head coach Tom Flores elects to kick a field goal on first down. John Kasay then promptly hooks the 33-yard kick. The Broncos prove to be equally incompetent, and on the Hawks' *fourth* possession in overtime, Kasay redeems himself with a 32-yard game winner, ending one of the most offensively inept games ever on *Monday Night Football*. The Hawks are banished from Monday night for the next seven years.

> **CHANGE THE CHANNEL!** While the Seahawks are in exile from the *Monday Night Football* landscape during the '90s, the Fox network valiantly tries to steal away some of ABC's viewers. The network plugs in a sitcom called *Lush Life*, which airs briefly opposite MNF in 1996. The show is about an artsy punk-rock girl who works at Hooters. No, I am not making this up.

When the Seahawks finally appear again on ABC prime time in 1999, it is at Lambeau Field against the Packers. The game's story line is too irresistible for the network: a coach who restored glory to a legendary team, prompting a street to be named after him, returns as the enemy after having left only 10 months earlier.

The Seahawks, on one of the game's early key plays, don't meet their past, but rather, their future. Packer kicker Ryan Longwell attempts a 50-yard field goal, but Hawk rookie Lamar King blocks the kick. The ball then takes a generous bounce right into the waiting hands of Seahawk Shawn Springs, who goes untouched for 61 yards the other way for a touchdown. Well, not exactly untouched, because, as he is celebrating in the end zone, he is shoved by Packer holder Matt Hasselbeck. Hass earns a personal foul call while Seahawk fans wonder, who's this knucklehead pushing Springs?

Packer quarterback Brett Favre has one of the worst nights in his storied career. He turns the ball over five times, and Seattle wins, 27-7. As the game ends Favre walks off the field with his hood hiding most of his face, making him look like a green version of Vincent Price's Prince Prospero character from *The Masque of the Red Death*. Meanwhile, the Hawks' coach rides down Holmgren Way in Green Bay, victorious.

At the turn of the century, the Hawks go on a three-game losing streak on Monday night. Included is an infamous loss at home to San Francisco in 2002. After hauling in the game-winning touchdown, 49er receiver Terrell Owens pulls a Sharpie pen out of his sock and signs the ball. Too bad Terrell didn't pull out some humility. Or at least a muzzle for himself.

The Seahawks return to their winning tradition on Monday nights during the Super Season of 2005. They venture to Philadelphia and encounter a snowstorm not unlike the ones General Washington's soldiers had endured in nearby Valley Forge some 230 years earlier. Seattle proceeds to smack the Eagles around like a band of unprepared British redcoats. Final score: Seahawks 42, Eagles 0. It's the biggest shutout in *Monday Night Football* history. Both Andre Dyson and Lofa Tatupu took the ball away from Eagle receivers on their respective interceptions returned for touchdowns. Lofa then looked like boxer Smokin' Joe Frazier when he punched the goal post base after his score. (Maybe Tatupu did it as an homage to Frazier, who lives in Philly.)

The crowd at Lincoln Financial Field was in a state of frozen shock most of the night, and all the schnapps in the City of Brotherly Love couldn't warm them up. Announcer John Madden even pointed out one guy in the stands who had passed out due to too many sips of the hard stuff and too many Seahawk touchdowns. When Dyson scored on a fumble return on the first play from scrimmage in the second half, even the angriest of Eagle fans was beyond booing. Still, it would've been hard to be Seahawk fan inside the Linc. Usually I love being at an opposing team's stadium for a Hawk win, but Philly doesn't take kindly to visitors celebrating. The temptation to be outwardly jubilant during the rout would've been too great for me. My celebratory antics would probably have gotten me thrown into a dumpster or the Schuylkill River.

CHANGE THE CHANNEL! After 35 years on ABC, the network moves *MNF* over to ESPN beginning in 2006. It means the 27 people in America who still didn't have cable or satellite television would not have access to the games. This list doesn't include my brother Hank and sister-in-law Janette, two TV Luddites who'd finally gotten cable a year earlier. Their lives are now complete.

Definitely the goofiest *MNF* fracas occurs in 2006 during a 16-0 victory against the Raiders at Qwest Field. After one play Raider end Tyler Brayton and Seahawk tight end Jerramy Stevens get into a scuffle. At one point, Brayton knees Stevens in the groin. I'd never seen anything like that before in football. Perhaps the two just wanted to give fans a little taste of the hatred that used to be commonplace between the Raiders and Seahawks. After all, they both grew up in Washington— Stevens in Olympia and Brayton in Pasco—so they knew the series used to be filled with fisticuffs. You gotta appreciate the kids keeping up tradition.

Three weeks later when the Seahawks play the Packers, what was once unthinkable becomes a reality in Seattle: snow falling during a Seahawk home game. Not just a few flakes but an all-out storm hits Qwest Field before the contest and continues throughout the first half. It's the first time I can recall snow falling during a major outdoor sporting event in Seattle. A surreal scene unfolds as the Qwest's FieldTurf turns from its perfect shade of green to a frosty white as play progresses. Matt Hasselbeck, starting for the first time in a month, shakes off a poor first half to lead the Hawks to a 10-point victory. Sales for Seahawk snow gear skyrocket.

In 2007 the Seahawks make *MNF* history when they blank the 49ers, 24-0. It is their fifth shutout on *Monday Night Football*, an NFL record for one franchise. Seattle also holds San Francisco to a team-record low of six first downs, another prime time performance that makes you glad you didn't switch over to see Jerry Springer's salsa steps on *Dancing with the Stars*.

Overall, the Hawks have one of the best winning percentages on *MNF*, as they have claimed victory in two-thirds of their total appearances. It's a testament to the franchise that it continually shines on prime time. Creative play-calling, dominating defense, and just a touch of theater have been the Hawks' modus operandi on Monday nights. I can almost hear the late Howard Cosell wax poetic about the Seahawks' entertainment value as he tips a few in the Afterlife Lounge.

06

MONSTER SCORES AND PHANTOM TOUCHDOWNS

Remember those touchdowns that had you jumping out of your chair and knocking your drink over, which shorted some outlets and caused an electrical fire that burned down your house? No? OK, maybe you remember the touchdowns that just made you really happy without having to consult your homeowner's insurance policy. Whatever.

GREAT SEAHAWK WINS: PART FOUR

SEAHAWKS 34, BEARS 21
Soldier Field, December 20, 1987

The Seahawks had been cruising once the legitimate season resumed following the players' strike of 1987. However, a crushing defeat by the Raiders on *Monday Night Football* and an ugly loss at Pittsburgh have left them fighting for a playoff spot when the team arrives in the Windy City for the second-to-last game of the regular season. Win, and the postseason is assured. No small task for an underdog in one of football's more storied stadiums. But a loss would put a playoff berth very much in doubt, especially since the final contest is at the always-troublesome Arrowhead Stadium in Kansas City. The Bears are two years past their Super Bowl season but still one of the elite teams in the NFL, with a 10-3 record. However, their oft-injured quarterback Jim McMahon doesn't even suit up for this game. Instead, McMahon is suited like PETA's Man of the Year, decked out in a ridiculous fur coat that features a fox carcass, complete with its head, draped around his neck.

A surprisingly sunny and mild December day awaits the teams as the fans at Soldier Field honor Walter Payton, playing in his final regular-season home game, in a pregame ceremony. The Hawks get on the board first when Daryl Turner does what he does best: score touchdowns. He makes a great catch behind a defender who is flagged for interference. (Not only is it the last touchdown reception of his too short and troubled career, but it's also Turner's last catch ever in the NFL.)

While the first half has little fireworks, with each team scoring just one touchdown, the third quarter is far different. On Chicago's first play from scrimmage of the half, fullback Neal

Anderson takes the pitch to the right for 3 yards to the 39. However, just as he is starting to fall backward, Brian Bosworth (who's already on the turf) strips the ball from him. Realizing that he is not down, The Boz gets up and starts heading toward the end zone. It looks like he is going to score, but a few Bears stop him, and he lands mere inches shy of the goal line, denying him his best chance to score a touchdown in his too short and troubled career. During the next play, Curt Warner shows The Boz how it's done as he goes over the top for 6. On the Chicago sideline, Bear coach Mike Ditka tells McMahon he looks like Huggy Bear, the pimp from *Starsky & Hutch*.

The capacity crowd at Soldier Field comes alive minutes later when "Sweetness" Payton ties the score at 14. Now, with the momentum shifted to Chicago, the Hawks need to answer. On their first play, which starts at the Seattle 25, Dave Krieg fakes the pitch to Warner and rolls out to the right, taking most of the defense with him. He then dumps a little screen pass to John L. Williams, who cuts toward the left sidelines. As John L. moves upfield, the play develops perfectly, with other Seahawks blocking out defenders, leaving him an open lane. At the Chicago 36 All-Pro linebacker Wilbur Marshall is in position to tackle Williams, but Steve Largent blocks him out, and John L. cuts back toward the middle of the field, where he eludes the last Bear defender and goes in for the touchdown. The 75-yard reception is not only the play of the game, it's the play of the season for the Seahawks.

After Seattle converts two Chicago fumbles into field goals, the Bears cut the Hawk lead to six points early in the fourth quarter when Payton again runs in for a touchdown. It is his 110th rushing touchdown and the final score of his long and untroubled career. The Bears again move the ball downfield on their next drive. It appears they have a chance to score the go-ahead touchdown, but Eugene Robinson picks off a Mike

Tomczak pass at the Seattle 14-yard line. Ditka can only stew on the sidelines as Warner scores another touchdown to make it a 34-21 final.

It is the Bears' only regular-season (nonstrike) loss at home all year. The Seahawks advance to the playoffs for the third time in five years. Meanwhile, McMahon and his coat are attacked by a den of rabid foxes.

SEAHAWKS 43, RAIDERS 37
Los Angeles Memorial Coliseum, December 18, 1988

The 1988 season was the definition of a roller-coaster for the Hawks. The team endured the trade and sudden retirement of defensive leader Kenny Easley prior to the campaign. There was also the transition to an uncertain future with OverBehring becoming the majority owner. While the team did stay relatively healthy, Dave Krieg's injury and absence for seven games was very detrimental. But Seattle perseveres, and the season comes down to the final game of the year at the L.A. Coliseum. Whoever wins this battle is going to be the AFC Western Division champ. For the Seahawks it would be a first in team history, as their other playoff appearances came from wild card berths.

The game starts awry as Krieg fumbles the second play from scrimmage, leading to a quick Raider touchdown. But Krieg, as he occasionally does after a mistake, rebounds on the Seahawks' next possession. Thanks to a key 34-yard John L. Williams reception and a 35-yard touchdown catch by Steve Largent, the game is tied. After an interception by Terry Taylor, the Seahawks take the lead on a Krieg touchdown pass to Brian Blades.

The game evolves into an old AFL-style shootout in which the defense is merely a supporting player to the starring role of the offense. A 51-yard touchdown pass from Raider quarterback Jay Schroeder to Willie Gault is followed by a 64-yard kickoff return by Bobby Joe Edmonds. Los Angeles counters with another 50-yard bomb to Gault, one of the great African American bobsledders. (No joke, Willie is an Olympic bobsledder.) The Hawks can only manage three field goals in the rest of the half. However, the Seahawk defense, no doubt taking umbrage to my above "supporting player" comment, holds the Raiders to a single field goal as Seattle leads 23-17 at the intermission.

The third quarter starts with a little razzle-dazzle from the Hawks as Krieg hands off to Paul Skansi on a reverse. Skansi in turn hands it off to Largent, who then hands it back to Krieg. A similar play went for a touchdown against the Broncos in 1987, but this time the coverage is too good downfield, so Krieg has to throw it near the sidelines to Blades. The pass still goes for 21 yards and is a crucial third-down conversion. On the following play Krieg hits Blades again, this time in the end zone for a touchdown.

Later, the Hawks' special teams fumbles a return deep in their own territory, but once again, the defense holds the Raiders to only a field goal. (I'm glad my demeaning comments inspired them.) Following the kickoff, the Seahawks start their next series at the 25. On first down Krieg fakes the pitch to Warner, rolls back, and throws a screen pass to John L. Williams. Just as he did on the same play in Chicago a year earlier, Williams goes 75 yards for the score. It's a beautiful play, one that will be recalled in a book some 21 years later. (Incredibly, it's the book you are currently reading.)

The Hawks now have a sizable lead, 37-20. But put that championship celebration on hold, because the Raiders drive the length of the field and score a touchdown on fourth and goal. (I guess another negative comment about the defense may be in order.) The third quarter ends with more trickery from the Seahawks, who run the old "flea-flicker" as a pitch from Warner is tossed back to Krieg, who launches a bomb to Blades inside the red zone for a 55-yard gain. Unfortunately a field goal, not another touchdown, is the Hawks' fate on this drive. The Raiders' fate is a spectacular 55-yard touchdown reception by Mervyn Fernandez (who, incidentally, is not an Olympic bobsledder). Seattle's former 17-point lead has now dwindled to less than a touchdown.

The rest of the fourth quarter moves too slowly for anxious Seahawk fans. Krieg throws an interception, but the defense doesn't allow the Raiders to convert. Norm Johnson ties his own team record with a fifth field goal of the day for the Hawks, but the Raiders manage a field goal of their own to make it 43-37. Despite the power backfield of Williams and Warner, the Hawks can't run out the last two minutes of the game clock. Nobody ever said it was easy to be a Seahawk fan.

The Raiders take over with one long minute to play. After two incompletions, Schroeder connects on a pass at the Seattle 46. The beleaguered Hawk defense, shelled for 440 yards on the day (not to mention my comments), then forces three more misses from Schroeder. It's now fourth down with only a few seconds left, and everyone within this galaxy knows Schroeder is going to throw a Hail Mary. He takes the snap out of the shotgun and rolls all the way back to his own 40-yard line, where he heaves a missile. Hawk defensive line coach George Dyer and many members of the Seattle sideline anxiously lean back as the ball sails toward the back of the end zone. As the ball falls to earth, cornerback Nesby Glasgow bats it out of play. For the very first time, the Seattle Seahawks are the AFC Western Division champions.

25 BIG-PLAY TOUCHDOWNS WORTH A MENTION

Many of the Seahawks' big-play touchdowns have been included in various other chapters in this book, but there are some that deserve to be acknowledged in a special chapter. "Big-play" scores are usually defined as offensive scoring plays that go for 40 or more yards, or defensive and special teams touchdowns. Here are some monster touchdowns not mentioned elsewhere. I've mostly limited them to games in which Seattle emerged victorious. For those scoring at home, sometimes more than one touchdown is included in a particular paragraph.

The First Big-Play Touchdown (1976)

You can't write about Seahawk history without mentioning this megaplay from the Hawks' first regular-season game ever. The St. Louis Cardinals are leading by 20 in the fourth quarter and probably taking the Seahawks a little too lightly when Jim Zorn, from his own 28, sends a missile downfield. Wide receiver Sam McCullum gets behind a dozing cornerback, catches the ball at the St. Louis 31, and heads for 6. The dozing defender dives at the 10 but is denied by McCullum's dancing feet. The result is a 72-yard touchdown. Seattle eventually pulls within six points and has a chance to win, but a Zorn interception in the end zone on the last play of the game squashes the hopes of a colossal upset. Still, it was a pretty good showing for a team playing its very first regular-season game and against the defending NFC Eastern Division champions.

Cause and Dufek (1976)

Don Dufek was the first in a long line of exceptional special teams players for the Seahawks. He made his presence felt in the Hawks' fifth-ever game when Seattle took on the Packers at the old County Stadium in Milwaukee (the Pack used to play a few games there each year). In the second quarter Green Bay punter David Beverly attempts a boot from his 29, but Dufek comes in to block the kick. The ball skips slowly on the stadium grass until Steve Raible scoops it up at the 27 and runs back nearly untouched for the first return score in team history. It's one of three blocked kicks that year for Dufek, and it helps the Hawks jump out to a 20-7 lead, which they sadly lose in the fourth quarter.

A Touchdown to Avoid Infamy (1977)

When the Seahawks and Buccaneers got together in 1977 it was called "Expansion Bowl II," but it really should've been titled the "Somebody's Gotta Win Bowl." Both Seattle and Tampa Bay had yet to be victorious on the season when they met in week five at the Kingdome. In fact, the Buccaneers had been winless for their entire history, marching their way into the NFL record books as the worst team ever (until the 2008 Detroit Lions). Naturally, the Hawks did not want to be the first victims of Buc coach John McKay's pathetic bunch. However, with Jim Zorn still injured, it was up to backup Steve Myer to save face for the boys in silver, green, and blue.

Late in the fourth quarter, with Seattle holding a precarious 24-23 lead, Myer dumps a pass over the middle to running back Sherman Smith. Evading many Buccaneers, Smith jets to the outside and heads for the end zone. The 44-yard touchdown reception helps secure a Seahawk victory, sparing embarrassment and giving them the momentum to win 5 out of their remaining 10 games, an impressive feat for a second-year team. I imagine Seattle's fortunes would have been a bit different had they lost this game.

Hunting for a Winning Season (1978)

Running back Al Hunter had few memorable games as a Seahawk; however, the final contest of the '78 season against the Chiefs was one of them. He rushed for 133 yards and two touchdowns. His second touchdown was the play of the game. In the second quarter, the Hawks punt on fourth and six. But Kansas City is called for an offsides on the play. Now Seattle has fourth and one at their own 45, and coach Patera decides to go for it. Zorn hands off to Hunter, who, after eluding a wall of Chiefs at the line, finds himself looking at a mostly clear field. He makes a nice move to avoid the safety, and then it's a straight sprint to the end zone. The 55-yard touchdown gives Seattle a 20-3 lead, and it proves to be the difference as the Hawks hold on, 23-19, and become the fastest expansion team to have a winning record with a 9-7 mark.

Green Acres (1979)

During the third quarter the Hawks are holding a 21-10 lead at Candlestick Park. The 49ers are knocking at the Seattle 6 when quarterback Steve DeBerg goes for the play action fake, spins around, and throws into the flat. However, his fancy football ballet fails him when linebacker Sammy Green cuts between two Niners and snags the ball at the 9. Green promptly goes the distance undisturbed, thanks to a late block by cornerback Cornell Webster on DeBerg. The Hawks win by 11. The 91-yard interception return is still the longest in Seahawk history.

Dial Doornink for Comeback (1981)

It is looking like another frustrating day for the 2-7 Seahawks as the Steelers (playing for the first time in Seattle) hold a commanding 21-3 lead. The Hawks have a third-and-six situation at the Pittsburgh 44 with under a minute to play in the first half. At the snap the Steelers blitz, but Jim Zorn is able to dump a pass off to Dan Doornink near the line of scrimmage mere milliseconds before future Hall of Famer Jack Lambert takes off Zorn's head. Upon catching the ball, native Washingtonian Doornink sees an open diagonal lane. He is aided by key blocks from Steve Raible and Sherman Smith and takes it all the way to the house. The touchdown helps ignite the Seahawks to their second biggest comeback in team history en route to a 24-21 victory. Also helping is the defense, which shuts out the mighty trio of Terry Bradshaw, Franco Harris, and John Stallworth in the second half.

Jacob's 73-yard Ladder (1983)

Defensive end Jacob Green scored four touchdowns in his brilliant 12-season tenure. The first came at Cleveland's old Municipal Stadium, aka "The Mistake by the Lake." With the Seahawks leading 17-9 in the fourth quarter, Cleveland quarterback Brian Sipe has the Browns driving in Seattle territory. However, Sipe throws up a lazy pass that Green grabs like a Subway sandwich at the 27, burning off 7,500 calories as he runs for six points. It turns out to be the longest NFL interception return in 1983. The Hawks win 24-9.

BlitzKrieg Bop (1984)

Dave Krieg was never confused with Jim Zorn in terms of mobility, but occasionally he did use his feet for positive gain. One of his more memorable runs comes in a win against the Chargers in the Dome. In the third quarter of a tie game, Krieg drops back to pass, but a blitzing San Diego defense forces him to take off to the right. With nothing but open greenery, Krieg does his best Curt Warner impression and chugs 37 yards for the go-ahead touchdown. It's the longest run in Krieg's 19-year career.

The Bomb (1984)

In 1984 Seattle battled the Broncos for first place the whole season but didn't face them until the last week of November in Denver. On the first play from scrimmage at their own 20, Dave Krieg launches a strike 46 yards before Daryl Turner stretches his arms at the Bronco 34. The ball bounces around his fingertips, but with the concentration of a doctor performing a triple bypass, Turner is able to pull it in on the run and sprint the remaining real estate. The 80-yard touchdown silences the Mile High Stadium crowd. It also helps propel the Hawks to a rare win in Denver and a tie for the division lead. Turner receives the nickname "Deep Heat," and the touchdown becomes one of the most memorable in Seahawk history. This was a very pivotal game, but if you're wondering why it's not included in a "Great Wins" chapter, it's because Bronco kicker Rich Karlis had a chance to tie the game at the end but missed a makeable field goal. One of my rules is that a great win never ends on a missed field goal. (Another rule: don't date actresses. Of course, I used to break that rule during my single days. I was an idiot.)

Ode to Bobby Joe (1986)

Bobby Joe Edmonds became an immediate special teams sensation in his rookie year. He had a 44-yard punt return in his first NFL game and continued to be a threat every time he touched the ball during the season. He led the NFL in punt return average in 1986 and was a consensus first-team All-NFL pick. His most memorable return is against Philadelphia when he receives a punt at the Seattle 25 and beats the entire Eagle special teams unit to the end zone for a 75-yard touchdown. The Seahawks eventually beat the Eagles, 24-20.

Th-th-th-that's All, Folks! (1986)

Quite possibly the most spectacular score to end a season comes in 1986 against Denver. The Seahawks need a win to keep their fragile postseason hopes alive. The Broncos want a victory to secure home field advantage throughout the playoffs. In the fourth quarter Curt Warner takes the pitch to the left side, threads through part of the Bronco defense, and then cuts to the right, where he beats one man near the Denver 40 and darts home free for a 60-yard touchdown. It makes the final score a 41-16 destruction of the Broncos, a team that would go on to win the AFC Championship. The run ties Warner's longest of his career. Seattle didn't make the playoffs, so the touchdown paraphrases one of Warner Brothers (no relation to Curt) cartoons' most famous characters, Porky Pig: "Th-th-th-that's all, folks, for the season." Never had the Hawks left the twelfth man wanting more than after this season: they ended the regular campaign as one of the hottest teams in the league, winning five in a row by an average margin of 18 points.

Ferrum's Finest (1991)

Occasionally, a player will join the Seahawks from a school most fans have never heard of; Dave Krieg's Milton College is probably the most well-known example. One of the best running backs in Hawk history, Chris Warren, came from Ferrum College, a school that the majority of Seahawk fans would be hard pressed to find on a map. (It's situated in the Blue Ridge Mountains of Virginia in the town of Ferrum. You're welcome.) Warren started as a special teamer in 1990 but eventually set

Curt Warner: the main ingredient in Ground Chuck.

the Seattle record for most career rushing yards. His lone punt return for a touchdown occurs against Indianapolis during his second season with the Seahawks. Warren takes a Colt punt at the Seattle 41 and backpedals to the 34-yard line as he crosses the field before he sees an open lane along the right sideline. Barely keeping his feet in bounds, he races his way to pay dirt to help the Hawks blow out Indy 31-3.

Lightning Rod (1993)

The Seahawks are down at Cincinnati, 10-9, with 4:38 remaining when Bengal running back Harold Green is grabbed and pushed back into the end zone by linebacker Kevin Murphy. Then linebacker Rod Stephens pops the ball from Green's clutch and recovers it for a game-winning touchdown. On the sideline, coach Tom Flores waits for the official acknowledgment of the score and then does the lamest celebratory "clap-jump" this side of a Norwegian gymnastic coach.

Double Reversal of Fortune (1995)

Facing third and seven from the Hawks' 14-yard line against Jacksonville, quarterback Rick Mirer fakes the handoff to Chris Warren heading to the left and instead gives the ball to rookie wide receiver Joey Galloway going to the right. Galloway moves near the sideline and zips upfield. However, four Jaguars trap him at the 16. Amazingly, he stays on his feet and makes an unbelievable lateral run across the field before finding daylight around the 20-yard-line hash marks. He then goes the distance, thanks to a terrific block by Warren, before sauntering into the end zone for the score. It is officially listed as an 86-yard rushing touchdown and the longest play from scrimmage in Seahawk history at the time. But when you take in account that the width of a football field is 53 yards, and Joey ran at least that much as he did a double reverse, he actually gained about 139 yards on the play. Galloway also has two receiving touchdowns in the Seahawks' 47-30 victory at Jacksonville and is named AFC Offensive Player of the Week.

Here's the Story of the Hurricane (1996)

Wide receiver Brian Blades played 11 years for the Seahawks and is number two in receptions and yards in team history.

Blades also grew up in Fort Lauderdale, Florida, and starred for the University of Miami Hurricanes. So it's appropriate that one of his biggest big plays occurs in South Florida. The Hawks and Dolphins endure monsoon-like conditions most of the day. Dolphin coach Jimmy Johnson's fabled bouffant is completely rain flattened, looking like trampled golf course rough. Despite the Dolphins setting a team record for fumbles in a game, the Hawks are down 15-14 with only 2:03 remaining. Seattle is staring at third down from their own 20 when quarterback John Friesz finds Blades at the 35. As Blades catches it, the defender covering him slips on the sopping grass. Blades runs to the outside and eludes another Dolphin at the 40, and then it's a 60-yard sprint to the end zone with other Fins chasing him to no avail. Seattle makes the two-point conversion and wins 22-15.

Most Miles Per Gallon (1997)

In the 10,000th game completed in NFL history, Steve Broussard puts a 10K hurt on the Tennessee Oilers (they were the Oilers for their first two years in the Volunteer State). He has two big-play touchdown runs that almost single-handedly win the game. The first occurs in the third quarter with the Hawks down 10-3 and on their own 23. Broussard goes up the middle for 10 yards before he breaks to the outside and makes half the Oiler defense miss him on the 77-yard touchdown run. In the fourth quarter, with the game still tied at 10, the former Cougar again burns the Oilers as he goes up the middle for 43 yards while breaking three tackles for the game winner. His box score reads 138 yards on six carries for a 23-yard rushing average. Not even a Prius is that efficient.

Moon Shot (1997)

After starting quarterback John Friesz went down on open-ing day, the Hawks turned to 40-year-old Warren Moon. The former Husky proceeded to have the greatest second-string performance in team history. Moon set a team record for pass-ing yardage in a season, and the Hawks led the NFL in pass-ing offense. Moon also had a streak of nine games in which he threw for at least 250 yards. One of these games came in San Diego. With 3:14 remaining in the contest and behind by four, the Seahawks are at the Charger 40. Moon rolls back, waiting for Joey Galloway to sprint to the end zone with the knowledge that his offensive line will give him time for the play to develop. Warren then demonstrates why he is Hall of Fame–worthy as he lays a perfect pass between two defenders and into Gallo-way's mitts at the 1. Joey's momentum carries him into the end zone, and the Hawks carry out a victory.

Rogers' Record Return (1999)

The Seahawks very quickly spoil the home opener for the Steelers. In fact, the Hawks take a 14-0 lead before their offense even sets foot on the field. The second touchdown comes cour-tesy of punt returner Charlie Rogers. Pittsburgh punter Josh Miller sends a booming kick 62 yards, which forces Rogers to catch all the way back at the 6-yard line. The kick outpaces the coverage, leaving Rogers a 10-yard buffer before a Steeler is near him. Charlie jukes his way around said Steeler and then cuts toward the sidelines, where he makes three more defend-ers miss. Rogers' speed is too much for two other Steelers, so by midfield, all that's between him and the end zone is Miller. The punter's feeble attempt to tackle looks more like a guy try-ing to pick up a lost contact lens, and Charlie sprints home free for a Seahawk team-record 94-yard punt return.

One-Man Show (2001)

Alex Bannister was a special teams force with the Seahawks, earning Pro Bowl honors in 2003. During his rookie campaign, he served notice to the rest of the NFL with one play against Denver. As the Broncos' Tom Rouen prepares to punt from his own 20, Bannister blows by the offensive line and blocks the kick. The ball bounces backward on the Husky Stadium FieldTurf until Alex scoops it up at the 9 and scurries in for the score. It is the Hawks' first blocked punt returned for a touchdown since 1987. Seattle defeats Denver by 13.

Even Republicans Would Go to This Left (2002)

Just inside the two-minute warning, the Seahawks are holding on to a slim 31-25 lead with the ball at the Kansas City 46. In these situations, it's always a good idea to run to the left behind one of the greatest offensive tackles of all time, Walter Jones. Shaun Alexander takes the handoff and heads left, where Jones and Chris Gray (who moved to the left after an injury to Steve Hutchinson) clear out a nice path that provides the running back with untouched access to the end zone. The touchdown proves critical in this wild offensive show in which the Hawks and Chiefs set an NFL record for most combined first downs in a game. Seattle emerges victorious, 39-32 at Seahawks Stadium.

St. Louis Swing (2006)

After a dismal first half, the Hawks are finally driving on the Rams in the third quarter. Unfortunately, a great Mack Strong 32-yard touchdown run is negated by a penalty, and the elation I had been feeling is suddenly replaced by a black hole of despair. But on the next play, Matt Hasselbeck rolls back and flings a pass about 60 yards to Darrell Jackson, who catches it between three defenders in the back of the end zone. And just as suddenly, my adrenaline is back up, with only a slight pause while I check to make sure there are no flags on the play. It is one of the more spectacular touchdown pass plays in Seahawk history, and it helps the team come back and win in St. Louis.

Mo-mentum (2007)

Maurice Morris has mostly been Shaun Alexander's understudy since he was drafted in the second round out of Oregon. In 2007, with Alexander having another subpar and injury-racked season, Morris produced a number of huge runs. The former Duck's biggest carry came against the Eagles when Mo takes a handoff at the Philadelphia 45, then cuts to the outside, where he shakes and bakes past a defender and into the end zone. It proves to be the game-winning score and makes Morris the most popular Oregon Duck in the state of Washington.

Seattle's Best (2007)

Nate Burleson comes from an elite Seattle football lineage. His father, Alvin, was an All-Pacific 8 defensive back at Washington in 1975. Nate himself was a football standout at O'Dea High School in Seattle. In 2007 he joined Charlie Rogers as the only Seahawk to return a kickoff and a punt for a touchdown in the same season (Rogers actually had his kickoff return touchdown in the postseason). Nate's two returns are pure gridiron artistry and occur on consecutive weeks. Some members of the twelfth man at the Qwest are still waiting in a concession or restroom line when Burleson receives the opening kickoff of the second half against the Rams. He catches the ball at the Seattle 9 and zigzags his way through defenders like he's Phil Mahre on a slalom course before cruising into the end zone.

The unlucky members of the twelfth man are overheard saying, "I missed *what*?!"

During the following week at Cleveland, Burleson has a more unorthodox return. Often, if the ball is going to land inside the 10-yard line, a punt returner will let it go, hoping/assuming it will roll into the end zone for a touchback. However, in the second quarter Nate grabs the punt at his own 6-yard line. Incredibly, he eludes five Browns before reaching the 10-yard line and another three by midfield. He is then home free for a touchdown. The 94-yard return ties Rogers' team record. Burleson also ran back punt returns for more yards than any other player in the NFL in 2007.

DREADFUL DEFEATS: PART THREE

49ERS 24, SEAHAWKS 22
The Kingdome, December 8, 1991

The Seahawks have to beat the 49ers to hang on to their playoff hopes. With both Joe Montana and Steve Young absent, defeating the San Francisco dynasty actually seems possible. The Hawks rally from an eight-point deficit in the second half to take a 22-17 lead. However, they can't convert a crucial third down late in the fourth quarter to ice the game. This enables third-stringer Steve Bono to hit John Taylor for the go-ahead score with 1:08 left. Seattle has one last chance to get within field goal range. With a little less than a minute to go, Dave Krieg makes a nice scramble upfield for 15 yards near the 50 before being hit from behind by Niner Tim Harris. The ball pops out, and San Fran recovers and kills the clock to end the game. Krieg breaks the NFL record for most career fumbles. The chance to end a two-year postseason drought is gone.

And the Hawks feel the loss for years to come because, by not making the playoffs, they give owner OverBehring an excuse to force out both coach Knox and Krieg, thus starting the Seahawks' worst era ever.

JETS 16, SEAHAWKS 10
The Kingdome, November 26, 1995

Amid a late-season, seven-game stretch that includes two three-game winning streaks by the Seahawks, stands this dog against the lowly Jets. Seattle starts perfectly inept, turning the ball over on their first three possessions; however, New York can only convert one of the turnovers into points. The Hawks can't convert much of anything until the third quarter, when they finally score on a Mack Strong reception. Down by only six, the Seahawks have the ball at midfield late in the game, but two Rick Mirer incompletions doom the rally. A sparse crowd of 41,000 diehards, already nervous that the Seahawks may be gone at the end of the season, is sent home with the disappointment and embarrassment of losing to a Jet team that scores its first road victory in over a year. The loss seriously hurts both the Hawks' chance at the playoffs and a winning record for the first time in five years.

JETS 32, SEAHAWKS 31
Giants Stadium, December 6, 1998

The Seahawks head into this game 6-6 and fighting for their playoff life. Meanwhile, the Jets are 8-4 and hold first place in the AFC Eastern Division. In the first half, the Hawks shock the faithful at the Meadowlands with three big-play touchdowns. Two Jon Kitna-to-Joey Galloway bombs and a 39-yard touchdown run by Ricky Watters on fourth and one stake Seattle to a 21-13 halftime advantage. The lead grows early in the third quarter when linebacker Anthony Simmons returns an interception for six points.

The score then progresses: 28-19, 31-19, 31-26. The Jets have a fourth-and-nine call at the Seattle 20 with 5:00 to go in the game, but the Seahawk defense comes up with a huge stop, making Jet head coach Bill Parcells look bad for not going for the safe field goal to cut the lead to two. However, the Seahawks can't run out the clock, and they give the Jets one last chance—which they take advantage of, making it all the way into the Seattle red zone.

With 0:27 remaining, it is fourth and goal at the 5. The full house at Giants Stadium is screaming as the Jets line up five wide receivers and an empty backfield. On the snap, Vinny Testaverde tries a quarterback sneak into the end zone. Initially, it looks like he is stopped just short as one official says he's down at the 1-yard line. However, head linesman Ernie Frantz, with not nearly the proper view, signals a touchdown. It's mayhem at the goal line as the Jets say they have a touchdown, while the Hawk defenders are waving it off. Referee Phil Luckett briefly runs into the picture, at which point the ball has made its way into the end zone. Luckett then stands back as if he were born without a spine while Frantz rules touchdown. Luckett does emerge to call unsportsmanlike conduct on Shawn Springs for throwing his helmet (probably the most understandable flag ever on a Hawk).

CBS Sports replays the supposed touchdown and announcers Kevin Harlan and Sam Wyche, like every football fan, are shocked over the call. With 100 percent certainty, Testaverde did not cross the goal line. How could crew of professional officials miss such a blatant call? After hearing from the coaches booth that it was a not a touchdown, Hawk coach Dennis Erickson stands on the sidelines helpless. I'm sick. As soon as the final seconds tick off, I walk outside into my backyard and stew in silence for about 20 minutes over this injustice my team has been served.

The fallout from the game is national news. The front page of the *New York Times* dated Monday, December 7, 1998, prominently features a color photo of Testaverde falling just short of the goal line with the caption, "Calls for instant replay continue." The front page of the *Times* sports section splashes the headline, "Officials Smile on the Jets" and four television freeze-frames showing Testaverde's knee down before the goal line. Below these stills is a large photo taken from behind the end zone right after Frantz ruled touchdown. Jet players jump jubilantly, but you can literally feel the anger radiating from the faces of the Seahawks, including Michael Sinclair, Terry McDaniel, and Fred Thomas, as they react incredulously to the call.

During his postgame press conference, Parcells says, "God's playing in some of these games, and he was on our side today." Parcells is a great coach, but a lousy theologian. God had nothing to do with the Jets winning; it was the incompetence of the officials that decided this game. If God had been involved, he would've easily ruled Testaverde short. Which brings up a pet peeve of mine: people giving credit to God for the wholesale outcomes of NFL games (and other sports contests as well). God has nothing to do with whether one team or another wins: God doesn't play favorites. If God really had a stake, wouldn't he have given Steve Largent at least one Super Bowl ring in his career? If God really had an influence on sporting events, would he have let the New Jersey *Devils* win a few Stanley Cups, while allowing the New Orleans *Saints* to languish for most of its NFL history? I will get off my soapbox now.

The loss to the Jets is a killer in that it significantly helps keep the Hawks out of the playoffs. Although the defeat didn't fully prevent the Seahawks from reaching the postseason (Seattle still would've had to defear the Broncos at Denver in the final game of the year to make the playoffs), a win against New York would've helped propel the team to a four-game winning streak coming into Mile High Stadium. It would also have meant that a guaranteed playoff spot was available for Seattle if they beat the Broncos. Denver already had home field advantage throughout the postseason, so it's entirely within the realm of possibility that the incentive of a playoff berth would've helped the Seahawks to a victory. As it turned out, the Hawks only lost by seven points, with no playoff motivation.

For Dennis Erickson, missing the playoffs meant unemployment at the end of the season. For the Seahawks, it meant the hiring of Mike Holmgren. For ref Phil Luckett, who two weeks earlier blew a *coin toss* in an overtime game between the Steelers and Lions, it meant more demerits that would hasten his demotion a few years later. For the NFL, it meant the return of instant replay. The Testaverde phantom touchdown became the rallying point for the pro-replay forces, and NFL owners almost unanimously voted to bring back instant replay for the 1999 season. The 1998 Seahawks became martyrs, taking a huge bullet in order to bring back some justice to the game.

THE FIRST BIG TRICK PLAY

It is the fourth quarter of a tie game against the Jets at Shea Stadium in 1978. The Seahawks line up for a 24-yard field goal. Coach Jack Patera senses a three-point lead won't cut it against New York, so he has the holder, Jim Zorn, pick up the ball on the snap and scurry his way to a first down at the Jet 3. Moments later, fullback David Sims takes the pitch from Zorn and scores the winning touchdown. On that late summer day Patera decides the fake field goal play is a keeper.

07

IT WAS THE WORST OF CHAPTERS

Hold on, did I just paraphrase part of the opening to Charles Dickens' A Tale of Two Cities? *My ninth grade English teacher Mr. Harry Apetz would be pleased. Admittedly, I was bored by the book and cheated by reading the CliffsNotes version instead (sorry Harry). Anyway, the Seahawks have had to endure some dark times in their history. Games and events that were as bleak as a Dickens novel. Hey, maybe Dickens wasn't so bad. After all, he inspired the opening of this section. Thank you, Harry Apetz!*

1992: STINK OR SWIM

In 1912 the RMS *Titanic* hit an iceberg and sank to the bottom of the North Atlantic Ocean. Eighty years later the Seahawks hit an iceberg of offensive futility and sank to the bottom of the NFL. The *Titanic* was designed by naval architect Thomas Andrews, who gave the ship a series of airtight compartments to prevent it from sinking in the event the hull was punctured directly by an iceberg. The Seahawk defense was designed by defensive coordinator Thomas Catlin, who gave the team various schemes to prevent NFL offenses from puncturing the end zone. Andrews' design was eventually betrayed by a series of mistakes and the ineptitude of the ship's ownership. Catlin's design was eventually betrayed by countless offensive mistakes and the ineptitude of the team's ownership. Yes, it may be a ridiculous reach to compare one of the great disasters of the 20th century with the worst season in Seahawk history, but only because Leonardo DiCaprio would never star in a movie about the 1992 Hawks.

The Seahawks went 2-14 that year, their worst record ever (the '76 debut expansion unit was 2-12). The '92 Hawks were notable for two things: an excellent defense and one of the most pathetic offenses to ever set foot on an NFL field.

It was a season of transition as team president Tom Flores came down from his Kingdome suite to take over head coaching duties from the guy he helped bump off, Chuck Knox. Longtime field general Dave Krieg was also let go, with Kelly Stouffer taking over as the starting quarterback. It started out well enough, with Stouffer moving the offense on an 80-yard opening touchdown drive in the first preseason game. But soon the Hawks ran into the iceberg.

The Seahawks set *offensive* offensive team records for fewest total yards, fewest first downs, fewest touchdowns, and most sacks allowed. Even worse, the team set an NFL record for fewest points scored in a 16-game schedule, with 140: a robust average of 8.7 points per game. The team was shut out twice (compared to 8 times in the rest of their history). They were also held to a single field goal three times and six points twice. The team never scored more than two touchdowns in a game. No player had more than three touchdowns the entire season. (Contrast that to Shaun Alexander, who scored three or more touchdowns in nine games alone.) The '92 Seahawk offense made even marginal defenses look like the '85 Bears.

The team's best receiver, Brian Blades, held out in a contract dispute for the entire training camp. He signed just prior to the start of the season, only to suffer a shoulder injury on his very first play on opening day against the Bengals; he was gone for 10 weeks. The only bright spot was running back Chris Warren. Amazingly, he rushed for over 1,000 yards on the season. However, Flores, offensive coordinator Larry Kennan, and their trio of quarterbacks (Stouffer, Dan McGwire, and Stan Gelbaugh) made sure most first downs were quickly followed with a punt.

The most pathetic offensive performance came during a 27-0 blowout against the eventual world-champion Cowboys. The Dallas defense limited the Hawks to 62 total yards. The closest the team came to scoring was when Eugene Robinson picked off a Troy Aikman pass and returned it 49 yards to the Dallas 18. Naturally, the offense couldn't move the ball, and John Kasay's field goal attempt was wide of the uprights. It appeared all the team's lifeboats left with Knox and Krieg.

This inept offense wasted one of the best defensive teams we've ever had. The unit, coordinated by Catlin and Rusty Tillman, set full-season team records for fewest first downs allowed, fewest total yards, and fewest touchdown passes. If you factor in touchdowns and safeties attributed to the offense and special teams, the defense never had more than 22 points scored against them in a game and only gave up 259 points (or 16.1 points per game) for the season. The star of this defense was third-year tackle Cortez Kennedy. After dedicating the season to his good friend, Eagles defensive tackle Jerome Brown, who was killed in a car accident in the off-season, Tez was a monster on the field. He racked up 14 sacks and 92 tackles—including 28 for losses—forced four fumbles, and had one fumble recovery.

A perfect illustration of the Hawks' dominating defense and impotent offense was the game at Pittsburgh in early December. The Central Division–leading Steelers came into the contest having thrown only seven interceptions in 12 games. However, the Hawk defense snagged five interceptions (including three by Eugene Robinson) in this game alone. These picks gave the Hawks the ball at their own 46 and the Pittsburgh 22, 24, 24, and 33. How did the offense take advantage of these gifts? By scoring absolutely nothing. Their failure to pick up even a single first down in these situations and John Kasay missing three makeable field goals were the main culprits in the Seahawks losing a game they had no business losing. Final score: 20-14. The Seahawk ship was sinking, and no amount of bailing by the defense was going to keep it afloat.

I attended 50 percent of our wins that season—a 10-6 squeaker against New England. It was in Foxborough, Massachusetts, where Tez Kennedy terrorized the Patriots and was tabbed AFC Defensive Player of the Week. He registered three sacks and four-and-a-half tackles for a loss and forced two fumbles. On one play Tez blew by two offensive linemen and stopped running back Leonard Russell for a 6-yard loss. Kennedy was in so fast, he almost arrived the moment Russell received the handoff. Later, Tez hopped over a Patriot

Unfortunately for the great Cortez Kennedy, Seahawk locker room celebrations were far too rare during his career.

lineman and sacked quarterback Hugh Millen, causing the former Husky to fumble. As the Foxborough Stadium crowd grumbled over this play, I stood up in my Largent jersey and yelled, "Hey, I thought everybody in Massachusetts loves a Kennedy?" Various scowls and screams of "Sit down, Seattle!" were soon directed at me.

For his outstanding play all season, Tez was named the NFL defensive player of the year by numerous organizations, including the Associated Press and ProFootballWeekly.com. Other accolades went to Catlin, who was named coach of the year by *Sports Illustrated*. I like that *SI* chose him over a head coach because the magazine recognized the amazing job Catlin did trying to keep the games close despite the anemic offense that foundered in every contest.

However, the defense notwithstanding, it really was the most dreadful season in team history. And what happened to Dave Krieg? He signed with the Chiefs. Interestingly, his first non-Seahawk scoring strike was a 72-yard touchdown pass against the Hawks in the second game of the season. Krieg beat Seattle twice in 1992, equaling the total amount of wins by Seattle. The team's atrocious 2-14 record was matched by New England. However, since the Hawks defeated the Patriots that season, New England had the first pick in the draft. They took Drew Bledsoe. Seattle, picking second, drafted Rick Mirer. Bledsoe lead the Pats to the Super Bowl four years later. After a promising start, Mirer led his career to a watery grave in the North Atlantic next to the *Titanic*.

A REAL HEARTBREAKER

In 1978 against Denver at the Dome, kicker Efren Herrera sends the Hawks into their first overtime game ever when he boots a 37-yard field goal with 0:53 remaining. The Seahawk defense plays the Broncos tough in the overtime, twice forcing punts. However, on Seattle's second possession, Jim Zorn is intercepted at the Seattle 36. The Broncos move down the field, but the defense makes a valiant goal line stand to force an 18-yard field goal attempt by Jim Turner. Amazingly, the normally reliable Turner misses the chip shot, sending the Kingdome crowd into blue-and-green hysteria. But then, just as suddenly, the crowd is hushed as a penalty flag appears. The Hawks are called for having 12 men on the field. A disheartening feeling seeps through the stadium as the Broncos get a second chance at a chip field goal, this one 18 inches closer. Turner makes the kick, thus avoiding a sure beatdown from his teammates. The frailty of mortality punctuates this contest as longtime renowned *Seattle Post-Intelligencer* sportswriter Royal Brougham (who helped push for pro sports in the city) suffers a fatal heart attack in the Kingdome press box near the end of the game. No doubt Brougham himself would have wryly called the game a heartbreaker.

HAWK HALL OF SHAME

Just as every team is guaranteed 16 games, the derision of sportswriters, and the unconditional adulation of 10-year-olds, every franchise is ensured their share of messes: the free-agent screwups, the injury-plagued, the guys who just couldn't get their act together, plus the suits who do more damage than any one player. Here are a few from Seattle's history. (Note: I have not included players whose sordid history was mostly either before or after their days in Seattle.)

Brian Bosworth

"Where's the $11 million lemon?"

—A sign at the Kingdome during a 1989 game against the Browns
with a picture of a lemon replacing the Boz's head

We all thought the football gods were smiling down on the Seahawks when the team won the lottery for first pick in the 1987 supplemental draft. Because he graduated from college early, Brian Bosworth was available for this little-regarded draft. He was an All-American linebacker and two-time Butkus Award winner from Oklahoma who combined the rebel flair of Yippie leader Abbie Hoffman with the marketing savvy of Madonna. Initially, Bosworth balked at playing for Seattle and inexplicably voiced a preference for Tampa Bay, a team that had won only 12 games during the previous four years. Bosworth eventually signed an $11 million, 10-year contract that caused some problems in the locker room, especially with linebacker Fredd Young. John Clayton in the Tacoma *News Tribune* reported that Jacob Green almost decked Bosworth during a meeting just hours before the players' strike ceased.

Most pro football experts predicted Bosworth was going to reinvent the position, like Lawrence Taylor. Marketers and kids everywhere loved "The Boz." Despite the team's many Pro Bowlers, The Boz instantly became the most famous Seahawk of all. The biggest-selling jersey of 1987 was Bosworth's No. 55 (and his NFL-rejected No. 44). He had a *Wizard of Oz*–themed poster titled "The Land of Boz," depicting Bosworth standing on the yellow brick road with "Bozkins" (kids dressed up like The Boz) and a *Playboy* Playmate as Dorothy. He sold Right Guard deodorant on television with the inarticulateness you would expect from a rookie linebacker.

He had been an amazing linebacker in college: quick off the ball, with the power to bring down even the strongest fullback by himself. In his first NFL year, he came close to living up to the hype. He was named by many organizations to the all-rookie team and was even the AFC Defensive Player of the Week for his performance against the Bears.

However, The Boz proved to be too brittle for the National Football League. He came back from a shoulder injury too soon in 1988 and was never healthy again. Some point to his acknowledged steroid use in college as the culprit in his demise. Whatever the case, he only played in 25 games (including one playoff) in three years before finally being put out to pasture. But the NFL's loss was Hollywood's gain as The Boz turned into a B movie actor, gracing such classics as *Stone Cold* and *One Tough Bastard*.

Daryl Turner

Man, I loved "Deep Heat." Maybe it was because of his last name. Maybe it was that he could outrun the fastest of cornerbacks. Or maybe it was the fact that when he caught the ball, good things usually happened. He was the Hawks' home run hitter. Their three-point shooter. During his rookie year in 1984, he caught only 35 passes, but those went for 715 yards and 10 touchdowns. He also finished third in the voting for AFC Offensive Rookie of the Year and caught the Hawks' only touchdown in their playoff win against the Raiders. The next year he led the NFL with 13 touchdowns and had 34 receptions, a crazy average of less than three catches per touchdown. In 1986 seven of his 18 receptions went for scores, including a pair of monster 72-yard touchdowns against the Eagles and Chargers. However, he lasted only four years in the NFL, due to admitted drug problems that destroyed his career. What a waste of Deep Heat.

Patrick Hunter

A solid cornerback for nine years but maybe more remembered for his off-the-field troubles. During the 1988 season Hunter totaled his Mercedes when he drove it over an embankment in Kirkland. He was cited for negligent driving and missed five games. In 1992 he was arrested for a DWI in Seattle but was granted deferred prosecution. The following year, he was again arrested for a DWI when he hit a Bellevue Fire Department aid car. He pleaded guilty to the DWI charge in Bellevue, which, in turn, reinstated his DWI in Seattle. Hunter further buried himself when he showed up drunk for a meeting with his parole officer. Consequently, the not-so-saint Patrick spent so much time in jail that he missed mini-camp in 1994. He played in only five games that season due to injury and then was done as a Seahawk. The roads in Western Washington were safe again.

Nate Odomes

You won't find his name on the team's all-time roster nor will you see him listed as a Seahawk in the official NFL player register, but Odomes was a Hawk in 1994 and '95. Not only that, he made a few million dollars courtesy of the Seattle organization. How? After co-leading the league in interceptions while with Buffalo, he signed a four-year, $8.4 million free-agent contract with the Seahawks in 1994. But that spring, he tore his ACL during a charity basketball game and was out for the entire season. The following year the cornerback wisely shunned basketball and made it into training camp. However, once there, he again injured his leg and was gone for the entire season. After having played seven healthy seasons with the Bills, he appeared in zero games with the Seahawks. The team cut him in the third year of his contract, before he could stub his toe and make another million bucks for not playing.

The Treatment of Sam McCullum

Wide receiver Sam McCullum is an integral part of Seahawk history. He scored the first touchdown ever for the Hawks (both pre- and regular season), had the first 100-yard receiving game for the team, and was a great complement to Steve Largent in Seattle's aerial attack for six seasons. He was also the NFL Players Association representative for the Seahawks, and this made him a target during the labor unrest before the 1982 season. Shockingly, he was released during that preseason. Both general manager John Thompson and head coach Jack Patera claimed it was a "football decision." But many players, fans, and sportswriters believe that McCullum was fired for his union connection. He was still a very productive player, having finished the 1981 season as the second-leading receiver for the team. (He was also voted the Seahawk MVP by his teammates in 1980.) A National Labor Relations Board judge also saw it that way, ordering the Seahawks to reinstate him. However, by that point it was too late: McCullum had joined the Vikings. The McCullum case was a mess all around. The franchise looked spiteful to the national media. Thompson and Patera, who did a tremendous job building the Seahawks in their early days, had their reputations permanently damaged and were fired during the players' strike by the Nordstrom family. And sadly, McCullum never again appeared in a Seahawk uniform.

Tom Flores

It came as a shock to me when the Seahawks announced Tom Flores as team president/general manager in 1989. After all, as a longtime Raider, he was the enemy. Flores may have been a Super Bowl–winning coach, but he had absolutely zero experience in running an NFL team from the top. This was quite clear during his six years in Seattle.

After bumping off Knox following the 1991 season, Flores took over as head coach. It only made the Seahawks go from bad to worse. I likened it to the Great San Francisco Earthquake of 1906: the earthquake trashed a lot of San Fran, but it was the fires following the quake that really destroyed the city. The hiring of Flores as team president was the earthquake; his becoming head coach was the inferno.

Prior to Flores taking over the coaching reins, the Seahawks had come in last place three times in its 16-year history. However, the team finished in the cellar all three years in the Flores coaching era. During this period, Seattle had a total of 14 wins. (If you take the *two worst* years during Knox regime, the win tally was 14.) Under his watch, first as team prez and then as the self-installed head coach, Seattle's record against the Raiders was 3-9. When you can only win a quarter of your games against the team's number-one rival, then you're not going to last long.

Flores the general manager wasn't much better. While he did well with the 1990 college draft, the selections in 1989, 1991, and 1992 were poor for the most part and helped doom the team during the first half of the decade. His free-agent signings were not any better. Kelvin Martin, Ferrell Edmunds, and Kirby Jackson are not names Seahawk fans recall fondly, if at all.

In defense of Flores, he was cursed with team injuries, especially during the '94 season that saw a promising 3-1 beginning deteriorate into a second straight 6-10 season. I also think the incompetent and dysfunctional environment created by OverBehring would've made it hard for any coach. However, the numbers don't lie: Flores is the worst head coach in Seahawk history.

Bob Whitsitt

Back in the early 1990s, Bob Whitsitt built the SuperSonics into one of the NBA's elite franchises. Unfortunately, when he became team president of the Seahawks, he only built a lot of ill will among the fans, Seahawk staffers, and head coach Mike Holmgren. It is no secret that relations between Whitsitt and Holmgren were not harmonious. Whitsitt was from the basketball world, while Holmgren was a football guy. You can see how this could be a problem, especially since the Seahawks don't play in a sport called "tackle hoop ball."

There was also the little issue of Whitsitt playing two of the NFL's greatest receivers off each other. When Jerry Rice came to the Seahawks in a trade, Whitsitt put both Steve Largent and Rice on the spot with regards to allowing Jerry to wear Steve's retired No. 80 jersey. This action showed not only great disrespect for two football greats, but for Seahawk history as well.

Whitsitt denies any wrongdoing, but reports from others indicate the contrary.

Possibly his most egregious error was his disdain for the fans. When Whitsitt was fired in January 2005, Les Carpenter in the *Seattle Times* recalled how the prez had once referred to season-ticket holders paying seat license fees as "suckers." His treatment of Seahawk superfan Mark Collins was also atrocious. It was Collins who'd organized the Save Our Seahawks campaign in 1996; he basically quit his job for a year and a half so could devote his time to keeping our team in Seattle. Collins told Doug Farrar of Seahawks.net that after the stadium vote was approved, Whitsitt essentially treated him like a second-class citizen. Such contempt for the twelfth man earns Whitsitt his own special seat in the Hall of Shame. And guess what, Bob? There's a seat license fee for you. Sucker.

OverBehring

In Baltimore, the name Robert Irsay elicits hatred. Art Modell in Cleveland inspires similar venom. Mentioning Bud Adams is akin to uttering an obscenity in Houston. These guys all stole their teams away from their rightful hometowns. Likewise, the name Ken Behring leaves a bad taste in the mouth of every Seahawk fan. It would be a far worse taste if he had been able to actually move the Hawks to Los Angeles. As it was, he came pretty close. Every good drama needs a villain, and the former Seahawk owner is the Darth Vader, the Lord Voldemort, the Hans Gruber in the story of the Seattle Seahawks.

In 1988 the Nordstrom family decided to sell their 51 percent stake in the Seahawks. (I believe two NFL player strikes in five years had something to do with their decision.) Soon different ownership groups began lining up to purchase the team. According to a *Seattle Times* article dated June 22, 1988, former Bronco running back Floyd Little headed a group of

Ken OverBehring. My mom once told me that if you don't have anything nice to
say about someone, then don't say anything . . . at least in a photo caption.
But by all means, slam him everywhere else.

black businessmen who wanted to buy the Nordstroms' controlling interest in the club. Little was also attempting to lure Bill Cosby into the group, which, if successful, would become the first African American–controlled ownership of a major pro sports franchise.

The Little-Cosby buyout never came to fruition. Instead, a former used car salesman–turned-developer from Northern California named Ken Behring bought the team just before the beginning of the 1988 season. Brokering the deal for Behring was Mike Blatt, a real estate wizard from Stockton, California, who later was accused of murdering a business associate. After both of his trials ended in hung juries, Blatt was set free. Seahawk fans were not so lucky.

The first act in OverBehring's reign of terror was the firing of general manager Mike McCormack in 1989. McCormack had orchestrated the rise of the Hawks in the '80s, but that wasn't enough for Behring. Instead, he hired Tom Flores as team president and general manager.

The change most affected Chuck Knox, a coach who had thrived in the nonmeddling world of the Nordstroms and the supportive McCormack atmosphere. Behring and Flores both favored a high-octane offensive approach that was contrary to Knox's more traditional ball-control game. After going 7-9 in 1989 (Knox's first losing year in Seattle), the team switched to a pass-oriented "spread" offense in 1990. No doubt this change came from the highly pressured urgings of Behring and Flores. However, the spread offense was an unmitigated disaster, and after going 0-3, the team switched back to Chuck Knox football and amazingly finished 9-7. Knox's reward for one of his best coaching performances? OverBehring left him hanging for four months before finally extending his contract.

The following spring college draft helped push Knox's front foot out the door. Under Flores' and Behring's control, the

1991 draft was a joke. The top three picks, quarterback Dan McGwire and wide receivers Doug Thomas and David Daniels, were taken without input from Knox. McGwire was drafted because Behring thought he could sign him cheaply. None of these players was considered an immediate help to Knox and the Seahawks. Following another 7-9 season that year, Knox's other foot, along with all NFL respect, went out the door as well.

The next four years saw the team sink to the lower depths of the NFL. Behring hired his son, David, as team president in 1993. (This happened after it was determined that Flores could be a lousy coach and a crummy president simultaneously.) The younger Behring, with no pro sports management experience, continued the philosophy of a commitment to incompetence. When Jacob Green was inducted into the Ring of Honor, he shook hands briefly with Son of OverBehring. However, when you look at footage of the ceremony, it appears Green was left with his hand out in the cold as he tries for an extended handshake with the oblivious Behring Jr. This moment truly epitomizes the clumsy nature of a guy who was completely unsuited to be president of the Seattle Seahawks.

It was during the Behring era that Kingdome attendance hit an all-time low and apathy toward the team spread throughout the Northwest. The team's lack of success and popularity were counter to the Seattle music scene, which was becoming a worldwide focal point for rock and roll. Bands such as Nirvana, Pearl Jam, Alice in Chains, and Soundgarden were selling out stadiums worldwide, while the Seahawks were being blacked out in Seattle and stuck in the cellar of the AFC Western Division. I felt the rage of Cobain and Vedder about what was happening to a team that used to be the pride of Puget Sound.

As much as I despised the contemptuous Californian and his failed ownership of my beloved Hawks, nothing could prepare me for the anger I felt in 1996. In the winter of that year I was feeling pretty good about the Seattle pro sports landscape. During the previous fall, the Mariners had saved baseball in the area with their incredible run, winning the American League West and advancing to the AL Championship series. The Seahawks had a great second half of the season and almost made the playoffs. The Sonics were in the middle of an amazing year that eventually saw them playing in the NBA Finals. However, in early February, a metaphoric bomb of epic proportions lands on the Pacific Northwest. OverBehring, with his ratlike facial features and a potbelly that makes him look like a rodent that swallowed half of Manitoba, announces he is moving the Seattle Seahawks to Los Angeles.

My biggest sports fear had been that Behring would destroy the franchise so it would be easy for him to move it to Southern California. Now that fear had become a reality. The most ridiculous part about the Dark Overlord's announcement was when he said the team was moving because of *earthquakes*! He claimed the Kingdome was not fit to withstand a temblor that would measure 8 to 9 on the Richter scale. Never mind that an earthquake of such size would probably trash most—if not all—other NFL stadiums. The comical irony of the Hawks' moving to Los Angeles because of earthquakes was not lost on Seattle leaders or the NFL. Everyone knew it was really about money: namely, the revenue that would come from a team in the second-largest city in the country. The NFL was not thrilled about the prospect of another team bolting from its hometown. It also wanted to control who went into the Los Angeles market. If Kenny Boy had his way, the league would not be able to plant an expansion team, with its highly lucrative admission fee, in Southern Cal.

As we all know, this story had a happy ending. Local son Paul Allen stepped in and bought the team, thus saving NFL football in Seattle. However, the twelfth man can't forgive OverBehring for screwing up the franchise. Objectively, just take a look at the Seahawks' record during the Behring era, 1988–1996: 61-84. Compare this to the Nordstrom era record of 90-96 during 12 seasons that included the brutal formative expansion years. Behring was around for only one playoff appearance, and that was in 1988 when the sale went through just before the start of the season, so he really had no full years of ownership with the team going to the postseason. Coincidence? I think not. Ken Behring was the biggest embarrassment to Seattle sports since serial killer Ted Bundy once appeared in court wearing a Mariners T-shirt. (Yes, that really did happen.)

ARROWHEAD: HOUSE OF 1000 MISTAKES

No stadium has given the Seahawks more nightmares and disappointments than Arrowhead in Kansas City. We lose during freezing Midwestern snowstorms, scorching late-summer sun, and Florida-like monsoons. We lose when the stadium has only 20,000 attendees and when the place is full with almost 80,000 red-clad crazies. We lose when KC has a good season and when the Chiefs are one of the worst teams in the league. Seattle's record of 5-20 at the place is equal to the dubious mark the Seahawks have in Denver. However, it's the *way* we lose in Kansas City that makes it like a roller-coaster train that hops the tracks and crashes into a crowd of people enjoying corn dogs at the state fair. Here are a few scream-worthy lowlights that feel like the horror flicks they used to play at the old Bel-Kirk Drive-In (which, coincidentally, was located near the old Seahawk headquarters).

I hate this place.

FROZEN ALIVE (1979)

The Seahawks are riding a three-game winning streak and need a win against the cellar-bound Chiefs to keep their postseason hopes afloat. But with the KC temperature hitting the freezing mark, the team is chilled to death, like the guy who crashed through the frozen lake in *Damien: Omen II*. They trail 24-0 in the first half and eventually fall, 37-21. The team also loses six regulars to injury during the course of the game. After going a career-high five games without an interception, Jim Zorn throws three picks in Seattle's first defeat at Arrowhead. The disaster officially freezes the Hawks out of playoff contention.

OPENING DAY OF THE DEAD (1983)

Playing in Kansas City on opening day is not good, since the Hawks had never won on the first Sunday of the NFL season. The game starts well, with Curt Warner running for 60 yards on the first play from scrimmage, but a frightmare soon follows. Just as a fire scorches a number of unlucky promgoers in *Carrie*, the 94-degree heat fries the team. Jim Zorn is burned by throwing two interceptions, and the Seahawks give the eventual-last-place Chiefs one of only six wins on the season.

THE DEFENSIVE BACKS HAVE EYES (1984)

Seattle goes into Kansas City 12-2 on the season and leaves resembling a partially digested victim of Hannibal Lecter. Krieg throws five interceptions; Zorn adds a sixth pick to tie a team record. It is also the only game in which the larcenous Seahawk defense fails to intercept a pass all season. The 34-7 bloodbath helps prevent the Hawks from winning their first division crown.

CHERRY BOMB OF DOOM (1985)

This display of gridiron grotesquerie plays as a sequel to the '84 contest with Seattle turning the ball over seven times. Chief defensive back Deron Cherry ties an NFL record with four interceptions. The Seahawks go down 28-0 before finally scoring a touchdown to make the final 28-7. The Daryl Turner touchdown reception is akin to combing the hair on a corpse before burial.

THE MISSOURI CHAINSAW MASSACRE (1986)

Another awful sequel as the Hawks dig themselves a 27-0 grave before scoring late in the game, when Largent makes a spectacular play on a tipped ball in the end zone. After replacing Gale Gilbert, Krieg is a zombie, going 2-12 for 13 yards and one interception. The mass homicide is devastating, as both teams finish the season 10-6, with KC winning the tiebreaker to make the postseason dance. Meanwhile, the Seahawks must stay at home and endure horrific special Christmas editions of *Webster* and *Mr. Belvedere*.

TEPEE OF TERROR (1987)

Needing a win to secure a home playoff game, Seattle is slaughtered 41-20 by a last-place team they had beaten earlier 43-14. Steve Largent sets the NFL career record for receptions in front of only 20,370 fans. In the horror movie world, this is equivalent to the disappointing box office receipts that same year for the classic film *Evil Dead II*. The mutilation is also incredibly costly. Not only do the Seahawks have to face the Oilers in the playoffs at the Astrodome instead of the Kingdome, but Curt Warner badly sprains his ankle in Kansas City and is lost for the postseason.

BLOOD BLIZZARD (1988)

With the Seahawks fighting for first place, a visit to last-place Kansas City seems like good fortune. But oh no, this is Arrowhead. A snowstorm hits the city the night before the game, prompting only 33,132 to make it inside the stadium. The Hawks strangle one opportunity when tight end Mike Tice fumbles at the Chief 7. Kansas City, which went the previous *10* games without a rushing touchdown, amasses *three* in this contest alone. It's as if the deceased Chief offense has been injected with the green reanimating liquid from the film *Re-Animator* and come back to life to murder the Seahawks. Unlike their previous four Arrowhead slayings, this time the Hawks keep it close. Terry Taylor returns an interception 26 yards for a touchdown that ties the game at 14. In the fourth quarter, Krieg evens it at 24 with a nice pass to Brian Blades. The touchdown is the 500th in team history. Unfortunately, Nick Lowery hits a 40-yard field goal with 0:46 to play to give the Chiefs the lead. The Seahawks have one last chance, but Kansas City blitzes Krieg and forces him to fumble. Tackle Mike Wilson briefly recovers it, but he too fumbles, and the Chiefs land on the frozen ball. Game over.

NIGHTMARE ON FUMBLE STREET (1989)

Cornerback Nesby Glasgow returns a fumble 38 yards on the third play from scrimmage to give the Seahawks a rare lead at Arrowhead. However, Krieg plays like he is being stalked by Freddy Krueger. He fumbles a team-record eight times, losing four and the lead to the Chiefs. To cap the carnage, Brian Blades catches and then fumbles the Hawks' last offensive play of the game. Seattle loses 20-10. It's the beginning of a very ugly four-game slide that sees the team outscored 93-34 and slashed from the playoff race.

SANTA'S SLAY RIDE (1995)

On Christmas Eve, with the Seahawks desperate to keep their playoff hopes alive, Chief returner Tamarick Vanover takes the opening kickoff 89 yards for a touchdown. Sadly for the Hawks, these are the only points KC needs. After scoring 75 points in the previous two weeks, Seattle manages only a measly field goal, much like the measly crumb the Grinch left for the folks in Whoville. Adding to this black Christmas is the fact that the offense has a mere 89 total yards. Even worse, the possibility of owner Behring moving the team makes this game potentially the last ever for the Seattle Seahawks. OverBehring is Ebenezer Scrooge but without the ghosts scaring redemption into him.

THE DROWNING (1998)

During this ESPN Sunday night telecast, two massive storms converge over Arrowhead, causing the field to become one big bowl of grass soup, a Bermuda Triangle on Bermuda grass where fumbles are frequent and players tread at their own peril. Midway through the second quarter with the score tied at three, Hawk quarterback Warren Moon has to eat the ball on a broken play and is taken down by four Chiefs. Before the

Seahawks are able to get off another play, the game is halted due to lightning. A very surreal scene unfolds as water comes gushing down the aisles and waves of rain water literally cross the field. After nearly an hour's delay, play officially resumes. Moon doesn't return due his ribs getting cracked on the broken play right before the game was suspended. It's also questionable as to whether the Hawk offense actually returns to the field, as they score only three points in the rest of the game. The only good play is Kerry Joseph's 66-yard punt return, which the offense fails to capitalize on. Seattle drowns, 17-6.

NIGHT OF THE LIVING BLOWN LEAD (2000)

After taking a 17-7 lead in the third quarter, the Hawks are beheaded. They give up 17 unanswered points and die on *Monday Night Football* for the first time in 13 years. With the Chiefs buried at their own 5-yard line late in the third, the Seattle defense allows Elvis Grbac to find Derrick Alexander for a 73-yard completion. Two plays later, Grbac hits Alexander again for 17 yards and a touchdown. The Chiefs score the winning seven points with 4:26 remaining by driving 51 yards in only four plays. It leaves Seahawk fans wondering why ABC would be so evil as to put the Hawks on *MNF* at Arrowhead.

RETURN OF THE LIVING DEFEAT (2006)

Without Matt Hasselbeck and Shaun Alexander, the partially amputated Seahawks head into Arrowhead for the first time in five years. However, backup quarterback Seneca Wallace, in his first NFL start, performs admirably considering the situation. He hits Darrell Jackson for a 49-yard touchdown to give Seattle a 28-27 lead with 6:30 remaining in the game. But the defense turns into one of those victims from *Saw*, tortured by their own foibles. They give up a long game-winning touchdown drive and allow an astounding 499 total yards for the game. Thankfully, another sickening sequel will have to wait until the year 2014.

Despite all the terror the team has endured at Arrowhead, there is a little positive Seahawk history in Kansas City. It is where both Curt Warner and Shaun Alexander scored their first NFL touchdowns. It's also the site of the greatest finish in team history (see "15 Freakin' Fantastic Finishes," page 58). Despite their 5-20 record, the Hawks actually won their first two games at Arrowhead and three out of the first four. This means the team has gone 2-19 since 1981. It also means Jack Patera has won more games in Kansas City than every other Seahawk coach combined. Truly horrifying indeed.

A SICK SEASON

After growing as the model expansion NFL franchise its first four years, the Seahawks took a nosedive in 1980, crashing like a wounded seagull into Lake Union. The team went 4-12 and finished with nine straight losses. During a season that saw the untimely deaths of John Lennon and Steve McQueen, Seahawk fans endured a number of untimely defeats as the team blew fourth-quarter leads in five home games. In fact, for the only time in team history, the Hawks were winless inside the Kingdome. I'm convinced the Dome was actually converted into Arrowhead Stadium for the season.

SEAHAWK SADNESS

I'd like to switch gears for a few paragraphs and talk about some of the real-life sadder moments in Seahawk history. Usually when we think of team losses, we are referring to what happens on the field. However, the Seahawks are not immune to tragic events that interrupt daily life.

Less than seven months before the Seahawks played their first game in 1976, tragedy struck when team owner Lloyd Nordstrom died of a heart attack while playing tennis in Mexico. According to Elmer Nordstrom's book *A Winning Team: The Story of Everett, Elmer & Lloyd Nordstrom*, it was Lloyd who spearheaded the Nordstrom family's decision to become majority owner of the Seahawks. His involvement in the creation of the team can't be overstated.

During the 1992 season, the longtime "Voice of the Seahawks," Pete Gross, succumbed to cancer. It is really sad Pete's last year had to be the Hawks' worst season in history. Pete called the first seven games before he became too sick to work. At least he was able to witness his induction into the Ring of Honor a few days before his death. Anyone who followed the Seahawks on the radio in the Northwest during the seventies and eighties will always remember Pete's signature "Touchdown, Seahawks!"

In 1999, there was the sudden illness and death of defensive coordinator Fritz Shurmur. Shurmur died prior to the start of his (and Mike Holmgren's) first season in Seattle. His death was a terrible blow, especially to Holmgren, both personally and professionally. Shurmur was his defensive rock. He was a brilliant tactician who had guided a great unit in Green Bay. His expertise made it that much easier for Holmgren to concentrate on the offense. I don't think it was a coincidence that the Seahawk defense struggled for a long time after his death. It is a sad coincidence that coordinator Ray Rhodes, the coach who finally steered the defense in a positive direction in 2005, dealt with some serious health issues himself.

A few days before the Seahawks faced the Redskins in the 2005 divisional playoffs, Ring of Honor inductee Dave Brown died of a heart attack. Dave was an original Seahawk, lasting longer than anyone else who set foot on the field for the first-ever Seahawk practice. After retiring from playing, he was a defensive coach with the team for seven years. From all reports, Brown was a classy guy who was always proud to be a Seahawk.

While stories of these gentlemen (along with the recent deaths of former defensive coordinator Tom Catlin and concessionaire Bill the Beerman) are simply a brutal part of life, there have been a few incidents involving Seahawk players that could have been avoided. During the 1994 season, running back Lamar Smith, after a night of drinking, crashed his car into a utility pole. Riding shotgun was running back Chris Warren, who suffered two broken ribs. He was the lucky one; sitting in the backseat was defensive end Mike Frier, who was permanently paralyzed from the crash. Barely seven months later, wide receiver Brian Blades accidentally killed his cousin during a family dispute. He was later acquitted of manslaughter charges.

The events of 1994 and 1995 were the subject of a *Sports Illustrated* article dated July 24, 1995. Titled "Luckless in Seattle," the story centered on the Seahawks' off-the-field troubles, including new coach Dennis Erickson's recent DWI arrest and the team's possible move to Los Angeles. A very bleak era in Seahawk history indeed.

THE SPECIAL TEAMS BOONDOGGLES OF '97

During the Chuck Knox era, Seattle special teams were a highlight reel. Thanks to the coaching of Rusty Tillman, the Seahawks had one of the premier special teams units in the league. Most older Hawk fans remember the sellout hits Fredd Young and Rufus Porter delivered and how they made it to the Pro Bowl as special teamers. Tillman's squads were also paragons of discipline, rarely vulnerable to giving up the big play. In fact, during Tillman's tenure on the Seahawk coaching staff between 1979 and 1994, special teams gave up only two kickoffs returned for touchdowns. In 1995 new head coach Dennis Erickson hired Dave Arnold as the special teams coach, and the Seahawks allowed two kickoffs returned for touchdowns in that season alone. Unfortunately, it was only a precursor to the 1997 season, when inept special teams play cost the Hawks four late-season games in a row and prevented a very good team from making the playoffs.

It starts in mid-November against the Saints at the Superdome. Regular punter Rick Tuten is sidelined with a pelvic injury, so coach Arnold brings in Kyle Richardson to punt. Not coincidentally, two punting unit mistakes lead to two Saint touchdowns: one on a fumbled snap, the other on a blocked punt. Then, using an unfamiliar holder in Richardson, kicker Todd Peterson misses a game-winning field goal in the waning seconds. The Hawks eventually lose by three in overtime.

The following week in the Dome against Kansas City generates more special teams problems. One Chief touchdown drive in the first half is aided by a fake punt, which turns into a 35-yard pass play. Then, early in the third quarter, Tuten, who was only active to be the placement holder, is forced to punt because Richardson suffered a concussion in the first half. I don't know what's more painful, Tuten's body language as he tries to kick with a pelvic injury or the fact that the punt went a negative-6 yards. (Sadly, this was the last punt ever as a Seahawk for Bootin' Tuten, the best punter in team history.) The Chiefs are able to turn this mistake into a touchdown drive. In the fourth quarter Richardson returns to the game and has a punt blocked and knocked out of the end zone for a safety. The Hawks lose by five.

Richardson is cut before the next game against Atlanta, but it isn't the punting that hurts the team. After the Hawks close the gap to 17-14 in the third quarter, the Falcons immediately answer with a 93-yard kickoff return for a touchdown. Despite a great second-half performance by the defense, which gives up only 29 yards and no first downs, the Hawks lose by seven.

Seattle makes its only appearance at Baltimore's old Memorial Stadium a special teams disgrace the following week. The Ravens' Jermaine Lewis returns two punts for touchdowns in the second quarter, tying an NFL record. These two returns are not little midfield scampers. They go for 66 and 89 yards. The Seahawks again lose by seven.

By the end of the year the Hawks are one of only four teams ranked in the top 10 in both offense and defense, yet they finish at 8-8 and out of the playoffs. Of the other three teams, two (Denver and Green Bay) face each other in the Super Bowl, while the third (Pittsburgh) reaches the AFC Championship game. Thankfully, the not-so special teams coach Arnold is soon shown the door. No doubt the door blocked him on his way out.

BURIED IN THE MEADOWLANDS

Legend has it that missing Teamsters president Jimmy Hoffa was buried in the foundation during the construction of Giants Stadium in the New Jersey Meadowlands. In 1983 the Seahawks fared better than Hoffa when they barely escaped with a victory at Giants Stadium after an apparent New York touchdown in the last minute was nullified by a holding penalty. Since then, the Hawks have lost five straight games in New Jersey to the Giants. The Meadowlands has also proven to be a shakedown to the Seahawks when they play the Jets. The Seahawks were 5-0 at Shea Stadium against their AFC foes, but since the Jets moved across state lines to play at Giants Stadium, Seattle has gone 0-5. Overall, the Seahawks have felt like they've been whacked by TV mobster Tony Soprano, with a cumulative record of 1-11 at Giants Stadium.

DREADFUL DEFEATS: PART FOUR

BUCCANEERS 16, SEAHAWKS 3
The Kingdome, November 28, 1999

You could actually pick from a number of losses down the 1999 stretch for this chapter, but I choose this one because it started the slide in a very promising season. The Seahawks are 8-2 and riding a five-game winning streak. The Buccaneers are in first place in the NFC Central, winning games with a superior defense. The old axiom "a good defense beats a good offense" is very true on this afternoon. Tampa Bay constantly pressures quarterback Jon Kitna, forcing him to have one of the worst days in Seahawk quarterbacking history. His mortifying stats: 19-44 for 197 yards, no touchdowns, and five interceptions (second only to Zorn's six picks back in the debut season of 1976). Tampa Bay has three sacks and one fumble recovery, which happens when Warren Sapp takes down Kitna and snags the ball in the process. Sapp then prances around the King-dome turf taunting the crowd with said ball. (This is an image that is periodically shown on ESPN. The sports network will probably show it during Sapp's television obituary.) The Buc-caneers beat the Hawks for the first time in team history.

The most critical aspect of the loss is that it exposed some of the Seahawks' offensive weaknesses, and every team who played Seattle afterward took note and adjusted accordingly (at least this seemed to be the consensus of football pundits across the land). Consequently, a team that looked like a Super Bowl contender in its first 10 games lost seven of its last eight, including a heartbreaking loss to the Dolphins in the playoffs that closed out the Dome's existence.

GIANTS 27, SEAHAWKS 24
Giants Stadium, December 23, 2001

The topsy-turvy 2001 season is moving in the right direction when the Seahawks take a 24-17 lead into the fourth quarter at Giants Stadium. The defense shows some fatigue as the Giants have a 12-play drive that results in a field goal early in the fourth to make it 24-20. Unfortunately, the Hawk offense can't sus-tain either of its fourth-quarter possessions. With under three minutes remaining in the game, the Seahawks have the Giants pinned at their own 4-yard line with the erratic Kerry Collins at quarterback. Somehow Collins manages to drive nearly the entire length of the field. Both Reggie Tongue and Anthony Sim-mons almost have interceptions on the drive that would've won the game for the Hawks. But "almost" doesn't mean squat in the NFL. New York scores the winning touchdown when Collins hits Ike Hilliard with a 7-yard pass with only 0:20 left on the stupid clock. The loss essentially keeps the Hawks from making the playoffs.

RAVENS 44, SEAHAWKS 41
M&T Bank Stadium, November 23, 2003

This game is eerily similar to the 1998 Jet contest in that the Seahawks make some big plays before blowing a comfortable lead and having the game ultimately decided by an officiating mistake. After a mostly uneventful first half, the Hawks score two touchdowns in the last 0:26 to take a 17-3 lead into halftime. In the second half Matt Hasselbeck absolutely takes apart the Raven's fierce defense. He is 23 of 41 for 333 yards with no interceptions and five touchdowns, including a 38-yard strike to Koren Robinson and an 80-yard bomb to Darrell Jackson. Seattle scores on six straight possessions, an amazing feat considering it's against Ray Lewis and company.

In the fourth quarter the Hawks let a 17-point lead slip away. Actually, they only give up 14 of the 17 points. With 0:58 to play and leading 41-38, the Seahawk offense is called for an illegal substitution penalty on third and one at the Baltimore 33. However, the officials realize offensive lineman Floyd Womack did report as a receiver, so the ref picks up the flag but then fails to reset the 40-second clock and start the game clock. (If he had, the Ravens would've had to burn their last time-out or let the clock run down 40 seconds.) The Ravens then stop the Hawks on third and one and call their last time-out with 0:44 left. They again foil the Hawks on fourth and one, and the clock stops for the change of possession. However, because the clock had not been restarted earlier, Baltimore has 0:39 left to mount a drive at their own 33 instead of what should have been only four seconds! They are given an extra 0:35 within the last minute of play. The Ravens are able to take advantage of this gift from the zebras and, aided by a key 44-yard pass interference call, manage to tie the game and send it into overtime. During the extra period, the Ravens prevail with a 42-yard field goal.

How an entire officiating crew failed to monitor the clocks correctly is beyond comprehension. (Maybe they were all watching *The View* on the Jumbotron.) It's interesting to note that if the crew had not mistakenly blown the illegal substitution call in the first place, the whole clock situation would have been moot. During this fiasco Holmgren was screaming on the sidelines, but the crew, perhaps blinded by their own incompetence, didn't see him wildly gesticulating like an angry Craig Stadler after missing a 2-foot putt. The 41 points are the most ever scored by the Seahawks in a loss, but what hurts more is that the defeat knocks the team out of first place, whereby they have no control over their playoff destiny.

08

YOU WIN SOME, YOU LOSE SOME, YADA YADA YADA

I considered calling this section "You've Got the Yin, I've Got the Yang," as a play on the Taoist expression for bad and good. But I thought this might be misconstrued as being racy, and I want to keep the book clean. My mom is going to read it. At least she will say she has read it, at which point I will have to quiz her on Seahawk trivia until she caves in and tells the truth that she isn't much interested in the Seahawks. Anyway, I digress. This section looks at some of the contrasts in Seahawk history.

TRICKS OF THE TRADE

Football doesn't engage in trading players with the frequency of baseball or even basketball. Often, football transactions involve players and draft picks. Obviously, these trades can be a gamble. If you trade away a decent draft pick for a player who succeeds, then the trade paid off. Conversely, if the player flops, then it will be deemed a bad move. Sometimes a team will trade draft picks to move up in the draft order. This strategy has worked well for the Seahawk front office on a few occasions. Here are some of the high- and lowlights from Seattle's trading history.

THE GOOD

1978. Fifth-round pick to Dallas for Efren Herrera. Efren was decent but not a great kicker. However, you couldn't find a better booter for trick plays.

1979. Seventh-round pick to the Giants for fullback Dan Doornink—there's something extra special about stealing from New Yorkers. In baseball, it was the Mariners getting Jay Buhner from the Yankees for Ken Phelps. In football, it was this trade for the former Cougar from Wapato.

1980. First- and third-round picks to Buffalo for the Bills first-round choice. This moved the Hawks up six spots in the draft and allowed them to take Jacob Green. I think the net cost of a third-rounder was a bargain for a guy who would one day be in the Ring of Honor.

1983. First-, second-, and third-round choices to Houston for the third pick in the draft. The Seahawks used it to select Curt Warner. I think the net cost of a second- and third-rounder

Jacob Green on the right (with Jeff Bryant). Yeah, he was worth an extra third-round pick.

was a bargain for a guy who became Seattle's first great running back and a future member of the Ring of Honor.

1990. Two first-round, a third-, and a 1991 fourth-round choice to New England for their first- and second-round picks. The Hawks used the Patriots' No. 3 slot to select Cortez Kennedy. I think the net cost was a bargain for a guy who would become one of the most dominant defensive tackles of the 1990s and a Ring of Honor inductee.

1997. Rick Mirer and a fourth-round pick to Chicago for their first-round choice. This extra first-round spot helped the Hawks maneuver into the third and sixth picks of the entire draft, who were Shawn Springs and Walter Jones. Springs was a solid player for seven years. Jones has become the best offensive lineman of his era. The trade also got rid of Mirer's huge salary. Thank you, Chicago.

2001. We basically swapped first-round picks (10th for 17th) with Green Bay, plus gave them a third-round pick, for Matt Hasselbeck. I think the net cost of a third-round pick was a bargain for a guy who—yeah, you know the story.

2002. Brock Huard to Indianapolis for a fifth-round pick. I like Huard. The Puyallup native is a good quarterback, but he was sitting on the bench in Seattle. The Hawks used the pick on defensive tackle Rocky Bernard, who has delighted the twelfth man with many a sack.

THE BAD

1976. Traded Ahmad Rashad to Minnesota for a fourth-round draft pick. Rashad, who grew up in Tacoma, came to Seattle as a free agent prior to the inaugural season. However, he clashed with coaches in training camp and was shipped to the Vikings, where he became a four-time Pro Bowler. In 1977 the Seahawks used that fourth-round pick on a receiver named Larry Seivers, who never played a down with the Hawks. I don't mind that the team traded Rashad, because they already had Largent and McCullum. However, I think a guy who married Bill Cosby's TV wife rated at least a third-round pick.

1984. Manu Tuiasosopo to the Niners for a fourth round pick in 1984 and a tenth round pick in 1985, who turned out to be Rickey Hagood and James Bowers, neither of whom played a down for the Hawks. Meanwhile, Manu had three good years with San Francisco.

1988. A first- and two fifth-round picks to the Cardinals for Kelly Stouffer (16 career Seahawk starts, seven touchdowns,

19 interceptions, 54.5 career quarterback rating, one stupid local Domino's Pizza commercial). Stouffer originally held out for the whole year after the Cardinals drafted him in 1987. I remember thinking at the time, "Who's this jerk from Colorado State holding out in the NFL?!" Lo and behold, he became a Seahawk the following season. I was really ticked off that Seattle originally wanted to trade Kenny Easley for Stouffer, but Easley's serious kidney problems prevented it. Even if the trade had ended up being a nonplaying Easley for Stouffer, I think the Cards would've had the better part of the deal. (On a more serious note, the original trade actually saved Easley's life. When he failed his Cardinal physical, doctors discovered he had a critical kidney ailment, which forced the safety to retire.)

1992. Second- and third-round picks to the Vikings for injury-prone Keith Millard. The former All-Pro missed much of training camp and then lasted only two games before being released. This was quite possibly the worst trade in team history, because the '92 and '93 Hawks were especially bad, and those high picks could've really helped.

1996. Eugene Robinson to Green Bay for Matt LaBounty. I understand Robinson was a victim of the salary cap, but the Seahawks should have found a way to keep him. I hope one day Robinson is enshrined in the Ring of Honor because he was the heart of the defense for many years. Nobody has more tackles in the history of the team than Eugene, and only Dave Brown has more interceptions. Robinson was the defensive captain for five years and the Seahawks' NFL Man of the Year four times; he was voted the MVP twice by his teammates; and he won the Steve Largent Award once. It really bothers me that many NFL fans remember Robinson mostly for his incredible lapse of judgment the night before playing for Atlanta in the

Super Bowl. But that act should not define his career. Stick him in the Falcons' hall of shame if you must, but also put him in the Seahawks' Ring of Honor.

2000. Ahman Green to the Packers for Fred Vinson. Holmgren hated Green's fumbleitis. Green Bay loved Green's production of over 7,000 rushing yards. I've played in as many regular-season games for the Hawks as Vinson.

THE CONTROVERSIAL

At the 1977 college draft the Seahawks held the number-two overall pick. When it came to Seattle's selection, NFL commissioner Pete Rozelle strolled up to the podium to announce that the Seahawks had traded the pick to Dallas. Cowboy fans quickly cheered this turn of events. Rozelle, after waiting for the Dallas contingent to quiet down (no Hawk fans seemed to be present to register their reaction), explained that Seattle would receive five choices in the first 54 picks. Basically, Seattle acquired the Cowboys' first selection (14th overall) and three second-round choices. Depending on your viewpoint, either this was a terrible trade or a necessary one.

With the second pick, the Seahawks had a chance of drafting All-American running back Tony Dorsett, but reportedly Dorsett's people had made it clear to Seattle management that he didn't want to play for the expansion franchise. In Dave Anderson's *New York Times* column dated May 1, 1977, Dorsett's agent, Michael Trope, was quoted as saying, "The Seattle club has been informed, formally, that Tony does not want to play there." Trope goes on to say, "Seattle is economically unattractive from a marketing standpoint." Seahawk general manager John Thompson denied he was forced to make the Dorsett trade and instead said the Cowboy deal had been too good to pass up. It's true that the trade gave the Hawks three players who were solid starters for years: Steve August, Terry Beeson, and Tom Lynch. Who's to say Dorsett would have put up Hall of Fame stats with the Seahawks? The Cowboys were already an elite team and in a position to make Dorsett a super-star. But think of what that offense could've done if it had Zorn and Dorsett in the same backfield.

THE GREATEST

A 1977 eighth-round draft pick to the Oilers gave the Seahawks Steve Largent in 1976. This was only the Hawks' second trade ever, but it turned out to be one of the greatest steals in sports history. Incredibly, Houston had actually *cut* Largent in training camp but still held the rights to him when Seattle inquired about his availability. The Oilers used the Seattle pick to draft a wide receiver named Steve Davis out of Georgia. Davis never played a down during an NFL regular-season game. Largent retired holding all three major receiving career records.

SAFETY DANCE

The Seahawks tied an NFL record with four safeties in 1993. Rod Stephens had two of the four, which also matched an NFL record. However, the team also gave up three safeties that season, so those of you scoring at home will realize it was a net of only two points.

A PERTURBING PATTERN: THE 1985 SEASON

If you like patterns, then you would've loved the 1985 Seahawks. They won two, lost two; won two, lost two; keeping this pattern all the way to a perfectly average record of 8-8. Me? I hate patterns. Maybe because I once had an art teacher at Enatai Elementary School in Bellevue named Mrs. Knapp, who insisted we use patterns in all our artwork. Every time Knapp would come to class, she would emphatically write the word "PATTERNS" on the chalkboard and say the key to good art was patterns. Coming from a family that included art teachers and artists, I found it odd that Mrs. Knapp appreciated a good flower bedspread design from Sears more than the work of Vincent van Gogh or Claude Monet. Well, there *is* more money to be made designing wallpaper than painting self-portraits after cutting off your ear, as poverty-stricken Vincent did. Seahawk fans didn't want to cut off their ears in 1985, but they felt like slashing their wrists at times.

The team entered the season with great expectations. They were coming off a 13-5 year and had the added bonus of a healthy Curt Warner. Despite the Hawks remaining relatively injury-free for the season, the team could never break out of the "win two, lose two" bondage. Blown leads, some anemic offensive displays, and game-changing fourth-quarter turnovers doomed the team to a .500 season.

There was one pattern I liked in 1985, and it was Daryl Turner scoring touchdowns. He had 13 touchdown receptions on the season, establishing a new Seahawk mark that still stands. He also set a team record with four touchdown catches in a shootout at San Diego. The game against the Chargers had a pattern of team records that continue to stand to this day. Charger quarterback Dan Fouts picked apart the Seattle secondary for four touchdowns and 440 yards (still a Seahawk opponent record), while wide receiver Wes Chandler had 243 receiving yards (still a Seahawk opponent record). However, the trio of Krieg, Warner, and Turner was even better. Warner had the third-best rushing performance of his career as he ran for 169 yards and two touchdowns, while Turner had the aforementioned record four touchdown receptions. Krieg threw for over 300 yards and had five touchdown passes (still a team record). The Hawks overcame a 23-14 halftime deficit by scoring 28 points in the third quarter (still a team record) and 35 points overall in the second half (still a team record) en route to a 49-35 victory. Mrs. Knapp would have approved.

SIZZLING HOT AND FROSTY COLD

To compare and contrast the absolute highs and lows in Seahawk scoring history, you need to look at the Hawk-Viking game on September 29, 2002, and the period between October 4 and November 22, 1992.

Airing on ESPN's *Sunday Night Football*, the Minnesota game is the first time most of the country has a chance to see the brand-spanking-new Seahawks Stadium. Late in the second quarter, Seattle creates one of the biggest scoring explosions in the history of the NFL. It starts with the Hawks beginning a drive at their own 20, leading 17-10. Quarterback Trent Dilfer picks up the blitz and dumps a pass to Shaun Alexander in the flat at the 18. Alexander finds the open field near the sideline and zips straight ahead. He cuts back toward the middle of the field near the Minnesota 30 to avoid a swarm of Vikings and races in untouched for an 80-yard touchdown.

It is Shaun's third score of the game. On the ensuing kickoff, special teamer Tim Terry lays a wicked hit on returner Nick Davis, who fumbles the ball back to Seattle. Three plays later Alexander walks in from the 1 to make it 31-10. It's déjà vu for the Vikes on the kickoff as Tim Terry again makes the returner, this time D'Wayne Bates, cough up the ball, which is recovered by Seahawk Alex Bannister. On the very next play, Alexander goes 14 yards for his fifth touchdown of the game. The Vikings manage to hold on to the ball on the next kick return. However, on second down, quarterback Daunte Culpepper is picked off by Reggie Tongue, who returns it 46 yards for the score and a 45-10 lead. Incredibly, the Seahawks put up 28 points in one minute, 47 seconds of play.

At halftime I contemplate the magnitude of the outburst. The 45 points are a team record for the first half and the third-highest total in NFL history. Alexander is within a touchdown of tying one of the NFL's great storied records: most touchdowns in a game. It was set by Ernie Nevers in 1929 and equaled by Dub Jones in 1951 and Gale Sayers in 1965. Alas, Shaun isn't able to tie the record in the second half, but he still sets the NFL record for most touchdowns in one half.

Now take a look at the ugly stepsister of that explosion, a six-plus-game stretch in 1992 in which the Hawks scored just 22 points in 375 minutes. Included in this sickening span is exactly one touchdown, a 13-yard Stan Gelbaugh touchdown pass to Tommy Kane that was set up after the Giants fumbled the second-half kickoff at their own 19. At no point during this putrid period did the Hawks put up more than one score in a quarter. It's hard to think that such a drought could exist in the modern-day NFL, but thanks to "offensive guru" Tom Flores, it was a reality.

SEAHAWK COACHING CAROUSEL

A brief *New York Times* story dated January 5, 1992, nearly covers the entire history of Seahawk head coaches. The article mentions that University of Miami head coach Dennis Erickson has turned down a chance to coach the Hawks and Seattle president Tom Flores appears ready to appoint himself as coach. The story also reports 49er offensive coordinator Mike Holmgren interviewed with the Los Angeles Rams, but team owner Georgia Frontiere is set to offer the job to Chuck Knox. Now if the article had somehow included Jack Patera, it would have been Pulitzer Prize material.

If the Viking explosion is akin to a porterhouse steak, then the anemic scoring spell of '92 is a crumb from an unsalted rice cake.

AND THE SEAHAWKS SELECT . . .

You don't need to be a football executive to know drafting can be a crapshoot. The Seahawks have had their share of second-round dogs (Andre Hines, Owen Gill, Doug Thomas, Anton Palepoi), but history shows the team has done much better with drafting linebackers in the second slot (Bruce Scholtz, Dave Wyman, Terry Wooden). When the Hawks traded with Carolina to move up and took University of Southern California linebacker Lofa Tatupu in the second round of the 2005 draft, there was some grumbling that it was a stretch. Nobody is grumbling now. It may be a cliché to say drafting ballplayers is an inexact science. However, being a cliché does not make it false. While most of the attention in a draft is focused on the higher rounds, success can sometimes come from those lower-round picks.

LATER-ROUND GEMS
(as defined by the sixth round or lower)
David Sims (seventh round, 1977)

The first in a long line of excellent Seahawk fullbacks and a great complement to Sherman Smith in the backfield, Sims led the NFL in touchdowns in 1978 despite missing four games during the season. Sadly, Sims had to retire prematurely 1979 when doctors discovered a congenital bone condition in one of his vertebrae.

John Harris (seventh round, 1978)

Harris was named to the All-Rookie team by many publications and then played eight more years with the Hawks. The safety started 112 out of a possible 119 games he was available. He is number three on the team's all-time list for interceptions. Interestingly, he was traded for a seventh-round pick to Minnesota, where he had three more productive years.

Robert Hardy (10th round, 1979)

The defensive tackle had a fine first year in which he won the Eddie G. Robinson Trophy as the NFL's MVP rookie from a black college. "Heartburn" Hardy started all but one game during his too brief four-year career.

Ron Essink (10th round, 1980)

The offensive lineman gained a starting job in week 13 of his rookie year and held on to it for the next five-plus seasons.

Eric Lane (eighth round, 1981)

A solid member of Rusty Tillman's stellar special teams unit. When Curt Warner went down in 1984, Lane was one of the running backs to pick up the slack. He had a 40-yard touchdown run to seal a victory against the Vikings and a 55-yard touchdown reception versus the Bears that season. He lasted seven years with the Hawks.

Dwayne Harper (11th round, 1988)

Took over one of the starting cornerback positions during his second year and kept it for the remainder of his six seasons with Seattle. His best year was 1991, when he made *Sports Illustrated*'s All-NFL team. He ended up playing 12 years in the league.

Derrick Fenner (10th round, 1989)

The running back had one very good year with the Hawks in 1990 when he led the league in touchdowns. The emergence of Chris Warren made him expendable, but he did play nine seasons in the NFL, a near-miracle for a 10th-round running back with off-field baggage.

Michael Sinclair (sixth round, 1991)

This was, no question, the best late-round pick in Hawk history, and ironically, it came during one of our worst draft years. The defensive end lasted 11 seasons in Seattle and was voted to three Pro Bowls. He had an amazing campaign in 1998 when he snagged at least one sack in 12 out of 16 games and finished the year with an NFL-best 16.5. He is second only to Jacob Green for career sacks as a Seahawk.

Josh Brown (seventh round, 2003)

Kickers are usually late-round picks if they are even taken at all. Still, Brown became a clutch kicker for the Hawks. He holds the record for the longest field goal in team history when he nailed a 58-yarder at Green Bay in 2003. He had two game-winning kicks in 2005 and four in 2006, a team record. However, he is not a favorite of the twelfth man since he bolted to St. Louis.

UNDRAFTED BUT NOT UNDERAPPRECIATED FREE AGENTS

You could almost build an all-franchise team out of some of the players we signed to free-agent contracts after they went undrafted: Norm Johnson, Dave Krieg, Bryan Millard, Joe Nash, Rufus Porter, Eugene Robinson, Mack Strong, and Jim Zorn.

FRONT OFFICE (MIS)FORTUNES

I have a vivid recollection of the draft missteps the front office has taken over the years. General managers and player personnel directors say you don't always know how an excellent college player will do in the pros. Fair enough. Injuries and bad coaching can hasten the decline of a player. And sometimes a guy is just a stiff, completely overrated by scouts. But those high-round flops do drive everyone nuts. So with my hindsight vision at a perfect 20/20, here are two draft year disasters.

The 1985 Draft

Although we didn't have a first-round pick that year, you would have thought Mike McCormack and company would've done better. The team had a total of 12 picks, yet only the seventh-round choice, Ron Mattes, logged significant time with the team. Two picks appeared in a total of six regular-season games,

Incredibly, the Hawks picked up Jim Zorn as a free agent in 1976.

none as starters. The other nine: zilch. Our top pick, second-rounder Owen Gill, was cut in preseason.

Maybe the best indication some scouts were sniffing glue is that the Hawks picked a *backup quarterback from Arizona*, John Conner, in the 10th round. Arizona, if you don't know college football, is not a quarterback factory for the NFL. This made the choice, in polite terms, even more ridiculous (and he was listed in the media guide depth chart as a quarterback, not converted to some other position). Then again, there was his name: John Conner. Maybe team prez McCormack was a big fan of the *Terminator* movies? John *Connor* was the rebel leader who fought against the machines in those films (and the TV show); the machines sent a cyborg back in time to assassinate him. Maybe Conner's drafting wasn't ridiculous. Maybe Conner's name is actually spelled "Connor"? Maybe, by drafting this obscure player, they could keep him from the rebel resistance? My God, Mike McCormack is in cahoots with the machines of the future! (Too bad the Terminator couldn't have come back in 1988 and prevented OverBehring from buying the franchise.)

The 1991 Draft

There was no such connection to a Schwarzenegger sci-fi flick with this draft. Nope, this one more resembled the *Police Academy* movies, although I think Steve Guttenberg could've run the Hawks better than the brain trust of Ken Behring and Tom Flores. OverBehring wanted offense. What he got was offensive (zing!). Despite having more pressing needs, Seattle selected quarterback Dan McGwire in the first round and wide receivers Doug Thomas and David Daniels in the second and third rounds, respectively. A mighty triumvirate of ineptitude. McGwire had all the grace and agility of an elephant on a miniature golf course. His career numbers with the Hawks:

12 game appearances with two touchdown passes, six interceptions, and 10 fumbles in four seasons. Thomas had 22 catches for 207 yards with no touchdowns and one fumble in a stellar three-year career. Daniels caught nine balls for 137 yards with no touchdowns and one fumble in two years. In other words, this trio had nine times more turnovers than touchdowns in their brief Seahawk history. Oh, by the way, there was another quarterback available in the draft when the Hawks selected McGwire. His name? Brett Favre.

OUCH! DRAFTED PLAYERS I WISH WERE NEVER ABLE TO LEAVE

Sometimes, the Seahawks draft quality players who later leave through free agency or are released. Here are three I wish the team had found a way to keep:

Michael Bates

He was a special teams standout, but the Hawks unwisely cut him before the 1995 season. After one year in Cleveland Bates went to Carolina, where he became an All-Pro kick returner. In fact, he was named to the NFL All-Decade team of the 1990s.

Steve Hutchinson

The Hawks tried to do the right thing with All-Pro guard Hutch. Unfortunately, he, his agent, and the Vikings all stabbed the team in the back with that ridiculous poison pen clause which meant the Hawks would have had to guarantee his entire contract if they matched the deal Minnesota gave him. I have since put a voodoo curse on the Vikings. The fact that I know nothing about voodoos beside the point.

SURREAL DREAM WEAVER

In 1979 Seahawk Herman "Thunderfoot" Weaver had a most unusual season for a punter. He completed three passes for 73 yards. He also had three punts blocked (which tied an NFL record at the time). Basically, he had the same chance of completing a pass as he did of having a punt blocked. I'm still debating whether the previous statement is praise or condemnation.

Kevin Mawae

Signed a deal with the Jets in 1998 to become the highest-paid center in the game. His six consecutive Pro Bowl appearances demonstrate he was worth it. He was also durable, at one point playing in 177 straight games. He returned to the Pro Bowl in 2008 as a member of the Titans.

TWO HOLDOUTS WHO INADVERTENTLY HELPED THE HAWKS

FREDD YOUNG

A great talent who complained (but not without merit) after Brian Bosworth got millions to sign with the Hawks. Young stayed away from training camp in 1988 and then missed the team plane to Denver for the opening game. Four days later, he was shipped off to Indianapolis for a pair of first round draft picks. One of these picks was used as part of the trade to move up in the 1990 draft and take Cortez Kennedy. After having 19 sacks and appearing in four Pro Bowls in four seasons as a

Seahawk, Young only had two more sacks and no Pro Bowls in his three seasons with the Colts before retiring. But had he never howled about The Boz, Seattle would've never had a chance to get The Tez.

JOEY GALLOWAY

Galloway made many amazing plays as a Seahawk, but he had some gall the way he acted during the 1999 season. Despite having never been voted to the Pro Bowl (the closest he came was as a "first alternate" in 1998), he wanted to become one of the highest-paid receivers in the NFL. So he held out the first half of the season, prompting the derision of Holmgren and fans alike. I spotted one guy at the Dome wearing a Galloway No. 84 jersey backward with Joey's last name altered: he'd taken out the two *L*s and switched the *A* with the *O* to spell out "Go away." When Galloway did finally return, it wasn't an All-Pro effort.

To illustrate Galloway's true selfish nature, he used to have a "favorites" page on his Web site, www.joeygalloway84.com, where he listed his three favorite moments of his career. He mentioned being drafted and beating Michigan (while at Ohio State). However, he also included playing quarterback in flag football during his holdout in 1999. Now what kind of self-respecting professional football player would list such a moment as a "top-three highlight"?! Even Joey must have realized how stupid it was, because the whole favorites page no longer exists on his site.

There is a happy ending to the whole Joey debacle. The Seahawks traded Galloway in 2000 to Dallas for two first-round draft choices. Seattle used one pick from the Cowboys on a running back out of Alabama named Shaun Alexander. Thank you, Joey.

OUR SILVER-AND-BLACK ENEMY

We are developing rivalries with other NFC West teams, most notably the Rams, but due to our relatively short history, it's extremely premature to put them on the level of the Bears-Packers, Giants-Eagles, or Cowboys-Redskins competitions. When it comes to rival teams for the Seahawks, however, there was really nothing like the Oakland/Los Angeles/ Oakland Raiders. The worst thing about moving to the NFC was dissolving these twice-annual clashes. The Raiders have great rivalries with other teams, especially the Chargers and Chiefs, but there was something very unique about the Raiders-Hawks games. It stems from the fact that the Raiders, along with the 49ers, are geographically the closest NFL franchises to the Seahawks. Before the Hawks came into existence, these two were the most popular teams in the Pacific Northwest, with many of their games broadcast on television and radio in Seattle. But with the Seahawks' inception, many people (like me, originally a Bengal fan) switched allegiances to the local team. Yet a number of Northwest Raider fans remained very loyal to Oakland. Even after the Hawks joined the league, Raider games could still be heard on numerous radio stations throughout the region. When the Hawks settled into the AFC Western Division, these local Raider fans were guaranteed a yearly visit by their beloved Silver-and-Black. Consequently, this made every Raider-Hawk game in the Kingdome quite a scene.

Raider fans are some of the most violently insane in the NFL (with the lobotomy scars to prove it). Therefore, they tend to mirror the outlaw image of the Raiders: mess with the other team before it messes with you. And no team has incited Hawk fans like owner Al Davis and Co., as evidenced by the Raider Hater T-shirts that sprouted during games in the Dome. Not only were there occasional fights on the field between the Raiders and Hawks, but also between rival fans in the stands. Usually it was a Raider fan recently out of prison who started the fracas. When I went to games at the L.A. Coliseum, I never wore Seahawk garb, for fear that I'd be sent to the hospital. This fear was not unwarranted. In 1990 I was at a Raider-Steeler game at the Coliseum in which an overly excited Pittsburgh fan suffered a serious brain injury when he was shoved to the ground by a Raider Nation goon. However, not all Raider fanatics are one strike away from a life sentence. One of my best friends since moving to Los Angeles, Shawmby, is a big Raider fan despite growing up in New Jersey. The rivalry has generated some interesting smack talk between us over the years.

WELCOME TO SEATTLE

The series starts in 1977 with a Raider rout in Oakland (44-7), but the rivalry doesn't really begin until the following year, when the Seahawks become full-fledged members of the AFC Western Division. The two teams begin their home and home division series at Seattle in late October. The largest crowd in the Kingdome's three-year history is on hand to see the first regular-season game between the two teams in the Jet City. There are a number of Raider fans talking crap at the start, but by the end they are covering their faces in shame. Not unlike when they leave their courthouse appearances in front of the news media.

Raider quarterback Kenny "the Snake" Stabler throws four interceptions, while the Seahawks' ball-control offense has possession of the clock almost three times longer than Oakland. Incredibly, the Seahawks lead 27-0 at the end of three quarters. In the waning moments of the blowout, Raider defensive end John Matuszak throws one of the first punches in series history when he takes a swing at Seahawk Steve August. No official sees the pop, and "the Tooz" is not flagged for a personal foul. (Instead, he is later awarded the role of the deformed Sloth in *The Goonies*.)

Later in the season the Hawks become the first team since 1965 to beat the Raiders twice in one season. Seahawk history is made in the fourth quarter when Zorn finds a wide-open Largent in the end zone for a 27-yard touchdown. It is the 100th touchdown in team history and very appropriate since it's produced by the most fabled tandem in Seahawk lore. What may be most satisfying about the victory is the fact that the Raiders came into this game with an 8-4 record, while the Hawks were 6-6. When the 1978 season ended, both teams finished at 9-7, and Seattle, on account of slamming the Silver-and-Black twice, is placed above Oakland in the official standings. Raider fans are almost as humiliated as when their names are misspelled in the police blotter.

Such humiliation becomes a more familiar feeling for Raider fans in 1979. The teams first meet in week three of the season in the Kingdome. Some of that lovely Raider-Hawk hostility appears in the second quarter when Zorn calls timeout as he lines up the Hawks near the Raider goal line. Oakland linebacker Phil Villapiano thinks Zorn is taking the snap and rushes in. However, Hawk center John Yarno immediately stands up and levels Villapiano. The Raiders argue that Zorn was messing with them. The Kingdome wants a penalty on the Raiders. In the end neither gets justice, but Villapiano did absorb a big hit, so I call it advantage Hawks.

A spectacular catch occurs in the third quarter when Steve Largent becomes Steve Austin from the TV show *The Six Million Dollar Man*. After a Terry Beeson interception sets up the Hawks at the Oakland 21, Zorn throws up a pass near the end zone, whereby Largent jumps up at the 3 and *flies* over Raider Lester Hayes into the end zone as he grabs the ball for a touchdown. Even Largent himself is amazed by the reception. Adding to the amazement is the fact that it comes against the All-Pro Hayes.

TIME-OUT I've seen thousands of receptions in Seahawk history, but few are as incredible as this catch. In fact, the only one that comes to mind that rivals it occurred in 1996 against the Oilers. Mike Pritchard made a nearly impossible diving one-handed grab that went for 44 yards. How he kept possession as his outstretched arm slammed onto the hard Kingdome turf is beyond my level of football comprehension. *Now back to the Raiders.*

With a little more than a minute to play and leading by 10, Patera calls a successful fake punt play that puts the Hawks at Oakland's 5-yard line. Seattle then scores on a Zorn touchdown on the final play of the game. Naturally, the Raiders are none too happy about the young Seahawks running up the score and vow revenge in their next meeting. (Normally, I would not condone the Seahawks' behavior, but it was against the Raiders, the dirtiest team in the league, so I have no problem with it.)

Their next meeting occurs during the final week of the '79 season in Oakland. Despite playing without an injured Largent, the Hawks prevail, 29-24. Surprisingly, there are no cheap shots or late hits by the Raiders. The loss is devastating for the Silver-and-Black, who are knocked out of the playoffs despite *never punting the ball in the game.* Even worse, they don't get their revenge on the Hawks for running up the score during the previous game.

CH-CH-CH-CH-CHANGES

The early 1980s are a dark time overall for the Seahawks, and the games against the Raiders are no exception. A blown

10-point lead on *Monday Night Football* in the Dome leaves the Hawks reeling in 1980. It's even worse inside the Kingdome in '81 when Seattle leads 24-3 in the third quarter and ends up losing 32-31. The Seahawks also lose that year in Oakland in front of only 45,725. I suspect the drop in attendance in Oakland is due to the new Reagan Administration policy of locking up more known felons. Owner Al Davis, not happy with the sparse crowds, moves the Raiders to Los Angeles in time for the 1982 season. The players' strike wipes out the game in Seattle, but the Hawks lose for the fifth time in a row to the Silver-and-Black in front of only 42,170 at the LA Coliseum. The meager crowd means either the City of Angels didn't care about the Raiders, or the town had more known felons locked up than Oakland.

With a winning attitude courtesy of new head coach Chuck Knox, the team reverses the losing trend in 1983. Twice, the Hawks are able to defeat a vastly superior Raider team, thanks to turnovers and special teams play. The two Seahawk wins account for exactly 50 percent of the Raider losses that season. However, the Hawks can't make it three victories over the Raiders when they lose in the AFC Championship game in Los Angeles to the eventual Super Bowl winner.

Following the 1984 regular season, the Hawks and Raiders again face each other in the playoffs. It is a game that features 15 of the 41 members of the AFC Pro Bowl squad. Surprisingly but brilliantly, Knox scraps the passing game that had carried them throughout the season. The reason? The Raiders feature one of the best passing defenses in the league. The Hawks run the ball five times as often as they pass. In fact, Krieg only attempts 10 passes, the lowest total in team history. The Seahawks knock the defending champion Raiders from the postseason, 13-7. Interestingly, Largent is held without a reception, but because this was a playoff game, it does not snap his consecutive-game streak of having at least one catch.

A MONDAY NIGHT MAULING

When the Raiders walk out onto the Kingdome turf for a *Monday Night Football* match against the Hawks in 1986, little do they know they are about to experience one of the worst losses in team history. The Silver-and-Black practically own *MNF*, coming into this game with an incredible 24-3-1 record. But the Seahawks have the twelfth man, who is poised to be extra boisterous since it's both a Raider and an *MNF* game.

The first play from scrimmage is a great harbinger: Raider quarterback Jim Plunkett tries to avoid Jacob Green, only to be sacked by linebacker Greg Gaines. Raider quarterbacks will be spending plenty of time on the Dome turf this evening, thanks to Seahawk sacks. Meanwhile, the Seahawk offense has no problem with sacks or moving the football. They put up 24 points in the first half while the Raiders are held scoreless.

The network displays a graphic showing Raider quarterbacks Plunkett and Marc Wilson have had identical starting records since 1981. Announcer Frank Gifford, known to occasionally fumble with his mouth, wonders aloud if you call that "charisma." (My friend Richie and I crack up over this Giff goof. We thought maybe he was thinking of the word "karma," but that doesn't make sense either. To this day, I can't figure out what Gifford meant.) Later, Plunkett is sent to the locker room with an injury, leaving Wilson to take over at quarterback. I don't know if it's charisma or karma or caramel, but Wilson, like Plunkett, is sacked on his first play.

TIME-OUT Marc Wilson was a standout quarterback at Shorecrest High School in Shoreline, just north of Seattle, who opted to go to Brigham Young University.

Due to the fact that he played his college ball outside the state of Washington and was a Raider, he may be the least celebrated superior hometown player in Seattle-area football history. *Now back to the Raider mauling.*

The Seattle defense eventually sacks Plunkett, Wilson, and Raider third-string quarterback Rusty Hilger a total of 11 times. This remains both a Seahawk team record and a *Monday Night Football* record. The final result is a 37-0 demolishing. It is truly one of the most dominating performances in Hawk history. I can only imagine the scowl Al Davis delivered to each player as they filed past him on the team flight back to LA. I wonder if he mentioned that it was the worst loss for the Raiders since 1961? Or did he make them all hitchhike their way home?

ON ENEMY SOIL

The Seahawk-Raider game in Los Angeles in 1989 is the first contest I attend on enemy turf. I heed advance warnings about how wearing Seahawk apparel to the Coliseum can be hazardous to your health. Raider fans are bad enough in Seattle. In their own stadium, it's like wearing a sign that says, "Please break every one of my 206 bones." No need to get beat up over a game, or worse, serious smack-talked if the Raiders beat my Hawks. So I go to the game with my friends Shawmby, Tom, and Tim and without my trusty Largent jersey. Once inside, Tom and Tim sit between Raider fan Shawmby and me to maintain harmony within the group. Occasionally, I do stand up and cheer a good Hawk play, but I am not obnoxious about it. However, there are a couple of times when a few very unhappy-looking guys send serious glares my way. Shawmby, who can look rather intimidating himself, motions to these Raider fans that it's "cool" and to just ignore me. That seems to the do the trick.

Coming into this game the Seahawks had lost 18 straight when trailing at halftime. However, thanks to Curt Warner's 102 rushing yards and some timely throws by Krieg, the Hawks turn a 10-7 midway deficit into a 24-20 win, and I walk out of the Coliseum in one piece. The next morning, Al Davis fires Raider head coach Mike Shanahan after only 20 games and then refuses to pay him the remainder of his contract. (To this day, the rift between Shanahan and Davis is one of the great NFL feuds. I would love to put those two in a room with only a couple of rubber mallets. It could make for a great reality show.)

Late in the 1989 season the two teams have their rematch in Seattle. The Seahawks are clinging to their remote postseason chances, while the Raiders are poised to clinch a playoff spot with a win, as the country watches this game on ESPN's *Sunday Night Football*. Meanwhile, I'm watching it in the LA apartment I share with Shawmby, who's fretting that his beloved Raiders need to win inside the Kingdome to get into the playoffs. In the first quarter things get a little nutty when Raider Bo Jackson jumps over a throng at the goal line and tries to break the plane for a touchdown. However, Hawk defensive back Melvin Jenkins knocks the ball out of Bo's hands, scoops it up, and runs it back 99 yards for a touchdown. The play goes upstairs to the instant replay booth, as both teams think they have a touchdown. But after further review, Jackson is ruled down at the 1. No score either way. Raider head coach Art Shell reacts in his usual stoic manner, while Knox is much more animated, slamming his hat to the turf. (Sadly, the hat was put on the injured reserve list for the rest of the season.)

The Seahawks let a 10-point halftime lead slip but are able to pull out a victory with a late Krieg touchdown pass to John L. Williams. After the game Shawmby spends the next half hour in his room stewing over missing the playoffs before emerging to watch the premiere of a new animated show on Fox called

The Simpsons. Although the Hawks eventually fail to make the playoffs, they do have the satisfaction of knowing they pulled the Raiders down into the abyss of disappointment. Raider fans are last heard exclaiming "d'oh!"

LAS HORRIBLE FLORES ERA

The early 1990s is the most dreadful period for the Hawks against the Raiders. Los Angeles swept Seattle from 1990 to 1993, an eight-game losing streak that is tied with the longest drought against a single NFL team in Seahawk history (set against the Chargers from 1977 to 1981). What is most frustrating is that we lost five of the eight games by a touchdown or less. As the Seahawks got progressively worse, Raider fan reactions to a twelfth man like me attending games in LA went from hatred to ridicule. Believe me, animosity from Raider fans is far more tolerable than mockery. When I would hear screams of "Go home, Seattle!" I knew Raider fans at least were worried about us. When they would simply laugh or have no reaction, then I knew the Hawks weren't feared.

However, going to Seahawk-Raider games in Seattle was, in some ways, worse. In 1993 I attend their annual battle at the Kingdome with Shawmby, along with my old friends Jay and Bri. It is a Sunday night game, shown nationally on TNT back when they split games with ESPN. To me the game represents a chance for the country to see a new Seahawk team ready to wipe away the stink of the '92 season. However, by the final gun, only Shawmby and his fellow Raider fans are stench free. Not only am I mad at the outcome, I'm also disgusted by what I see inside the Dome: a less-than-enthusiastic home crowd. How could the fans, who helped set every conceivable NFL noise record in the '80s, suddenly become passive—or worse, apathetic? Where was the fire? Where were the thousands of Raider Hater T-shirts? Where was the passion of the twelfth man? Part of the answer was not hard for me to find. He was standing on the Seahawk sideline. Back when he was the head coach of the Raiders, Tom Flores often got his butt handed to him by the Hawks. Now running the Seahawks, he was still getting his butt handed to him, only it was the Raiders that were doing the butt-handing. In fact, Tom Flores never beat the Raiders in the Kingdome during his tenure as head coach. Consequently, the twelfth man's bite had been defanged considerably.

The Seahawks are finally able to break free from the bondage of the eight-game losing streak to the Raiders in week two of the 1994 season in Los Angeles with a convincing 38-9 victory. However, in what turns out to be Flores' last game in the Kingdome as the Seattle coach, the Hawks lose the rematch to the Raiders. John Kasay blows a 43-yard field goal attempt with 0:09 left that could have won the game. It wastes a great effort by Chris Warren, who has 122 yards for the day and breaks Curt Warner's single-season team rushing record. It is also the last time the Seahawks play a team from Los Angeles, as both the Raiders and the Rams flee the city after the '94 season.

A DOWN AND UP 1995

The Seahawks' first game with the once-old, now-new Oakland Raiders in 1995 has the least amount of attention in series history in the Seattle area. The reason? The Mariners play the Yankees in the deciding game five of their playoff series in the Kingdome an hour after this game ends at the Oakland Coliseum. It's just as well there's not a lot of interest because the Seahawks don't convert a third down all day and lose 34-14.

However, when the Seahawks face the Raiders in Seattle later in the season, as Robert Zimmerman (who also goes by the name Bob Dylan) says, the times they are a-changin'. The Hawks have won five of their last six, while the Raiders, once 8-2 for the season, are on a four-game skid. This contest harkens back to an earlier era when late-season games between the two teams had major playoff implications. Also making a return are the high-decibel cheers of the twelfth man. Adding to the drama is the talk around Seattle that Seahawk owner OverBehring is seriously considering moving the team at the end of the season, so this could potentially be the last Seahawk game ever inside the Kingdome. But I don't want to think about that possible nightmare. I just want to think about beating the Silver-and-Black. Shawmby (who wasn't my roommate by this point) makes the trek to my house for the Sunday night game.

The Seahawks score at a brisk pace in the first half. Two Chris Warren touchdowns cause Shawmby to drown his sorrows in a couple of Bacardi and Cokes. Then a Joey Galloway touchdown reception forces him to pour another Bacardi with only the slightest amount of Coke. At halftime Shawmby wonders if his Raiders can overcome a 27-3 deficit. I tell him it's possible, mainly because I don't want to jinx the Hawks and say the game is in the bag.

The Raiders open the second half by fumbling the ball, which is in turn picked up by Seahawk cornerback Corey Harris and returned 57 yards for the touchdown. Shawmby doesn't even add Coke to his freshly poured glass of Bacardi.

Later in the third quarter Billy Joe Hobert takes over at quarterback for the Raiders. The former Husky, who led the University of Washington to the national championship in 1991, is greeted with a cacophony of boos from the Kingdome. (Maybe it has something to do with him taking outside money during his college days, thus helping to put the UW on probation and causing legendary head coach Don James to take an early retirement.) The only time Hobert will hear cheers in the Dome is when he is sacked.

Despite being one of the best running backs in team history, Warren rarely had a chance to display his skills on national television. But he did in this game. His best run occurs in the third quarter, when the Hawks have the ball at the Oakland 35. Warren takes the handoff and moves to the left. However, he sees no room to move upfield, so he cuts back to the middle and then beats the entire Raider defense to the end zone for his team-record 15th rushing touchdown of the season. Shawmby doesn't bother with the glass this time and instead just pours what remains in the bottle of Bacardi down his gullet. The Hawks destroy Oakland 44-10.

IT'S NOW ALLEN'S TOWN

In 1996 Paul Allen places an option to buy the Seahawks, but the team returns to their losing ways against the Raiders in Seattle. Twice, the Hawks are stopped on fourth down in Oakland territory during the last seven minutes and lose 27-21. The teams then face off in Oakland in the final game of the season. If the stadium vote doesn't pass the following June, this would also be the last Seattle Seahawks game ever. Stan Gelbaugh, who began the year as the third-string quarterback, starts but only lasts seven plays before succumbing to injury. This forces coach Dennis Erickson to call on his old quarterback at Miami, Gino Torretta, who was signed five weeks earlier when John Friesz went down with a season-ending injury. Torretta throws the one and only touchdown pass in his NFL career, a 32-yard strike to Joey Galloway. However, it's the defense that wins this game for the Hawks, recording seven turnovers and seven sacks, including a team-record-tying four by Michael McCrary in the 28-21 victory.

The following year, with the Hawks securely in Seattle thanks to Allen and the Washington state voters, 40-year-old Warren Moon defies age and the Raider secondary in the Kingdome. Moon throws for 409 yards and five touchdowns while quieting any AARP jokes. Oakland actually has a 13-point lead in the third quarter, but Moon, along with Joey Galloway and James McKnight, helps Seattle come back for a 45-34 victory.

Late in the season, the teams square off on a rainy afternoon in Oakland. It does not start well, and the Raiders jump to a 21-3 halftime lead. Seahawk quarterback Jon Kitna, making his first NFL start, looks shaky in the first 30 minutes. But the second half is a whole different screenplay. The Raiders fumble the opening kickoff, and Seattle takes advantage with a Kitna touchdown pass to Galloway. Seattle scores 13 more unanswered points and wins, 22-21. This ties for the second-largest comeback in team history and is the biggest blown lead ever by the Raiders. After only one game, Kitna becomes the greatest Central Washington University graduate to ever play in the NFL.

The largest crowd ever inside the Kingdome (66,400) is on hand to witness the 21st and final Seahawk-Raider game indoors in 1999. The Raiders usually lead the league in personal foul penalties, and this sort of enterprising spirit is often beneficial to opponents. The Hawks benefit when defensive back Charles Woodson stupidly shoves tight end Christian Fauria and is flagged for unsportsmanlike conduct. The penalty sustains a drive that leads to a touchdown, and Seattle wins by one point. Thank you, stupidity!

On the final Sunday of the 1999 season, I suddenly find myself becoming a passionate Raider fan. After the Jets beat the Hawks in one of the early games, Oakland needs to beat the Chiefs at Kansas City to give the Seahawks the AFC Western Division championship. I'm sulking as the Jet game ends, and my mood worsens as the Chiefs go up on the Raiders 17-0 in the first quarter. But Oakland scores three straight touchdowns to take a 21-17 lead. The contest seesaws for the rest of the day. Raider kicker Joe Nedney ties the game at 38 with only 0:45 remaining. But the weak Raider defense allows the Chiefs a chance to win it in regulation. As I'm screaming at my TV for a miss, KC kicker Pete Stoyanovich obliges. Oakland wins the coin toss in overtime and moves into position for a 33-yard field goal attempt. I squat on the floor in front of the television and send all my positive energy to Nedney. His kick sails right through, and I go nuts. Never have I been so crazy for a non-Seahawk game in my life, and it comes courtesy of our biggest rivals.

NEW MILLENIUM, NEW STADIUM

The turn of the century brings controversy to the series. While the first game is a blowout win for the Raiders, the second contest, at Husky Stadium, is a tight and crazy affair. Conditions are miserable as a driving rainstorm and swirling winds coming off Lake Washington give the annual game in Seattle a new look. Despite the weather, a record Seahawk home crowd of 68,681 is on hand (admittedly, the extra attendance is likely generated by Raider fans creeping in from the backwoods of eastern Oregon).

The Seahawks post a 13-10 lead at halftime, thanks to a 52-yard field goal by Rian Lindell at the gun. It's just your standard Northwest sports irony to see the former Washington State University Cougar Lindell elicit a huge ovation from the crowd at the UW stadium.

In the closing minutes of the game, the above-mentioned controversy appears. From the Seattle 18, Seahawk running back Ricky Watters breaks through for a gain of 53 yards before Raider Charles Woodson slaps the ball from his arm. The ball hits Watters' leg, which causes it to propel down the wet Field-Turf toward the Oakland goal line. Raider Marquez Pope dives on the ball on the 1-yard line but slides into the end zone, where he is tackled by wide receiver James Williams for what is ruled a safety. Raider coach Jon Gruden is livid. He thinks

Pope's momentum carried him into the end zone, thereby creating a touchback. The officials tell him the rule is different for a fumble than for an interception. The safety makes the score 24-21, Raiders. Taking advantage of the free kick, the Hawks march 60 yards in two minutes and score the winning touchdown when Jon Kitna throws 9 yards to Darrell Jackson in the end zone with only 0:28 remaining. The NFL changes the "fumble momentum" rule in the off-season.

Sadly, the Seahawk-Raider divisional rivalry comes to a close on the Sunday evening of November 11, 2001, as realignment in the NFL moves the Hawks to the NFC West the following year. But what a way to finish the division series. In the third quarter the Seahawks start a drive at their own 12. They need only one play to score. Shaun Alexander takes the handoff to the left side and, after eluding a few defenders, cuts back toward the center of the field at the 20. In front of him is an open Husky Stadium field and a pitch-black Lake Washington in the distance. Behind him are 11 burned Raiders. The 88-yard touchdown run is the longest in team history. By the end of the game, Alexander has had quite possibly the single most dominating offensive performance in Seahawk history. He finishes with 266 rushing yards, at the time the fourth-highest total ever in the NFL, and the Hawks win 34-27.

The victory propels Seattle to finish the season on a 6-3 run. However, the Seahawks fail to make the playoffs, partly because the Raiders can't beat the Jets at home in the final game of the season. But Hawk fans get the last laugh: if the Raiders had beaten the Jets, they would've had home field advantage over the Patriots in the second round of the playoffs. As it was, they had to travel to New England, where they lost in the snow in a game that featured the infamous Tom Brady tuck/fumble. That terrible call essentially enabled the Pats to win the game. No doubt the officials wouldn't have made that controversial call

MOONSTRUCK

As early as 1983 there was talk of bringing quarterback Warren Moon to Seattle, but he didn't become a Seahawk until 14 years later. In between, the Hall of Famer played in the Kingdome three times and generally had a miserable experience. He never won as an Oiler or a Viking inside the concrete cocoon. In a 1988 loss he was 13 of 22 for 182 yards with one touchdown and one interception. Terrible numbers for the Houston run-and-shoot offense. He played slightly better in 1990, throwing for 232 yards. However, this was still a low number for a quarterback who led the NFL in passing yardage, averaging nearly 300 yards a game. In 1996 with the Vikes, he was 14 of 30 with two interceptions before being pulled from the game. He fared much better with the home team inside the Dome, going 7-5 as a starter during parts of the '97 and '98 seasons in Seattle.

at the Oakland Coliseum. The zebras are sometimes none too bright (see Super Bowl XL), but they are smart enough to realize the stadium's nickname, "The Black Hole," should be taken literally—as in, they would be sucked into a region of space and never return to human civilization if they ruled in the Patriots' favor. Or end up in an Oakland hospital administered by the Raider Nation. Whichever would be worse.

COMEBACKS, COMEDOWNS, AND A QUIZ

I lied earlier at the beginning of the second chapter. There is a test in this book. Of course, you probably don't remember reading that line so many pages ago, making this the lamest recall in literary history.

POP QUIZ, SEAHAWK STYLE

Note: This quiz is not intended to be given to fiancées, like in the film *Diner* where one of the characters makes his future wife correctly answer a slew of questions about the Baltimore Colts before he will marry her. However, if you want to make sure your future spouse is a true Hawk fan, then be my guest.

1. Who was the first-ever starting Seahawk quarterback?

2. Who scored the first regular-season touchdown for Seattle?

3. Who is the only undefeated starting quarterback in Seahawk history?

4. What two running backs have thrown touchdown passes for the Seahawks?

5. Who was the first Seahawk to return a kickoff for a touchdown?

6. Who returned the first punt for a touchdown in team history?

7. What was the longest game in Seahawk history?

8. How many days of the week have the Seahawks played regular-season games?

9. In what two NFL cities have the Seahawks never been victorious?

10. In what city will the Hawks always have a 5-0 record?

11. Besides Steve Largent, what two NFL Hall of Famers finished their careers in a Seahawk jersey?

12. When did the Seahawk defense record its first shutout?

13. What was most unusual about the Seahawk home game against the Steelers in 1994?

14. The Hawks have played twice outside the United States. In what cities were these games played?

15. Name the four stadiums where the Seahawks have played NFL games in the state of Washington.

(Answers are at the end of this section. No peeking! What do you think this is, the SATs?!)

GREAT SEAHAWK WINS: PART FIVE

SEAHAWKS 31, BRONCOS 27
Mile High Stadium, December 10, 1995

For the first nine football seasons I lived in LA, I rarely was able to watch the Seahawks on local television. This forced me to seek out sports bars that would show the Hawk games on satellite. It was always a tough task because Seattle wasn't a popular team in Southern California in the '90s. During the 1995 season, I discovered that my neighborhood bar, the Foxfire Room, had acquired one of those new small satellite dishes and the accompanying NFL Sunday Ticket subscription. (I would get it myself the following year.)

I thought it was odd the Foxfire would pay for such a service, because the place was in no way a sports bar, unless you count having a few dartboards as the only requirement for such a designation. But who was I to argue? It was mere minutes from my front door. The Foxfire had two very different clienteles: At night, it was mostly a younger group who like hanging out in a rather unpretentious setting. The daytime crowd was a decidedly older crowd of sauce monkeys and chain smokers who would fit nicely in a Charles Bukowski novel. (Not to get all Dennis Miller *Monday Night Football*-speak, but Bukowski was an LA novelist who liked to write about drunks almost as much as he liked to drink.) The Sunday afternoon Foxfire gang was an especially mellow but hearty bunch that didn't care much about football but thought of drinking as a recreational sport. This allowed me to turn one of the televisions to many Seahawk games in 1995. I'd park myself in the back corner booth and comfortably watch the game, nursing either a Coke or, if the locals insisted, a Sierra Nevada Pale Ale, which was always on tap at the Foxfire.

When I walked away from the sunshine of this December Sunday and into the dark den that is the Foxfire, I wasn't expecting much from the Hawks, because they were playing at Mile High Stadium. Success for the Seahawks at that stadium is about as unlikely as Mormons hanging out at the Foxfire. Like Kansas City's Arrowhead Stadium, Mile High in Denver has been the site of many a Seahawk disaster. In the 1987 season opener, the Seahawks led 17-7 at Denver in the second quarter. But the momentum swung the Broncos' way after Hawk linebacker Fredd Young, in the process of returning a fumble for a probable touchdown, was tackled by John Elway. (Elway?! It's still hard to believe he could take down Young.) The play ignited the Broncos, who scored 33 unanswered points and won 40-17. In 1989 Seattle trailed 38-0 at halftime, statistically the worst half in team history. And then there was 1979, when the Seahawks blew a 24-point lead and a postseason berth (see "Dreadful Defeats: Part One," page 27).

Seattle catches a break with the weather as the temperature goes from 10 degrees on Saturday to a rather balmy 56 at kickoff. However, the Hawks' Mile High curse rears its ugly head in the first half. The 7-6 Broncos play like a team still fighting for playoff spot (which they were) while the 6-7 Seahawks play

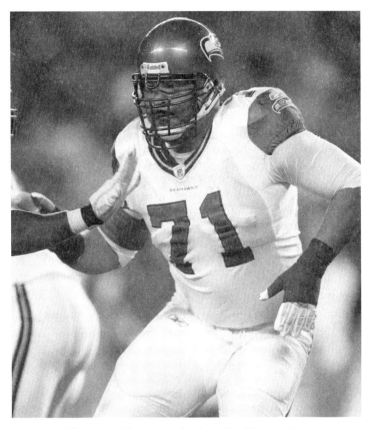

Walter Jones: The greatest offensive tackle of his generation.

like their season was done (which it wasn't). Denver returner/
running back Glyn Milburn takes apart the Seahawk special
teams, piling up all-purpose yards while Rick Mirer and the
Seattle offense sputter.

When the Broncos kick a field goal to create a 20-0 lead
with five minutes remaining in the half, I slump in my Foxfire seat. Never in their history had the Seahawks come back
from 20 points. The Hawks do manage to put together a field

FOR ONCE I WOULD LIKE A BROADCASTER TO OMIT THE FOLLOWING DURING A GAME TELECAST FROM THE JET CITY:

1. The words "coffee" and "Seattle" in the same sentence.
2. Shots of fish being thrown in Pike Place Market.
3. Mispronouncing a Washington city such as Puyallup, Yakima, or Federal Way.

goal–scoring drive near the end of the half. However, Mirer (who earlier in the week surprisingly had his $8 million option picked up) is lost for the game when he separates his shoulder.

On the opening drive of the third quarter, the Broncos move down the field with ease, thanks to Milburn and Elway. Things are looking pretty sweet for the Denver denizens when the Broncos have a first-and-goal situation at the Seattle 6-yard line. I'm thinking a 27-3 score is just too much to overcome. The Broncos call a passing play, and as Elway looks for a receiver in the end zone, he fails to see cornerback Robert Blackmon come in unblocked from his right side. Blackmon nails Elway, causing the ball to pop loose and land generously at the feet of defensive end Antonio Edwards, who scoops it up. Edwards, defying the image of a huffing and puffing lineman, moves rather briskly down the field toward pay dirt. Meanwhile, I'm screaming "Go! Go!" and forgetting momentarily that I am inside a rather quiet bar and not in my living room. I get even louder as Edwards crosses the goal line. The 83-yard touchdown is the longest fumble return in Seahawk history. (It remains the longest fumble return to this day, although there is some discrepancy over whether it was 82 or 83 yards. Announcer Jim Lampley and later ESPN call it an

83-yard return. The 1996 media guide has it at 83 yards in the game summary section, but somehow it's listed as 82 in the team records chapter. Consequently, every Seahawk media guide since then has it at 82 yards, but if you look at the play, it's apparent the return is 83 yards. Maybe the official scorer changed the distance way after the fact. Who knows? I'm outing my dorky statistician side by even mentioning it.)

It's now a 20-10 game with most of the second half remaining and most of the Foxfire patrons realizing a football game is on. Unfortunately, Seahawk backup quarterback John Friesz struggles throughout the third quarter. One player who is not struggling in this game is Milburn. When he is not killing the Hawks with his returns, he's hurting them with big rushing plays.

As with all late-season games in Denver, nightfall engulfs Mile High by the start of the fourth quarter. Friesz finally finds his rhythm and quickly moves the Hawks down the field. Seattle faces a critical third-down situation at the Denver 24. Friesz hands off to Chris Warren, who cuts to the left and then goes upfield, making every Bronco miss as he runs all the way to the end zone. This disturbs the Mile High crowd, who were not expecting the Seahawks to pull within three points. It also disturbs some of the Foxfire regulars from their *Dawn of the Dead* drunken stupor. Apparently, they were not expecting me to yell "Yes! Yes!"

My celebration is short-lived as that Milburn guy returns the kickoff 45 yards. Announcer Lampley mentions Milburn is approaching the NFL record for most all-purpose yards in a single game. I am reminded of another record-breaking contest against the Seahawks on the road featuring a tough AFC West opponent: the 1990 Chief game at Arrowhead when Derrick Thomas set the NFL record for most sacks in a game. I am also reminded the Hawks still won that game (see "15 Freakin'

Fantastic Finishes," page 58). While I'm reminding myself of all this, Elway scores a touchdown to make it a 10-point margin again. Elway emphatically spikes the ball while Bronco fans let out a thunderous cheer, as normalcy has returned to Mile High. They figure it's next to impossible for Seattle to score two unanswered touchdowns in the last seven minutes of the game. I wonder if they will be correct. After all, this is Mile High Stadium, and the Hawks have a terrible history here. But I remain optimistic despite someone at the bar saying, "Denver's got this one in the bag." What do these drunkards know, anyway?

Friesz, the former University of Idaho Vandal from Coeur d'Alene, again has the Hawks driving. He makes some key passes to Brian Blades while Warren runs through the Denver defense. The cool Friesz even keeps his composure when confusion between the field officials and sideline chainsmen cost the team a down. On first and goal at the 5, a big slice of luck befalls the Hawks. Friesz tries to sneak a pass to Joey Galloway in the end zone, but safety Steve Atwater is poised to pick it off. However, the ball comes in so hot that it bounces off Atwater's fingertips and miraculously into Galloway's mitts for a touchdown. I let out a big scream and actually get a high five from one Foxfire barfly.

The Seahawks kick off to Milburn, but this time they stop him at the 17. Interestingly, this return, one of his shortest of the day, allows him to break the NFL single game record for all-purpose yardage that was set 34 years ago to the day by Billy Cannon of the Houston Oilers. For the first time all day, the defense then steps up and completely shuts down the Broncos.

Seattle takes over at their own 44 with 2:47 remaining and down by three. Three clutch catches by Blades and a great second effort by Galloway give the Seahawks the ball at the Denver 20. On second and ten with only 0:57 remaining, the Broncos all-out blitz. Warren, who, after missing a block on a safety, instead runs into one of his own lineman and then moves to the outside, where Friesz dumps a pass to him mere milliseconds before getting pummeled by said safety. I jump out of my seat and start yelling as Warren takes the ball at the 23 and scampers all the way to the end zone. Warren makes the run look so effortless that he slows up before crossing the goal line for the game-winning touchdown. I start applauding the victory while the Foxfire juiceheads return to their Seven and Sevens and smoke their Pall Malls.

In the same stadium where 16 years earlier they blew their biggest lead ever, the Seahawks have the greatest comeback in team history. Just like the 1990 game in Kansas City, the Hawks win in one of their toughest stadiums despite an opposing player setting a single-game NFL record. Seattle just misses going to the playoffs in 1995, but victories like the one in Denver start to restore pride to the team.

The Foxfire Room? Well, it's still around. It even reached stardom itself a few years after this game, when it was prominently featured in the film *Magnolia*. This would raise the hip value of the place so high that it had a doorman for a while. I'm sure the daytime drinkers had a good laugh about that development.

SEAHAWKS 24, 49ERS 17
San Francisco Stadium at Candlestick Point, December 27, 2003

After a promising 5-1 beginning to the 2003 season, the Hawks fizzle in the second half of the campaign, losing some key games on the road. In fact, the team is winless in other stadiums since week two. So they come into their last regular-season contest at San Francisco with their road woes hanging over them. Compounding this is the fact that they have to win this Saturday afternoon game and then wait for either Dallas or Minnesota to lose on Sunday to make the playoffs. There's a lot of discussion that a loss could cost Mike Holmgren his job. Matt Hasselbeck, who had to leave the Arizona game the week before, is still hurting with a sprained ankle and a shoulder injury. Plus he and some of the other players have been battling the flu. Meanwhile, I'm battling the nauseous thought of my team being dismantled and rebuilt once again.

The Seahawk road horrors continue through much of the first half. Seattle receivers drop balls, the running game with Shaun Alexander is nonexistent, and Josh Brown misses a field goal. Then the Niners put up 14 quick points, with the second touchdown set up by a Seahawk turnover. This forces me to start chugging Pepto-Bismol. My stomach can't handle another rebuilding period.

But then the Hawks start playing like they want to make the playoffs. They gain yardage in tidy double-digit chunks. With the Hawks at the San Fran 31, Hass calls an audible and then looks at various routes before launching a pass to Alex Bannister, who catches it just as he's streaking at the 2 and flies in for six points. A surge of adrenaline fills my body, replacing the stomach pain. Adrenaline feels a lot better than nausea.

Celebrating Christmas two days late, the two teams exchange gifts in the form of turnovers. The Hawks take advantage of their present with Hasselbeck orchestrating a perfect West Coast offense drive, in the stadium where said offense was perfected years earlier by Bill Walsh and Holmgren. Hasselbeck also breaks Warren Moon's team record for passing yardage in a single season before Alexander ties the score at 14.

San Francisco responds with a nice drive of their own. Eventually, the Niners have a first and goal at the 2. But after a penalty and a fine play by Seahawk safety Ken Hamlin, 49er head coach Dennis Erickson decides not to take any more chances and brings in his old Seahawk kicker Todd Peterson on second down for a 29-yard field goal with 0:07 left in the half. This does not go over well with the crowd, who wants them to take another shot at the end zone. Peterson then shanks the chip shot to the right, where it hits the upright. The sound of the ball clanking off the post followed by a stadium crowd moan that morphs into a tremendous boo is sweet music to my ears and relief to my stomach. The camera shot of Erickson afterward makes me realize that his NFL luck is worse than the Hawks'. Poor Dennis, the Niners went through three kickers that season. Upon replaying the missed kick, the camera finds Erickson's immediate reaction: he pulls off his headset in disgust and is about to slam it into the turf when he thinks better of it. (Maybe he thought the 49er ownership was going to charge him if he broke the thing.)

The Niners open the second half with a successful Peterson field goal for a 17-14 advantage. Later in the quarter the Hawks respond when Hasselbeck throws a 30-yard bullet to Koren Robinson, who makes an incredible catch in the back of the end zone. In a season where dropped balls are common, Robinson reverses the trend. The Seahawks take the lead for the first time in the game.

The Seattle defense, erratic all season, picks a very opportune time in the second half to step up. Chad Brown and Shawn Springs combine to sack Niner quarterback Jeff Garcia on third down, killing a drive. Seattle is able to move the ball into scoring position, but Hass is picked off deep in San Fran territory. The ghosts of other road games, namely critical turnovers, haunt again.

With 7:48 remaining and holding a slim four-point lead, the Hawks start their next drive from their own 15. Hasselbeck, battling through illness and injury, not to mention a hostile crowd, coolly directs the Hawks downfield. Darrell Jackson picks up a big third-down conversion. Matt barely escapes a sack two plays later and dumps a pass off to Itula Mili. The tight end doesn't pick up the first down but gains positive yardage when a loss was very likely. Alexander then has a few big running plays that move the ball to the San Fran 16. The Hawks can't go much farther, but Josh Brown knocks down a 33-yard field goal to make it a seven-point game. It's a team-defining drive, as the Seahawks move 70 yards and eat up six minutes of the clock. Incredibly, Alexander, who had been limited to 27 rushing yards in the game, racks up 57 on this possession alone.

The Niners, with no time-outs left, need to move 70 yards in only 1:51 to tie the game. They manage to get to midfield when receiver Brandon Lloyd makes a spectacular one-handed circus catch. But they go no farther, and the Seahawks pick up their first road victory in three months.

My elation is tempered by the fact that the Hawks have not yet clinched a playoff spot, but the victory does make me confident enough to think there will be no rebuilding in Seattle in the off-season. By early Sunday afternoon, the Seahawks are guaranteed their first postseason berth in four years when the Cowboys lose to the Saints. There will be no more upset stomach—at least until the next critical game.

ALL-TIME OPPONENT LEADERS . . . MAYBE

The following are purely guesses: educated guesses, but guesses nonetheless. The quarterback with the most career passing yards against the Seahawks? John Elway. The running back with the highest total of rushing yards in history versus Seattle? Marcus Allen (with both the Raiders and the Chiefs). The all-time leading receiver against the Hawks? Tim Brown. Now, somebody prove me wrong.

DREADFUL DEFEATS: PART FIVE

RAMS 33, SEAHAWKS 27
Qwest Field, October 10, 2004

Right after this loss I wrote on the *Seattle Times* Seahawk Forum that this wasn't going to be one of those devastating defeats that sends the team on a downward spiral. Uh, my prognosticating skills were a wee bit off. The team, saddled with Super Bowl expectations, proceeded to lose two more in a row and were never the same. But how did we lose this game? How did we snatch defeat from the jaws of victory? There was a series in the fourth quarter whereby if Shaun Alexander had only muscled his way for another yard, we would've had a first down. Therefore, we could've taken a few precious minutes off the clock and more than likely prevented the Ram comeback. But this loss wasn't only Alexander's fault. True, the offense couldn't sustain a drive when it needed to, but the defense collapsed as well, giving up almost as many points (17) in the last 5:30 as they had for the first 234:30 minutes of the season (20). In hindsight, this game was a crushing defeat, but at the time I was more in shock than angry. Plus our record was still a respectable 3-1. To me, the really historic demoralizing loss didn't occur until two months later, against the Cowboys.

COWBOYS 43, SEAHAWKS 39
Qwest Field, December 6, 2004

This is the devastating loss that stayed with me for the rest of the season. A Monday night meltdown of epic proportions that cemented our national reputation as a team that blows leads and featured the most schizophrenic quarter in team history. The game begins well enough, with Jerry Rice adding to his *Monday Night Football* record for touchdowns. The newly acquired Rice has an amazing game, bringing joy to 42-year-olds everywhere as he catches eight passes for 145 yards. But the hated (at least I hate them) Cowboys score 29 unanswered points in the second and third quarters.

The Hawks start to play some of their best football of the season in the fourth quarter. It commences with Terreal Bierria picking off Dallas quarterback Vinny Testaverde at the Seattle 20 with 12 minutes to go and the Seahawks down by 12 points. The Hawks proceed to score 22 points in less than seven minutes, thanks to a second Testaverde interception and a 32-yard touchdown run by Alexander on fourth and one that puts us up by 10 with only 2:46 to play. You think this is going to be one of the all-time classic games for the Seahawks, sorely needed for a team that has been disappointing most of the season. But the lead evaporates like the stock values in my retirement account. First, Keyshawn Johnson scores on a very questionable touchdown reception (and isn't it interesting Testaverde is involved in another phantom touchdown?). Then the Cowboys recover the onside kick and win the game with Julius Jones' 17-yard touchdown run with 0:32 remaining. This in turn forces Hawk fans everywhere to consume Prozac like Skittles.

RAMS 27, SEAHAWKS 20
WILD CARD PLAYOFFS
Qwest Field, January 8, 2005

Playoff loss. Again. Jerry Rice's final NFL game ends in defeat. There's Bobby Engram's dropped ball in the end zone and the image of Hasselbeck on his knees, pounding his fists into the FieldTurf. 'Nuff said.

ANSWERS TO THE POP QUIZ

1. Neil Graff. He started the first preseason game against San Francisco in 1976. Graff was quickly supplanted by Jim Zorn and never played in a regular-season game.

2. Sam McCullum. In the Seahawks' first-ever regular-season game, he caught a low pass from Zorn as he fell across the goal line in the third quarter against St. Louis. McCullum also snagged the first touchdown in the inaugural preseason game versus the Niners. I actually mentioned these facts earlier in the book, so if you had been paying attention and not daydreaming, you would've gotten this question correct.

3. Glenn Foley, who won his only start against Chicago in 1999.

4. David Sims in 1977 and Ricky Watters in 1998.

5. Zachary Dixon, with a 94-yard sprint against the Cardinals at St. Louis in 1983.

6. Will Lewis. He had a 75-yard punt return in 1980. In 1999, Lewis had a different kind of return: he came back to the team as the director of pro personnel.

7. Hawks-Eagles, December 13, 1992. They played the entire overtime period, and the game ended on a last-second Philadelphia field goal.

8. Five. Obviously the Hawks have played on Sunday and Monday, but they have also had games on Saturday, Thursday, and even one Friday night contest against the Broncos in 1985. We lost that game to Denver, so don't expect a *Friday Night Lights* book/movie/TV show about the Hawks.

9. Baltimore (0-2 against the Ravens, never played the Colts there) and Charlotte (0-2 versus the Carolina Panthers).

10. New York City. The Hawks were 5-0 at Shea Stadium before the Jets moved to New Jersey. This answer was also available earlier in the book, so if you got it wrong, then you really need to quit trimming your nose hairs and pay attention while reading.

11. Carl Eller and Franco Harris. After retiring, former Viking great Eller clinched his Hall of Fame credentials by appearing in the first television episode of *The Fall Guy*. Franco never fit in Seattle in 1984, especially since he had to wear No. 34 instead of his celebrated No. 32 from his Steeler days. Hall of Famer Warren Moon is not included here because he finished his career in Kansas City. (Jerry Rice will join this group once he is inducted into the Hall of Fame in 2010. Cortez Kennedy and John Randle are two other players likely to be included soon.)

12. On November 13, 1977. The Hawks shut out the Jets at Shea Stadium 17-0. It was the first time in NFL history that a second-year expansion franchise blanked an established team.

13. The kickoff time. Due to the Kingdome closure, the game was at Husky Stadium on the campus of the University of Washington. Because there was a UW freshman convocation at Hec Edmundson Pavilion on Sunday morning, game time was moved to 3 p.m. The Hawks won, so I say, let's have more games at this time!

14. Tokyo (1990) and Vancouver (1998). The Seahawks played preseason games in both cities. They lost both times, so I say, let's never play outside the country again!

15. The Kingdome, Husky Stadium, Qwest Field, and Joe Albi Stadium in Spokane, where they played a preseason game in 1976.

10

THAT WAS CLASSIC

The Hawks have played in 533 regular and postseason games through the 2008 season. Some are neither great Seahawk wins nor dreadful defeats but were very memorable nonetheless. Here are a few that fall into that category.

A RECORD AND A FREE ETIQUETTE LESSON

SEAHAWKS 24, BENGALS 17
Riverfront Stadium, December 10, 1989

When Steve Largent broke the NFL record for career receptions in 1987, it came during an ugly loss at Kansas City. Likewise, when he eclipsed the NFL record for receiving yardage in 1988, it occurred during an awful defeat at San Diego. As he approached his final season in 1989, there was only one major career receiving record not owned by Steve: Don Hutson's mark of 99 touchdown receptions. Injuries prevented Largent from playing in six games during the season, but he did tie Hutson's record during a hideous trouncing at Denver in late November. Two weeks later, the Hawks were back on the road at Cincinnati, the site of a disappointing Hawk playoff game the previous year.

For most of the first half, the Seahawks are inept on offense, and one wonders if Largent will ever get the record. With the team trailing 10-0, Dave Krieg and the offense finally show a pulse in the last three minutes of the second quarter. Krieg starts to make some key passes, mostly to rookie Brian Blades, to move the team deep into Bengal territory. With 0:49 remaining, the Hawks face a second and seven at the 10-yard line. Working out of the shotgun, Krieg looks to the left and goes to his right, and hits Largent falling backward in the rear of the end zone to break Hutson's record. The catch is classic Largent. Lining up in the slot, he is able to sneak by three Bengal defenders and is wide open and in position to make NFL history.

Steve Largent scoring one of his 100 touchdown receptions. I'm going to go out on a limb and say he was a very good player.

One of the more memorable NFL coaching outbursts occurs in the fourth quarter. Some Bengal fans take their nickname of "The Jungle" to heart and start pelting the Seahawks with snowballs as the Hawks are backed up near their end zone. The officials stop the game and ask for security. Cincinnati head coach Sam Wyche jogs down the sideline to confer with the zebras. He then runs across the field to the Seattle bench, where he is handed a microphone hooked up to the public address system. Wyche proceeds to scold the unruly fans at Riverfront Stadium by exclaiming, "You don't live in Cleveland, you live in Cincinnati!" thus pitting Ohioan against Ohioan in a battle of manners.

Wyche's tirade apparently fires up his team because, two plays later, they return a Krieg interception for a game-tying touchdown. But the Hawks come back on their next series. On third and eight at their own 26, Krieg lofts a ball down the left sideline, where Largent makes another one of his incredible "How on Earth Did He Make That?" catches. Steve had to jump and turn around between two defenders to grab the ball before landing on the turf. The play goes for 34 yards to the Cincinnati 40. Seattle scores the winning touchdown when Krieg drops a little 1-yard pass to Curt Warner in the end zone. It is Warner's last touchdown as a Seahawk. Largent's touchdown is his last ever in a Hall of Fame career. It's also the last day Wyche is a spokesman for the Cleveland Chamber of Commerce.

A MOST UNUSUAL WIN

On a late October afternoon in 2002, the Seahawks, losers of four out of their first five games, play on the road at one of the most famous stadiums in the NFL. Their starting quarterback is injured and lost for the remainder of the season early in the second quarter. Their best wide receiver is also injured during the game and then suffers a frightening seizure afterward in the locker room. Their opponent's future Hall of Fame running back sets an NFL career record, which pumps up the sold-out stadium. This has all the ingredients of a Seattle defeat. However, somehow the Seahawks beat the Cowboys 17-14. Despite the season-ending injury to Trent Dilfer, the devastating hit Darrell Jackson absorbed, and Emmitt Smith breaking Walter Payton's NFL career rushing yardage record, the Hawks use 5:10 of the remaining 5:35 on the clock and win it with a 20-yard field goal by Rian Lindell.

OUR BEST LOSS EVER

VIKINGS 27, SEAHAWKS 21
Metropolitan Stadium, November 14, 1976

During their inaugural season, the Seahawks put a scare on a number of established teams. Against Roger Staubach and the Cowboys, they had a 13-0 second-quarter lead before losing. The Hawks led the Packers 20-7 in the third quarter until finally succumbing 27-20. The biggest scare occurs when the Hawks visit the old Metropolitan Stadium in Bloomington, Minnesota, to face the NFC power Vikings. Captained by All-Pro scrambler Fran Tarkenton, the Vikes are massive favorites to blow out the lowly expansion kids. But the Hawks are riding a nice emotional high after beating the Falcons the week before, and Jack Patera, who used to be the line coach for Minnesota, wants to make a good showing against his former employers.

A crisp, yet sunny afternoon greets the clubs, thus ensuring the more savage weather elements that chilled many a Viking opponent will not make an appearance. Each team scores a touchdown in the first quarter. Jim Zorn has one of his soon-to-be-famous scrambles of 12 yards to tie the game at seven. Tarkenton throws a touchdown strike in the second quarter to make it 14-7 at the break. This halftime score sends shockwaves to the bewildered oddsmakers in Las Vegas, who expect the Vikes to cover the sizable spread.

The bewilderment continues in the third quarter. With the Hawks at their own 20, Zorn launches a bomb that Steve Raible catches on the run at the Minnesota 43, sprinting to the end zone to tie the game at 14. An 80-yard touchdown. The Metropolitan faithful are not just surprised, they are infuriated. How dare an expansion team stay in the game this long?! Their anger is slightly abated after two Fred Cox field goals put the Vikes up by six after three quarters. However, the Viking fans' venom soon returns when Seahawk Don Dufek blocks a punt deep in Minnesota territory. It multiplies as the Hawks take the lead on a Zorn-to-Sam McCullum 7-yard touchdown. Suddenly, the scoreboard reads Seahawks 21, Vikings 20, fourth quarter. An upset the size of Minnesota's legendary son, Paul Bunyan, is a-brewin'. Unfortunately, Tarkenton is able to rally his team with a fourth-quarter touchdown for a 27-21 lead. The Hawks don't give up and have a chance to win it late after Zorn hits the former Viking McCullum on a 58-yard pass to the Minnesota 8. Seattle gets near the goal line, but Zorn's fourth-down pass is off target, and the crowd at the Met is saved from utter humiliation.

Against their toughest opponent of the year, the Hawks take a big step toward respectability that afternoon. Minnesota finishes the season 11-2-1 and goes on to win the NFC championship. And what became of Metropolitan Stadium? It was demolished to make room for the nation's largest shopping center, the Mall of America, where there are more places to buy chicken fingers than anywhere else on earth.

THE BOTCHED HOLD

SEAHAWKS 21, COWBOYS 20
NFC Wild Card Playoffs
Qwest Field, January 6, 2007

Rational thought can't explain the incredible ending to the Seahawk-Cowboy NFC Wild Card playoff game. More than even the 2005 Giant contest, this one had probable defeat replaced by improbable victory. A loss to the Cowboys is in hand with 6:42 remaining when the Hawks are stopped on fourth and goal at the Dallas 2. This sickens me, especially since we originally had a first and goal at the 1. So now the Cowboys have the ball at the 2 and lead 20-13. On their very first play, quarterback Tony Romo throws a little screen pass to Terry Glenn at the 1. But right after catching it, Glenn fumbles the ball, and a few Hawks try to dive on it. The ball squirts into the end zone, where it looks like Lofa Tatupu keeps it in play so Michael Boulware can recover it for what is judged a Seattle touchdown. Cowboy coach Bill Parcells challenges the call, and upon further review, the ball is ruled a fumble but also just a safety. I wonder if this is better than a touchdown, because now we will have the ball in good field position after the free kick with a chance to take the lead.

It does turn out to be a godsend: four plays after the safety, Hasselbeck hits Jerramy Stevens with a 37-yard touchdown for the go-ahead score. Unfortunately, Seattle is unsuccessful on the two-point conversion. I worry that the Hawks' failure to score on short-yardage plays will really cost us, but I also have faith our defense can stop Dallas. However, the dreaded poor rushing defense that showed up too often during the regular season returns, and Julius Jones runs rampant, including a clutch jaunt that takes Dallas into easy field goal position. On third and seven at the Seattle 8, Romo drops a short pass to his tight end Jason Witten. It appears to me that the Hawk defense stops him short of the first down, but the refs give the Cowboys a generous spot. I go nuts and start ranting about the city of Dallas, including blaming the place for JFK's assassination. I'm then reminded that the replay officials can and will look at the spot. I calm down—slightly. After some anxious moments, the ref returns to the field and announces that the receiver was short of the first down. Thank you! I knew I was right.

Martín Gramática comes in to kick what could very possibly be a 19-yard game-winning field goal with 1:19 on the clock. I've seen some pretty goofy events in all my years of watching the NFL, but the following play ranks at the top, especially considering the importance of the situation. On the snap, Romo, who's the only starting quarterback in the league these days to be the holder, can't grab the ball and place it. Realizing the kick isn't happening, he gets up and starts to go to the left side toward the end zone. As he runs with the ball, three scenarios could happen on the play, and two of them would be bad for the Hawks.

1. He could run it in for an unlikely touchdown, forcing Seattle to go the length of the field in about a minute with no time-outs.

2. In an even worse scenario, Romo could pick up the first down but be just short of the end zone. This would give Dallas the chance to kill most of the clock before either punching it in or kicking a game winner with just a few seconds left.

3. The Seahawks cash in some serious karma chips.

Miraculously, the third scenario occurs as cornerback Jordan Babineaux brings Romo down just shy of the first-down marker. As he hits the ground Romo fumbles the ball, which the Hawks recover. It takes a few moments for me to realize exactly what happened. I wonder if there is some sort of flag on the Hawks. But the referee rules it Seattle's ball. I'm suddenly in a Seahawk blue–colored straightjacket and headed to Happyland. Meanwhile, Parcells is so despondent over the loss that he quits his $5 million a year job.

It's not often that a game or a play becomes part of the NFL lexicon with a few words. "The Ice Bowl," "The Catch," "The

Drive," "The Holy Roller," "The Immaculate Reception": add to this list "The Botched Hold."

REPEAT WHEN NECESSARY II

In 1984 Kenny Easley set a team record when he intercepted three passes in a win against the Chargers. This record was matched in 1992 by Eugene Robinson and again in 1997 by Daryl Williams. Then, in 2007, the record was equaled in consecutive weeks. Lofa Tatupu picked off three passes at Philadelphia that essentially won the game. The following week Marcus Trufant put his name in the record book when he intercepted three passes against the Cardinals.

KRIEG BATTLES THE CHIEFS AND THE TWELFTH MAN

SEAHAWKS 51, CHIEFS 48
The Kingdome, November 27, 1983

The term "scrappy" often refers to a person who relies on determination to overcome limited skill or seemingly insurmountable odds. David Krieg was often described as a scrappy quarterback. Not blessed with a prominent university pedigree (he went to tiny Milton College), Krieg was a classic example of an underdog. He is one of 64 undrafted free agents when he arrives in camp in 1980. Odds on him making the team are only slightly better than me dating Jessica Alba. But when longtime backup Steve Myer goes down for the year with a back injury during an intrasquad scrimmage, Krieg beats out three other free-agent quarterbacks for the third-string slot.

The following year Jim Zorn is lost for the season in the 13th game, and Krieg takes over. In his first NFL start against the Jets, Krieg makes it memorable. He throws three interceptions but also completes 80 percent of his passes to his teammates, including a game-winning 57-yard touchdown bomb to Steve Largent in the fourth quarter. Krieg also has a 29-yard run and one rushing touchdown himself. Not a bad debut. Krieg is actually named the starter prior to the 1982 campaign, but an early-season thumb injury thwarts his progress.

He has another chance to be the full-time starter in 1983 when new head coach Chuck Knox replaces Zorn with Krieg midway through the year. Dave is erratic in his first four games. He becomes the first Seahawk quarterback to throw for over 400 yards in a game, but he also has a number of devastating turnovers that doom the team to defeat at Denver. The loss against the Broncos is part of a Seahawk two-game losing streak just prior to a critical late-season matchup versus the Chiefs in the Kingdome. Krieg's inconsistency leads to speculation around Seattle that coach Knox is strongly considering replacing Krieg with Zorn.

In the first half the turnover bugaboo hits Krieg again when he fumbles a botched shovel pass at the Seahawks' own 1-yard line. Kansas City immediately takes advantage with one of the shortest touchdown drives imaginable: a whole 36 inches. This brings out some booing by the twelfth man while Knox contemplates bringing Zorn into the game. All is forgiven with the twelfth man a few minutes later when Krieg zips a touchdown pass to Byron Walker. However, this forgiveness is short-lived, and the boo birds among the twelfth man return on the next Hawk drive when Krieg throws a pass in the middle of three Chiefs. Nickelback Albert Lewis does the honor of accepting the gracious gift and returns it to set up another Kansas City touchdown. Knox again contemplates bringing in Zorn.

Dave Krieg: the scrappy man from Milton.

The teams go into halftime with the Hawks hearing a significant chorus of jeers and Kansas City leading 28-14. Normally, that size of an intermission score would give way to a lower-producing second half. Normally.

Krieg comes out to start the second half, much to the dismay of some members of the twelfth man, who want their old favorite Zorn back at the helm. The Seahawks don't do much on their first drive, which has some fans wondering not if, but when, Knox will replace Krieg with Zorn. After the defense intercepts a Chief pass deep in Kansas City territory, the beleaguered Krieg comes back on the field and is immediately sacked for a 7-yard loss. He actually fumbles the ball, but the officials are very kind and rule he was in the grasp of the defensive player (and therefore sacked) at the time of the fumble. This enables Seattle to keep possession. Krieg then badly overthrows a potential touchdown pass to Paul Johns. On the sideline Zorn can be seen putting on his helmet. Of course, as the holder, he is probably just prepping for a possible field goal attempt, but it does make fans wonder. So now it's third and seventeen, and Krieg is not just battling the Chief defense but his own future as the starting quarterback as well. The Seahawks line up in a shotgun formation that has the quarterback 5 yards behind the center. Krieg picks up the blitz and dumps a pass off to Dan Doornink at the 20. Dr. Dan grabs the ball and hauls himself untouched into the end zone. Scrappy Krieg's job is saved, at least for one series.

While a new fan phenomenon known as "the wave" circles around the Kingdome, the teams continue to put up points, with the Chiefs leading 35-31 after three quarters. Normally, such a tally would be an above-average final score. Normally.

The Hawks have a chance to take the lead early in the fourth quarter, but disaster strikes our hapless hero again. On second and goal at the 8, Krieg drops back but then has to go forward to avoid the rush. However, he starts to fall and uses the ball as a brace. Not a good idea. The ball pops out, and defensive tackle Dino Mangiero scoops it up and stumbles off the other way to the Seattle 45. Once again, Krieg's fumbleitis is very costly, and the twelfth man is cheesed off. It takes KC exactly three plays to score another touchdown and push their lead to 11 points.

On the next Seahawk possession, Krieg returns to the field, but even more boos greet him as he goes into the huddle. Fortunately for Dave, a key pass to tight end Charle Young near midfield brings the crowd back to his side. A few big Curt Warner runs move the ball deep into Kansas City's side of the field. Then with 8:30 remaining in the game, Seattle faces a fourth-and-four situation at the Chief 12. Knox decides to go for it with four wide receivers and an empty backfield, with the exception of Krieg, who operates out of the shotgun. During the count Largent runs behind the line in the backfield. Right after Krieg takes the snap, he hands it off to Largent. Steve rolls out to the right, pivots, and then flings the ball to the other side of the field, where Krieg makes a jump-ball *catch* at the 6 and runs before being tackled at the 1. The Dome goes bonkers. At the most crucial of times, the conservative Knox channels Jack Patera with one of the zaniest trick plays in team history. Warner's touchdown plunge on the next play almost seems anticlimactic.

After the defense finally shuts down the seemingly endless Chief attack, the Hawks drive via Warner's feet to the Kansas City 14. On third and six, Krieg rolls out to the left and throws the ball out of the end zone. This is a big mistake, because he easily had room to run for the first down. It brings up another critical fourth-down call with 2:27 left. Knox takes a time-out to make sure Krieg is absolutely sure he knows what the coach wants. On the shotgun snap Krieg rolls around the backfield for what seems like an eternity (or the length of a David Lean film, for you old movie buffs). He finally spies Johns coming across the back of the end zone, and Krieg lofts a perfect pass to him in the left corner to give the Hawks the lead, 45-42.

The Kingdome explodes, thinking there can't possibly be more scoring in this game. But the Chiefs have a few more tomahawks in their arsenal. They drive 80 yards in less than a minute and score on Bill Kenney's fourth touchdown pass of the game. The touchdown is controversial because it appears Hawk defensive back Gregg Johnson wrestled the ball from Chief running back Theotis Brown in the end zone. The side judge at first rules it an interception but then changes his mind. This enrages both players and fans. With boos from the twelfth man raining on the field, the Chiefs' All-Pro kicker Nick Lowery attempts the extra point. He shanks the kick wide left. Must've been the noise bouncing off the concrete roof that caused the miss. This gives the Hawks a chance to tie or win the game in regulation with 1:30 remaining.

The Seahawks start with lousy field position at their own 17-yard line. On first down Krieg drops back, only to see the pocket quickly collapse. He breaks out of a tackle, maneuvers to the outside, and throws a short pass to Doornink at the 24. Doornink makes it to the 35 before being tackled by three defenders. It's a play that encapsulates both this game and the roller-coaster football life of Dave Krieg. With everything closing in on him in the most dire of circumstances, he manages to convert a play that may not look pretty but works nonetheless. But Dave's work is not done. He knows he must either score a touchdown or set up a field goal. If not, Seahawk coaches, fans, and reporters will point to his critical turnovers as the main reason for defeat. A place on the Seahawk bench awaits his failure.

Two incompletions are followed with another clutch Doornink catch. Krieg then hits veteran Harold Jackson for reception at the KC 25. (Jackson, a star with Knox's Rams, only had nine catches for Seattle but earned his roster spot with this reception alone.) With 0:07 remaining and no time-outs, Knox sends out Norm Johnson. Only in his second year, Johnson had never attempted a game-winning or -tying field goal in the NFL. But Norm calmly boots the 42-yarder to make it an astonishing 48-48 tie after 60 minutes.

Famed Chicago Cub first baseman Ernie Banks may have liked to say, "Let's play two," referring to doubleheader baseball games, but NFL players rarely enjoy playing extra time. Their bodies are already beaten up, and a trip to the whirlpool is much more appealing. But play they must. As with all overtimes in the NFL, possession is determined by that most arbitrary game of chance: a coin toss. Luckily, the Chiefs call tails, and the coin comes up heads. The tired Chief defense is dejected, while the equally exhausted Seahawk defense smiles at its fortune. Lowery kicks off to Zachary Dixon, who returns the ball all the way to the Kansas City 47. The whirlpool is beckoning the Chiefs.

Curt Warner continues his amazing day as Knox calls his number on three straight plays. Warner becomes the first Seahawk in team history to go over the 200-yard rushing mark. Knox then brings in Johnson to win the game. The attempt is nearly identical to the game-tying field goal he'd converted only moments earlier. It's the same distance and on the same side of the field. Thankfully, the result is also the same, as Norm kicks the first of what will be many game winners for Seattle. Now, everyone in the whirlpool.

The 51-48 final score is the third highest in NFL history (it has since been bumped to number four). The Chiefs fly back to Kansas City with the harsh reality of scoring 48 points and *losing.* The Seahawks build on their good fortune as they make the push to the playoffs during their magical 1983 season. Despite his erratic play the embattled Krieg (whose name literally translates from German as "war") is never again in serious jeopardy of losing the starting job that year and would fight off potential successors for the next eight seasons. During this era, he would be called "scrappy" approximately 487,563 times.

YET ANOTHER FLUKY SEAHAWK HISTORICAL NOTE

Player strikes caused the cancellation of eight Seahawk games in 1981 and one in 1987. Three of those battles were against the Chargers. Apparently, Hawk players really hate the city of San Diego. Maybe it's all that sunshine.

11

WHAT A POSTSEASON!

Let's have another 2005, except change the ending this time.

DREADFUL DEFEATS: PART SIX

STEELERS 21, SEAHAWKS 10
Super Bowl XL
Ford Field, February 5, 2006

I should be writing about how the Seahawks overcame a terrible push-off call against Darrell Jackson that resulted in three points instead of seven in the first quarter. How they overcame the Roethlisberger phantom touchdown (shades of Testaverde) in the second quarter that gave the Steelers seven instead of three points. I should be writing about how our defense overcame a few massive mistakes, such as allowing the Steelers to convert a third-and-28 situation and Willie Parker's 75-yard touchdown run. About how Jerramy Stevens overcame his mouth and early dropped balls with both a touchdown reception and a critical catch in the fourth quarter. About how Seattle overcame two missed 50-yard field goals and some curious clock management.

I should be writing about the incredible Seahawk drive of 98 yards that bridges the third and fourth quarters. A drive ending with an Alexander touchdown plunge to give the Seahawks a lead they would not relinquish. A drive that would be remembered up there with the Giants' clock-killing possession in Super Bowl XXV and Montana's last-minute march against the Bengals in Super Bowl XXIII. I should be writing about all these events, but I can't.

I can't because of the gross incompetence of referee Bill Leavy and his crew. If this game had been a car accident, the other driver's insurance company would've had to buy you a new vehicle. If this game had been a surgical procedure, you could've sued for malpractice and won. If this game had been a marriage, you could've divorced your spouse and taken all her/ his money. But this was a football game, and you can't right a wrong. Super Bowl XL will forever be remembered as the championship decided by the zebras, not the players. A good team can usually overcome one or two bad calls. However, so many horrible flags hit the Seahawks in this game, not even a team like the '72 Dolphins or the '85 Bears would've survived to hoist the Lombardi Trophy.

There are a few parts of this contest I fondly remember. The Kelly Herndon interception would've been the key play of the game if the Hawks had officially won. The Steelers had a third-and-six call at the Seattle 7, trying to make it 21-3. Roethlisberger, experiencing one of the worst games in his pro career, throws a lazy pass that Herndon steals at the 4. At first it appears the safety may be able to go the distance, but Herndon loses his footing near the 30 and is tackled at the Pittsburgh 20. The 76-yard interception return is the longest in Super Bowl history. It's a play that silences most of the partisan Ford Field crowd. Three plays later, Hasselbeck hits Stevens for a touchdown.

When the fourth quarter started, I was strapped in, anticipating the ultimate in football nirvana. It was only a four-point game, and the Hawks were driving for the go-ahead touchdown. I didn't have the dread that had accompanied me during many games in the Seahawks' 30-year existence. I was just in the moment, feeling like every Seahawk play was destined for NFL greatness. An Alexander run for 5 moves the Hawks into Steeler territory. A clutch third-down reception by Engram goes for 17 yards to the Pittsburgh 30. Two more Alexander runs result in 11 yards. The Seahawks were doing to the Steelers what they had been doing to teams all year: crushing them with their two-pronged offense. Hasselbeck then completes an 18-yard pass to Stevens at the Pittsburgh 1. But—and this is the biggest "but" in Seahawk history—a flag is thrown on Seattle. Offensive tackle Sean Locklear is called for holding. When I watch the replay, I'm five miles past livid. There is absolutely no reason Locklear should've been flagged. Now, there were a few times during the season when Locklear got away with holds (what offensive lineman doesn't?). However, the time to even out the calls is not during the most critical drive in the entire history of the Seattle Seahawks. There is no way he should have been flagged. If there was any penalty on the play, then it was offside on the defense. All hyperbole aside, it's the second-worst referee call in the history of professional football.

The capper—and of course there has to be a capper—occurs a few plays later when a justifiably distracted Hasselbeck throws an interception and then is flagged for a chop block as he tackles the intercepting party. The officials say Hasselbeck went low on a blocker, but the replay clearly shows he was going near the ground only on the return man. All hyperbole aside, it's the *worst* referee call in the history of professional football. This most generous of gifts from the zebras to the city of Pittsburgh adds 15 yards to the interception return, which enables the Steelers to score the knockout touchdown.

Like every other twelfth man, I am inconsolable after the game. I sit outside feeling 100 times worse than after the Testaverde phantom touchdown cost us the Jet game in '98. My friends tell me this game will be most remembered for its appalling officiating, but that is small comfort. The way we lost gnaws on my soul. Rather than losing due to our own foibles, the Hawks' destiny was determined by a group of NFL part-timers who clearly were not up to the task of calling the biggest game on Planet Earth. The Seahawks and the twelfth man are denied the opportunity of playing "We Are the Champions" by Queen; instead, we're reduced to Tanya Tucker's "Highway Robbery."

In his speech during the postgame ceremony at the Qwest, Mike Holmgren tells the crowd he didn't realize that the team was going to have to play against both the Steelers and the officials. Many members of the national sports media also rip the officiating. Then I learn that the back judge, Bob Waggoner, is from Pittsburgh. Waggoner is the guy who called D-Jack for the push-off of what should have been a Seahawk touchdown. To alleviate any concerns about impropriety or safety, the NFL should never have had an official from one of the Super Bowl cities. (Can you imagine if Waggoner had made a controversial call against the Steelers? He wouldn't be able to live in Pitt anymore.) The kicker was probably Roethlisberger going on *David Letterman* and admitting he didn't think he crossed the goal line.

One of the maddening ironies of this game is that the Steelers almost didn't make it to the Super Bowl because of bad officiating. Their playoff battle against the Colts a few weeks earlier was marred with lousy calls against them. It wasn't their own talent that helped them overcome the injustice, but rather a case of domestic abuse. You may remember that during the final minutes, with the Steelers up by three, Jerome Bettis' career almost ended when he fumbled near the Indianapolis goal line. The ball was scooped up by the Colts' Nick Harper, who ran the other way toward one of the most inconceivable touchdowns in NFL history. But Harper wasn't running at full speed, because he had been stabbed in the right knee by his wife the previous afternoon. This allowed Roethlisberger to tackle him at the Indy 42-yard line. Then after the Colts were in scoring position, the most accurate kicker in NFL history proceeded to badly shank a game-tying field goal, and the Steelers escaped with a victory. If Indy had won, Steeler fans would be screaming forever about that game and would've been on

Seattle's side if all those bad calls in the Super Bowl had been in the Colts' favor.

In the weeks following the game, some members of the national sports media (and Pittsburghers) called Seahawk fans "whiners." They said we should just get over it. Well, I can't "just get over it." How many chances will I have in my lifetime to experience a Seahawk Super Bowl victory? No one knows for sure, but I do know Bill Leavy and his band of IQ-challenged zebra mates took away one real opportunity. I defy fans of another NFL team to act differently if their club had been treated like the Hawks were during the game. Followers of any other franchise would be just as furious, if not more. I imagine Jet fans would've probably trashed the NFL offices if their team got jobbed in the Super Bowl. Raider fans? I don't even want to think about the carnage that would've ensued.

Time has lessened my anger toward this game—slightly. I don't think I'll ever be able to watch NFL Films tell the story of Super Bowl XL, but I don't obsess often about the biggest sports crime since the 1972 men's Olympic basketball final (Google it if you don't know that story). As for the Steelers, I don't hold any direct animosity toward them. It's not their fault the officiating was atrocious. I mean, what are they supposed to do? Return the Lombardi Trophy? Hold on, that's not such a bad idea.

GIANT MISSTEPS

In 1981 Joe Danelo set a Giant and Seahawk opponent record with six field goals at the Kingdome. Apparently, he used up all the good kicks in Seattle, because Giant kickers have had a miserable time since then. In New York's next appearance five years later, a botched snap dooms an extra point. Then Raul Allegre misses a 42-yard attempt despite the ball being in the favorable middle-of-the-field placement. Consequently, the Giants have to go for a touchdown late in the game instead of a potential game-winning field goal; they lose, 17-12. The Giants didn't return to Seattle again until 1995, but it was too soon for the kicker. With the Hawks leading 30-28, New York's Brad Daluiso pushes a 48-yard field goal to the right on the last play of the game. And then there's the G-Men's next appearance in 2005. Jay Feely, who had only missed two field goals all season, fails on three game-winning attempts. Feely's futility was soon the subject of a sketch on *Saturday Night Live*. I doubt Jay saved it on his DVR.

GREAT SEAHAWK WINS: PART SIX

SEAHAWKS 20, REDSKINS 10
NFC Divisional playoffs
Qwest Field, January 14, 2006

In the days leading up to this game, it seemed all I ever heard about the Seahawks was the fact that the team hadn't won a playoff game in 21 years. When you are in possession of the longest postseason-victory drought in the NFL, it's going to shape your image around the league. In the past broadcasters have occasionally brought up the playoff losing streak, but it becomes just ridiculous this week. Naturally, that creates corkscrew knots in my stomach that last well into the actual game.

In the first quarter the demons of postseasons past make their way onto the FieldTurf at Qwest Field. The Hawks move the ball into Washington's red zone on the opening drive, only to see a rare fumble by Shaun Alexander. Even rarer is that the first quarter has a total of 10 drives. This means our defense is doing its job. It also means our offense can't move the ball either. The quarter gets much worse when Alexander is knocked out of the game with a concussion. There's a feeling of dread because Shaun almost never leaves games. Then Darrell Jackson is sidelined with a back injury (his return questionable), and I'm convinced the football gods take particular joy in crushing the hopes of Seahawk fans.

This cruel joke continues into the second quarter. Hawk returner Jimmy Williams muffs a punt return. Thankfully, the defense holds the Skins to just a field goal. The Hawks' next drive almost begins disastrously when Matt Hasselbeck is nearly picked off by the Redskins' Carlos Rogers. If Rogers had intercepted, he would've had a clear path to the end zone and a 10-0 lead. The near-miss quiets the Qwest, and Redskin defenders mock the twelfth man. It's not good to goof on the twelfth man, especially when you didn't actually do anything, Skins!

Two plays later, it's third and 10 for the Hawks. Jackson miraculously returns to the game and makes a great diving catch for a first down. It may be the most important play of the game, if not the 2005 season. A 10-yard gain may not seem like such a huge deal, but it had the timing of an 80-yard bomb. If Jackson hadn't made that catch, who knows how the game would've turned out? Jackson's back problems may have been considered minor, but anyone who has ever had a back injury will tell you it is the most debilitating pain you can suffer. With Alexander out, D-Jack buried that pain. Later in the drive Jackson caps his return with a 29-yard touchdown reception, as he falls backward in the end zone with a defender all over him. He then runs up and jumps into the stands. All I can think is,

"People be careful, he has a bad back!" (Jackson eventually sets a team record for receiving yards in a playoff game.)

> **TIME-OUT** I feel this was Jackson's second-greatest performance in a Seahawk uniform. His best came in 2004 at Minnesota. He posted excellent numbers against the Vikes in the Hawk win: 10 receptions for 137 yards and one touchdown. But what made his performance so amazing is that it came less than 24 hours after his dad died. *Now back to the game.*

Not to be overshadowed by D-Jack is our fearless offensive leader, Hasselbeck. His play reminds me of the last game in the 2002 season (see "The Maturation of Mr. Hasselbeck," page 29). Alexander left that game in the fourth quarter with an injury, which necessitated a few key runs on Hass' part. The same thing happens in this game. On the Hawks' first touchdown drive in the second quarter, Hasselbeck has scrambles of 9 and 6 yards to help move the ball. But the run that will always be remembered happens in the third quarter. It's third and five at the Washington 7. Matt rolls out but doesn't see anyone open in the end zone, so he takes off to the right and angles himself just inside the pylon to make it 14-3.

Equally important is the play of the defense. On nearly every series it dispatches Washington with nary a point. (In fact, the only points given up in the first three quarters were on a field goal after the Williams punt return fumble.) The pass rush makes quarterback Mark Brunell hurry. The secondary befuddles and intimidates the receivers. The team allows only 11 first downs, a team postseason record.

I'm a little sick when Seahawk Josh Scobey fumbles the kickoff after Washington had made 17-10 with 12 minutes to go in the game. But again, the defense bails out special teams by limiting Washington to just a field goal *attempt*. I put the

Strong as a Mack truck, Mack Strong clears the way for Shaun Alexander.
Both went to the Pro Bowl in 2005.

emphasis on "attempt," because Redskin kicker John Hall hooks his kick to the left like so many of my tee shots on the golf course. Unlike my hooks, which I greet with contempt and shouts of "Fore!" this one is as welcomed as a 75-degree April day in Seattle.

Mack Strong, the longest-tenured Seahawk, puts the game away by rumbling 32 yards on a third-and-six call from the Seattle 48. Strong's run sets up a Josh Brown field goal to make it 20-10 with just under three minutes remaining.

When Brunell's last pass in the end zone falls incomplete, the knot that has been sitting in my stomach finally unravels. As Hasselbeck takes that last knee, there are equal amounts of joy and relief coming from this twelfth man. Never again do I have to hear "21-year playoff drought" and "the Seahawks" in the same sentence. I don't think I could be prouder of a team. Adversity and history. Often a lethal combination, but not on this day for the Hawks.

SEAHAWKS 34, PANTHERS 14
NFC Championship
Qwest Field, January, 22, 2006

It is the single most important sporting event to occur in the city of Seattle. I was hoping to attend this game, but my brother Milt couldn't secure me a ticket. Instead, I am watching it 1,000 miles away at my friend Stan's house, along with my old Seahawk viewing buddy, Richie. I'm a deluxe pizza of emotions, with toppings of anxiousness, excitement, nervous energy, and anchovies. Before the game even starts, the noise level inside the Qwest is at an all-time high. Appropriately, it is owner Paul Allen who raises the twelfth man flag prior to game time.

When Josh Brown kicks off, I'm in complete Seahawk mode. Nothing else matters for the next three hours. There could be an earthquake in LA. Beams could be falling by my head. Gas could be leaking. But as long as the television is working, I won't be getting up from my chair (except during moments of extreme excitement).

The defense holds the Panthers to three and out on their first drive. Rich and I renew our tradition of giving "low-fives" following a good Seahawk play. The twelfth man at the Qwest gets louder, if that's even possible. I wouldn't be shocked if people in Renton can hear the noise from the stadium.

The first big offensive play of the game occurs on the Hawks' second drive. Seneca Wallace makes a great over-the-shoulder 28-yard catch inside the Carolina 20. It's the first time I can recall a Hawk backup quarterback making a reception. On the very next play Matt Hasselbeck hits Jerramy Stevens for the touchdown. Of course, I jump from my chair with joy and give a low five to Rich and a high five to Stan.

The Seahawks quickly get the ball back when Lofa Tatupu intercepts a Jake Delhomme pass. Seattle drives inside the 10 but then stalls when the officials fail to see a blatant face mask penalty on the Panthers. While the Hawks set up for a field goal, the mood at the Qwest turns sour when they see the non-call on the big screens. It really should be first and goal at the 3, which most likely would lead to a touchdown. Instead, Brown makes the field goal, and I can't help but wonder if the potential four-point difference will, in fact, make a difference.

My mood, and that of every other twelfth man, brightens considerably on Carolina's next drive. Seattle's brilliant defensive strategy of concentrating on Panther star receiver Steve Smith pays off like early shares of Microsoft stock. Delhomme throws into coverage, where Seahawk Marquand Manuel snags the ball at the Carolina 49 and returns it 32 yards. This leads to Shaun Alexander following Walter Jones and Steve Hutchinson into the end zone and a 17-0 lead early in the second quarter. Rich and I can't keep up with the amount of low-fives this game is producing.

The Seahawk defense continues to fluster Carolina. After scorching the Bears the week before, Smith is getting a goose egg in this game. Apparently, he does not like eggs, because he cracks on the sideline, yelling at every coach within earshot. He is slightly appeased when he returns a punt for a touchdown, but the Seattle defense allows little else in the first half. Meanwhile, the Seahawk offense moves the ball on its possessions. One drive leads to three points, while the other ends on a missed field goal. The Hawks walk off with a 20-7 halftime lead. The still-angry Steve Smith walks off the field and screams at the camera about something like four guys are covering him so that means someone else must be open. It's either that, or he is saying he's going to Disneyland.

Whatever trepidation I had about the lead being only 13 points at halftime quickly sinks to the bottom of Elliott Bay. The Hawks take the opening drive of the second half and march over the Panthers. When Hasselbeck double-pumps and hits Darrell Jackson for a 20-yard touchdown, I allow myself to feel that we are going to win this game. I try to get back my "one play at a time" attitude, but the defense makes it hard as it continues to play its best football of the season. Rocky Bernard has a big sack. The unit forces another three and out by the Panthers. Delhomme later throws another interception, this time to Michael Boulware. At one point, Fox announcer Joe Buck points out Hasselbeck's quarterback rating is 127.8, while Delhomme's is an awful 1.6. This is made even more incredible because the Carolina quarterback had the highest rating in postseason history coming into this game.

When Alexander scores on a 1-yard run with six minutes remaining, the victory celebration by the twelfth man officially begins. The scoreboard reads 34-7, Seahawks. A Panther touchdown a minute later does nothing to dampen the party at Qwest Field. Longtime fans such as Patti "Mama Blue" Hammond are joined by kids who weren't even alive when Chuck Knox coached the team. Television cameras catch former Hawks Dave Krieg, Charle Young, Cortez Kennedy, and Jim Zorn on the Seahawks' sideline. Then a graphic lists the seven teams to never reach the Super Bowl. A Telestrator pen crosses Seattle from the list.

As Hasselbeck takes a final knee, I fall to my knees. I break down. I didn't know how I was going to feel when the game finally ended, and now I know: I am a big, blubbering, happy mess.

The sky over the Qwest rains blue and green confetti on the twelfth man. It is the apex of Seattle Seahawk history. Former Seahawk president Mike McCormack presents Paul Allen with the George Halas NFC Championship Trophy. Allen raises it up, a fitting coda to raising the twelfth man flag before the game. I am impressed by how well the Hawks played in the biggest game in franchise history. For a team that often makes it so hard, it went so easily. I can finally utter a sentence I've been waiting 30 seasons to say: the Seahawks are going to the Super Bowl.

12

ONE ERA CLOSES, ANOTHER BEGINS

Am I finishing this book by focusing on the 2008 season because it is Mike Holmgren's last year? Or did Holmgren retire from the team because my book is coming to an end? I don't think we will ever really know the answer.

HOLMGREN'S SWAN SONG BECOMES AN UGLY DUCKLING

2008 was a banner year for sports. It started with the New York Giants beating the previously undefeated New England Patriots in the final minute in one of the best Super Bowls of all time. That June, an ailing Tiger Woods and Rocco Mediate battled for an extra 19 holes to decide a classic U.S. Open golf championship. The following month Rafael Nadal and Roger Federer dueled in the finals of Wimbledon. It was a match that more than a few tennis experts called the best of all time. Michael Phelps had the greatest Olympic Games ever individually when he won eight gold medals in China later that summer. Yes, 2008 was a great year for athletics. That is, unless you were a Seattle sports fan.

Historians, psychologists, and barroom philosophers all looked at 2008 as not only being the worst year in Seattle sports history but perhaps the most awful any one city has had to endure, period. The Mariners, who were picked by a few sportswriters to win the pennant back during spring training, instead became the first baseball team with a $100 million payroll to lose 100 games. The Washington Huskies football team, formerly a premier national college program, sunk to the unimaginable depths of a winless season. Their cross-state rivals, the Washington State Cougars fared only slightly better with only one conference win (in overtime to the above Huskies, no less). The SuperSonics finished their worst season in team history by winning a franchise-low twenty games. However, that paled compared to what happened to the Supes after the season ended. New Sonic owner Clay Bennett became the new Ken Behring when he moved

the team to Oklahoma City. (Albeit a little more successful than the old Behring because Bennett was actually able
to transfer a Seattle team.) Meanwhile former Sonic owner
Howard Schultz played the part of Judas by selling out his
home city. Seattle's sports futility was so monumental that
many national sports outlets including *Sports Illustrated* and
ESPN.com had multiple articles on the subject.

It's no wonder then the Seahawks were also afflicted with
this losing virus. It almost seemed inevitable the Hawks
were going to have a down year. The team had been going
through the most successful era in its history and it's extremely
hard to maintain elite status in the NFL. But the Hawks' troubles had more to do with injuries and disappointing play than
any inevitability.

Injuries. I don't know about you, but I hate that word.
Before the season even started, the team was depleted at the
wide receiver position. Deion Branch, recovering from a torn
ACL he suffered in the playoff loss at Green Bay the previous
January, was not available until the fifth week of the season.
Bobby Engram got hurt during the first preseason game and
was gone for a month of the regular campaign. Ben Obomanu
broke his collarbone during the last preseason game and was
lost for the year. This left the Hawks with only one receiver
with any real experience on opening day: Nate Burleson.
During that first game of the year at Buffalo, Burleson scored
Seattle's first touchdown of the season with a spectacular catch
in the end zone. However, in what would be one of the many
cruel jokes during the season, Burleson injured his knee in the
second half and was gone for the year. Courtney Taylor, with
all of five career receptions for 38 yards, became the receiver
with the most team experience.

Mike Holmgren, who before the season started, announced
this was going to be his last year coaching the Hawks, scored

the waiver wire for available receivers who had at least caught a few balls in the NFL. He found one in Billy McMullen, a player who hadn't made a reception in almost two years. Holmgren's band of band-aid receivers took more hits in the home opener against the 49ers. Back-up quarterback Seneca Wallace, who was being pressed into wide receiving service, got hurt during pregame warm-ups and was scratched from the game. Then Logan Payne (who was originally sixth on the depth chart but moved up to number two thanks to all the injuries) was hurt early in the contest and done for the season. It became difficult to count all the casualties at the wide receiver position. The total may have been some sort of NFL record for injuries to one team's wide receivers.

The Seahawks then make a call to a player I never thought they would: Koren Robinson. I originally had Robinson listed in my Hall of Shame chapter because his drinking cost him a job in Seattle four years earlier. But K-Rob appeared to have turned his life around and team president Tim Ruskell, along with Holmgren, gave him another chance. I felt Koren had the potential for a rebirth like former receiver Cris Carter. It was Carter who partied his way off the Philadelphia Eagles, only to clean up his act and become a star in Minnesota. Unfortunately the injury bug hit Robinson before he could play a single down. A sore knee kept him from the field for nearly a month. I stopped counting all the casualties at the wide receiver position. Now I know the Hawks established some sort of NFL record for injuries to one team's wide receivers.

When Robinson was finally able to play, he was inconsistent. He dropped a sure touchdown in the end zone at Miami in the third quarter, forcing the Hawks to settle for a field goal. Seattle eventually lost by two points. However, Robinson also made some Seahawk history during the season. On the Hawks' first offensive play against the Eagles at the Qwest, quarterback

Seneca Wallace connected with Robinson for a 90-yard touchdown. It was the longest touchdown pass play in team history, besting an 82-yard strike from Jim Zorn to David Sims that stood as the record for 31 years. Robinson's reception was also the longest offensive play of any kind in the Seahawks saga, surpassing his own 83-yard record reception against the Rams from 2002 (which did not go for a touchdown) as well as Shaun Alexander's two 88-yard record runs for touchdowns.

The Seahawks finally were able to get Branch and Engram in the line-up for a week five encounter against the Giants. Unfortunately the team encountered more injuries, namely to quarterback Matt Hasselbeck who hurt a knee and his back. The Seahawks extended their horrible luck at Giants Stadium. Hasselbeck was gone for five weeks.

> **TIME-OUT** During Hasselbeck's absence, a much more serious and sad event took place in the Seattle sports scene. For many years, Seattle fans were entertained by the melodic sounds coming from Ed "Tuba Man" McMichael. With his gray beard and Dr. Seuss-style hats, the Tuba Man greeted fans as they walked into Qwest Field, Safeco Field, KeyArena, and the Kingdome. *Sports Illustrated* once even called him a "super fan." But on one late October night, McMichael was assaulted and robbed by a group of youths. McMichael died a few days later, a direct result of the attack. A tragic and pointless end for one of the city's more colorful people. *Now back to the football season.*

With their field leader sidelined, the Hawks managed to win only one of five games. By the time Hasselbeck returned, Seattle had already lost more games than all of the previous regular season. The Seahawks were holding a 2-7 record when the Cardinals came to town. Arizona had a four-game lead in the division but I had faith in the Seahawks. We were finally healthy at wide receiver. Plus, the Hawks and Cards still had to face each other twice. If Seattle won those two games, and gained two more games elsewhere then—bam! We would win the NFC West and be on a roll heading into the playoffs.

Uhhhh, it didn't work out that way. As you have probably surmised, this is a non-fiction book. A series of heartbreaking defeats at Qwest Field turned the season into a disaster. The team won more games in January 2008 (one, against the Redskins in the playoffs) than in November 2008 (zero).

Enough of the negativity. Let's end this chapter on a snowy Sunday in December. Officially, it is the first day of winter but for everyone in the Puget Sound region, the season was already here. Western Washington is in the midst of the storm of the century. (Alright, a little hyperbole since we are less than a decade into the century.) The city of Seattle is paralyzed and the words "snow plow" becomes a political hot potato. Over at Qwest Field, snow plows are inaccessible to a number of snowed-in seats in the Hawks Nest. Instead, the snow there will be used to make a few "twelfth snowman."

On the other end of the stadium Kathy Holmgren raises the twelfth man flag before the game against the Jets. She receives great applause from 67,000 frosty souls. How many wives of NFL coaches get such an ovation? As her husband prepares for his final game in Seattle, standing on the opposite sideline is his most storied student, Brett Favre.

The Jets move with ease on their opening possession, going 78 yards before being stopped at the Seattle two. New York head coach Eric Mangini elects to kick a field goal instead of going for it on fourth and inches. (It is one of a few curious decisions that will hasten Mangini's demise in the Big Apple.)

Mike Holmgren (seen here in 1999, either deciding which play to call or what to order from the Applebee's take-out menu) is the winningest and longest-tenured head coach in Seahawk history. Next stop: the Ring of Honor.

Most of the first half plays like one would expect in a snowstorm. The Hawks fumble twice including once inside the New York five-yard line. Favre himself throws an incredibly bad interception. Near the end of the first half, the Hawks finally hold onto the ball and score when Seneca Wallace hits John Carlson for a two-yard touchdown. (Second round pick Carlson was one of the pleasant surprises of 2008. By necessity, he was turned into a primary target early and responded by setting Seahawk records for receptions and yardage by a tight end. He also became the first rookie to lead the team in receptions since Steve Largent in 1976.)

The snow continues to dump on the twelfth man in the second half but the Hawks don't go down the toboggan run of defeat. They add three points in third quarter while staying turnover-free. After giving up the opening drive field goal, the defense, which underachieved most of the year, holds the Jets scoreless for their remaining ten possessions. Olindo Mare (who took the sting out of losing Josh Brown), boots another field goal late in the game to make it a 13-3 final.

Quite possibly the most bittersweet victory in Seahawk lore was the last game of the 1991 season against the Rams. Chuck Knox was resigned to the fact that he was going to resign as head coach after the win. There was a sadness on his face as he walked off the Kingdome turf for the final time. Now, almost exactly seventeen years later, Holmgren waves goodbye to the twelfth man. But unlike Knox, Holmgren has no sadness because he is able to leave on his terms. His final season was a disappointment but his career in Seattle certainly was not. Amid snowfall (and a few snowballs), the winningest coach in Seahawk history takes a victory lap around the Qwest before disappearing into the tunnel. Coach Holmgren has left the building.

A FINAL NOTE FROM A TWELFTH MAN

No doubt Seahawk fans recognize the second half of the Holmgren era to be the greatest period in team history. The Hawks won four consecutive division titles and accumulated five straight postseason appearances from 2003 to 2007. Winning has brought great expectations, but more importantly, it has brought incredible pride to the franchise and to the fans.

This recent run of success seemed nearly impossible during the OverBehring era. As we know, Seahawk fans almost lost their team in the mid-'90s when the Hawks had one foot in Southern California. Generations of future members of the twelfth man were almost denied the opportunity to cheer on the Hawks, either live or on television. I think because we survived such an ordeal, we can appreciate the team that much more. We don't take the Seahawks or their success for granted. We're grateful for every Sunday afternoon at the Qwest. We give thanks every time we turn on the TV and see an opening kickoff with the *Seattle* Seahawks. We're happy that we can add to the 33 years of Hawk history and memories. (Sadly, with the demise of the SuperSonics, the Seahawks will have to take on an even bigger role in sports stewardship for Seattle.)

I have faith Jim Mora will be able to continue the winning tradition established by Holmgren. We have the best owner in NFL, someone who wants the organization to be first-class in every way. This is evident in the new Hawk headquarters and training facility in Renton. We also have the best stadium in the league, a place truly feared by opponents. And of course, we have the best fans. It's good to be a twelfth man.

ACKNOWLEDGMENTS

"A book doesn't write itself, it has a lot of help." A well-worn expression that has been used a thousand times to lead the acknowledgment section of a book. Make that a thousand and one.

First of all, a big thank you goes to my buddy Stan Evans who gave me the encouragement and advice to make this book the best it could be. I also need to give shout-outs to Jon Brooks and Big Boy Medlin, both of whom took the time to read earlier drafts and give me valuable notes.

I would be remiss if I didn't mention my group at Sasquatch Books who believed *Notes* was of interest to more than just my imaginary fan base. Main editor Terence Maikels now knows more about the Seahawks than he ever thought was possible. Production editor Kate Kershner endured my numerous changes and phone calls without once hanging up on me. Copy editor Diane Sepanski and proofreader Lisa Hay both watched my back. Designer Rosebud Eustace put together an outstanding layout. Publicist Tess Tabor, to whom I apologize in advance if I become a pain while promoting this book. I would also like to thank the sales and marketing team at Sasquatch Books for their efforts.

A huge thank you goes to Lance Lopes of the Seattle Seahawks for all his help. I want to also thank Rich Gonzales and Sandy Gregory along with everyone else at the Seahawks who assisted in this project.

A tip of the hat goes to Fred Moody, Northwest writer extraordinaire and a great guiding light. Also to my brother Hank and my sister-in-law Janette Turner for their assistance. Legal help came from William Hochberg.

I would also like to acknowledge the following people (in no particular order) who in some way or another helped me through my literary excursion: Shawmby Harper, Tom Lazaroff, Milton Turner, Joyce Turner, Betsy Nunley, Art Thiel, Robb Weller, John Henson, John Anderson, Kenny Mayne, TC Senn, Max Bishop and everyone else at SeahawkBlue, Matt Ward, Kenn Lear, Dan Dunn, and Steve Largent.

And finally, a gargantuan thank you goes to my lovely and incredibly intelligent wife, Terry, who put up with many nights of me being camped out in our home office, only emerging on occasion to grab another glass of iced green tea. Her tolerance to my fanaticism must be noted. In other words, she has yet to strangle me over my obsession.

INDEX

INDEX

INDEX